The Afghan-Central Asia Borderland

Based on extensive, long-term fieldwork in the borderlands of Afghan and Tajik Badakhshan, this book explores the importance of local leaders and local identity groups for the stability of a state's borders, and ultimately for the stability of the state itself. It shows how the implantation of formal institutional structures at the border, a process supported by United Nations and other international bodies, can be counterproductive in that it may marginalize local leaders and alienate the local population, thereby increasing overall instability. The study considers how, in this particular borderland where trafficking of illegal drugs, weapons and people is rampant, corrupt customs and border personnel, and imperfect new institutional arrangements, contributed to a complex mix of oppression, hidden protest and subtle resistance, which benefitted illicit traders and hindered much needed humanitarian work. The book relates developments in this region to borderlands elsewhere, especially new borders in the former Soviet bloc, and argues that local leaders and organizations should be given semi-autonomy in coordination with state border forces in order to increase stability and the acceptance of the state.

Suzanne Levi-Sanchez is a Visiting Scholar in the Department of African, Middle Eastern, and South Asian Languages and Literature (AMESALL) at Rutgers University and Central Asia Course Chair at The U.S. Department of State's Foreign Service Institute.

Central Asian Studies

For a full list of titles in this series, please visit www.routledge.com.

The Afghan-Central Asia Borderland

The state and local leaders

Suzanne Levi-Sanchez

Routledge
Taylor & Francis Group

LONDON AND NEW YORK

First published 2017
by Routledge

2 Park Square, Milton Park, Abingdon, Oxfordshire OX14 4RN
711 Third Avenue, New York, NY 10017

Routledge is an imprint of the Taylor & Francis Group, an informa business

Firstissuedinpaperback2017

British Library Cataloguing in Publication Data
A catalogue record for this book is available from the British Library

Library of Congress Cataloging in Publication Data
Names: Levi-Sanchez, Suzanne, author.
Title: The Afghan-Central Asia borderland : the state and local leaders /
   Suzanne Levi-Sanchez.
Description: Abingdon, Oxon ; New York, NY : Routledge, 2017. |
   Series: Central Asian studies series ; 30 | Includes bibliographical
   references and index.
Identifiers: LCCN 2016003134| ISBN 9781138912892 (hardback) |
   ISBN 9781315691718 (ebook)
Subjects: LCSH: Badakhshåan (Afghanistan)–Boundaries–Kåuçhistonåi
   Badakhshon (Tajikistan) | Kåuçhistonåi Badakhshon (Tajikistan)–
   Boundaries–Badakhshåan (Afghanistan) | Local government–
   Afghanistan–Badakhshåan. | Local government–Tajikistan–Kåuçhistonåi
   Badakhshon. | Political stability–Afghanistan–Badakhshåan. | Political
   stability–Tajikistan–Kåuçhistonåi Badakhshon.
Classification: LCC DS374.B25 L49 2017 | DDC 958.1–dc23
LC record available at https://lccn.loc.gov/2016003134

ISBN: 978-1-138-91289-2 (hbk)
ISBN: 978-0-8153-5621-9 (pbk)

Typeset in Times New Roman
by Taylor & Francis Books

For Dani, Rebecca, Taina, Harper, David

Contents

List of illustrations

Acknowledgments

The following is only a partial list of the many people I have to thank for their kind assistance with my fieldwork, analysis, many drafts of chapters, and support. For those I leave out, it is not my intention to do so.

The usual caveat applies: all mistakes are my own.

For better or worse, my academic advisers at San Francisco State University, Sophie Clavier and Sanjoy Banerjee, planted the seeds of my current vocation. As awkward and out-of-place as I felt in academia at the time, they guided me and encouraged my intellectual development. They forever changed my life.

Rutgers University, where I received my PhD, gave me a homebase for my research. The Department of African Middle Eastern and South Asian Languages and Literature Department at Rutgers University invited me as Visiting Scholar for two years and I am grateful to Professor and Chair of AMESALL, Charles Haberl for giving me this opportunity. This allowed me access to a much-needed research library, community of scholars, and institutional support. Without AMESALL finishing this project would not have been possible. Also, the Department of Geography, and specifically Mike Segal, worked with me closely on developing the maps for this book.

The many fruitful arguments I had with my dissertation adviser at Rutgers, Jan Kubik, forced me to re-conceptualize my project repeatedly and to improve in ways I would not have accomplished alone. Cynthia Daniels guided me through my entire dissertation process at Rutgers and offered words of advice and an empathetic ear. She believed in me. Ambassador Robert Finn started supporting me and talking with me about Persian literature, language, and Central Asia even before I arrived at Rutgers. His calm voice, vast field experience, language ability, and mentoring, helped me through many unexpected obstacles over the past six years. I am equally grateful to Paul Poast, who inspired me to not only believe I could write this book, but who also convinced me it was an important body of research. My book would not have been completed without our many discussions about the different drafts of the chapters.

Mark Kleiman, along with UCLA, awarded me my first grant for conducting fieldwork in Afghanistan. Since our first phone conversation, Mark has introduced me to countless experts in the field, academics, and given me advice on my writing, analysis, and research. Stephen Amster and Jeffrey Miller advised me during my Title VIII Award from University of Delaware. Stephen has become a true friend and I have been so grateful for his shoulder. Tom Sanderson, Christine Fair, and Vanda Felbab-Brown supported me early on in my project advising me about the research design, fieldwork, and analysis. Wolfgang Danspeckgruber, LISD, and the Woodrow Wilson School at Princeton University provided institutional support and a place to develop my book prospectus and early versions of my maps. Nurmamadsho Nurmamadshoev, Faizullah Faizullah, Mohammadnur Pana, Dr. Shams Ali Shams, Dagi Dagiev, Barnett Rubin, Jonathan Kulick, Jonathan Caulkins, Angela Hawkins, Eckart Schiewak, Soultan Khodjanizorov, Hy Rothstein, Kalev Sepp, Sean McFate, Larry Sampler, Thomas Willard, Leonard Crane, Khurshed Konunov, Dvora Yanow, Parviz Mullajonov, Randall Jarrell, Patrick Thaddeus Jackson, Miguel Centeno, Jennifer Bryson, Paul Sprachman, Andrew Carney, Judith Stiehm, Dipali Mukhopadhyay, Dvora Janow, Andrei Tsygankov, Mahmood Monshipouri, have all provided expertise which helped me develop my book and keep my analysis in-line. Many people at Rutgers provided advice including David Hunter Walsh, Tom Glynn, Mary Hawkesworth, and Jill Richards. I received generous support (financial and logistical) from The American Institute for Afghan Studies, The International Research and Exchange Board, The Rupani Foundation, UCLA, Rutgers University of Delaware, The Aga Khan Foundation and LISD and The Department of Sociology and GIS at Princeton University.

The administrative office at UCLA's school of Public Policy assisted me in ways too many to detail here. The LISD team at Princeton, including Trisha Barney, Beth English, Angella Matheney, and Ankit Panda, also provided support and advice during my time there. Beth English was kind enough to share her office with me for a semester before I went back to Tajikistan and Afghanistan for further fieldwork. The many phone calls I had to make in Beth's office in order to plan all of my logistics for 11 months overseas with my daughter must have been distracting and her patience was much appreciated.

Andrew Williamson, Ambassador David Fischer, Yasaman Babaloo, Amir Hussein, Montgomery McFate, Bri Hurley, Laura Sjoberg, Frederik Coene, Michael Bauer, W.L. Pickens and so many others have supported me and advised me along the way and continue to do so. They are all close friends to whom I will remain in debt. I owe a special thanks to Danielle Pritchett whom I met on my first day in the PhD program at Rutgers University. She has been there for me emotionally, intellectually, and as a fellow traveler in a terrain that may well have been Mars.

There are those in the field, most of whom cannot be named, who supported me, guided me, taught me, and traveled with me. Some of the people I can include are: Ambassador Henri and Mrs. Guenvieve Fabian De Zipper, Jonathan Andrew, Chris Pickens, Sabzali Shukrolloev, Malika Abdulasieva, Iqbal

Safi, William Lawrence, Inayat and Mohabbat Ali, Don Van Atta, Christian Bleuer, Eric Hamrin, Christopher Tatum, Azita Ranjbar, Ali Mohammad Ali, Rodolph Oberle, Paul Minshull, Anne Johnson, and Ashley White. Also, all of the border guards, commanders, customs agents and officials, government workers and other border personnel, and the local leaders and people of Khorog, I owe you my book and only hope it is worthy of the support and time you have given me. There are so many people from Tajikistan and Afghanistan (and Gorno-Badakhshan and Badakhshan in particular) who I would like to mention here, and to whom I will always count as some of my closest friends but, given the sensitivity of my subject matter, at this point, I will have to leave their names out. Suffice it to say, without their guidance and mentoring in the field and in their region, my book would not have been possible. A very close friend, Doug Foster, died in an unexpected accident while I was writing this book. We were both IREX IARO fellows in Tajikistan together. I miss him terribly and see him smiling down on me as this book finally makes it to print!

A number of organizations supported me in my research including the United Nations, the European Union, the Organization for Security and Cooperation in Europe, International Alert, Cesvi, GIZ in Khorog, Girls International, International Organization for Migration, most importantly, the Khorog State English Program (now closed), the Aga Khan Lycée, and the Aga Khan Foundation (and of course the staff and administration of both organizations). Also, the incredibly helpful and patient editorial team and staff at Routledge who made this book possible.

Last and definitely not least, is my family, who has given me love, support, patience and encouragement during the entire process. I know my lengthy absences while I was in the field along with my many hours in my office afterwards have not been easy on my daughters. Watching them grow up into such wonderful and strong young women has been the greatest gift I will ever receive in this short life. As a new grandmother to a beautiful granddaughter, these gifts just keep getting better!! I am also so very lucky to have such an understanding husband who has believed in me at every turn, no matter how crazy the next bend in the road might have seemed at the time.

Abbreviations

AKDN	Aga Khan Development Network
AKF	Aga Khan Foundation
AKF-A	Aga Khan Foundation, Afghanistan
AKHS	Aga Health Services Program
ANC	Anti-Narcotics Committee
ASSR	Autonomous Soviet Socialist Republic
BBP	Badakhshan-Badakhshan Project
CHC	Community Health Center
DCA	Tajik Drug Control Agency
DDRP	Drug Demand Reduction Program
EUBOMBAF	European Union's Border Management Program for Badakhshan, Afghanistan
FATA	Federally Administered Tribal Areas
FDGs	focus discussion groups
GBAO	Gorno-Badakhshan Autonomous Oblast
GIZ	Deutsche Gesellschaft für Internationale Zusammenarbeit
GKNB	Tajikistan's State Committee on National Security
ICRC	International Committee for the Red Cross
IGOs	inter-governmental organizations
IMU	Islamic Militants of Uzbekistan
IOM	International Organization for Migration
IRPT	Islamic Revival Party of Tajikistan
ISIS	Islamic State in Iraq and Syria
ITREC	Ismaili Tariqah and Religious Education Committee (now known as ITREB)
KEPP	Khorog State English Preparatory Program
MSDSP	Mountain Societies Development Support Program
NGOs	non-governmental organizations
OSCE	Organization for Security and Co-operation in Europe
PDPA	People's Democratic Party of Afghanistan
SBC	Sarhad-e Breughel Village Cluster

SSRs	Soviet Socialist Republics
UN	United Nations
UNDP	United Nations Development Programme
UNMOT	United Nations Mission of Military Observers in Tajikistan
UNODC	United Nations Office of Drug and Crime
USSR	Union of Soviet Socialist Republics

1 Introduction

Borders define the periphery of the places they mark. They are the beginning, the end, and the point of transition. Borders delineate territory physically, symbolically, culturally, and economically. They serve as markers to order our world and provide a context within which to make and enforce laws. The state would not exist without its borders and neither would the symbolic representation of each nation. Yet, as much as we might want borders to order our

Figure 1.1 Map of the borderlands in Tajik/Afghan Badakhshan
Source: This map was created by the Rutgers Department of Geography and Suzanne Levi-Sanchez.

world, many borderlands are anything but clear zones of delineation. Border-lands are often rife with smuggling, illegal crossings, safe havens, and resistance groups living at the margins of the state.

A simple definition of a state is given in Article One of the Montevideo Convention of 1933. A state is defined by its having: (a) a permanent popu-lation; (b) a defined territory; (c) government; and (d) capacity to enter into relations with the other states. Borders define the territory and delineate what is included in and excluded from the purview of the government's reach—who is an insider and, more importantly, who is an outsider. Institutions at the border control who gets in and who stays out.

Border institutions are often part of the basic infrastructure assumed to be necessary for the development of a stable state. In fact, since the fall of the Soviet Union, state formation largely has been studied and implemented based on the assumption that formal institutionalization of the rule of law—including "free and fair" elections, border controls and institutions, and legitimate security forces in the form of an army and police—will lead to a developed state. In fact, the international community has spent billions of dollars on border development projects in Afghanistan alone over the past decade. These development projects are designed, funded, and imple-mented around the belief that a secure border will create a secure state or, more precisely, that stabilizing the periphery will make the center stronger. But has this theory held up in reality? Does securing the border of a state automatically mean the state will become more stable? Are secure borders a necessary component of a "developed" country? Does it ever backfire? That is, does the formalization of the border and its institutions ever result in *less* stability and *less* security for both the border and the state in the long-term?

The challenge of institutionalizing a border without negative blowback becomes especially difficult along a porous border with a marginal rule of law regime on both sides of the border where insiders and outsiders blur as informal networks permeate state institutions. In this case, increasing the institutional infrastructure might inadvertently increase instability since it institutionalizes laws ill-matched for the context in which they are to be enforced. Moreover, law-enforcement personnel who lack legitimate local authority might be unable to enforce new laws and regulations, choose not to enforce them for reasons of personal security, or increase their rent-seeking behavior toward locals, forcing them to buy their way out of arrest or jail. In this way, "securing" a border may accomplish just the opposite by pro-viding avenues for informal networks to cooperate more easily and creating institutional systems that are doomed to fail from the start. This only further marginalizes the local people and local leaders by creating a more distinct, more entrenched disconnect from the country in which they live.

When citizens living at the border realize that state security institutions are actually undermining their own security, they inevitably look for protection and justice elsewhere. This appears to be the case with Badakhshan, two autonomous, adjoining regions in Tajikistan and Afghanistan. The result is a negative spiral of increased outside enforcement coupled with progressively more organized local resistance to outside interference.

My research starts with a simple question: How important are local leaders and local identity groups to the stability of state borders and, ultimately, the state itself? I then expand the discussion, asking how formalizing security institutions along a border connecting two weak states impacts security and cooperation along that border? In other words, how does increasing security along a nearly impossible-to-control border affect cooperation at that border? How does this negative and/or positive cooperation impact the borderlands of that state, which are an inherently weak part of any nation-state? Ultimately, does this cooperation affect the stability of the state? Conversely, does allowing autonomy in coordination with the state actually increase overall security? These questions cut across a number of areas theoretically and conceptually.

Other important questions encompass the definition of the border itself, identity and the border, and institutions/organizations and local leaders. These include:

1 How do local and domestic identity(ies) interact with border institutions and the laws the border personnel are tasked to enforce?
2 What roles do local leaders and local organizations have within the context of the border and how do they impact border stability?
3 Since the border is inherently the beginning and end of the state, how do local, domestic, and international actors conceptualize the border itself physically and symbolically as well as within the context of the institutions that secure or control it? For example, if there are tensions or disagreements between the local and domestic leaders about what the border means symbolically, how does this impact the stability of the border?
4 How do the border and the border institutions operate *in situ* as opposed to what the state and/or international community assert is going on at the border? The dissonance between the goals versus the actual application is primary to the study of any border since research often analyzes what programs are hoping to do as opposed to what they actually have accomplished.
5 Lastly, how do border formalization schemes within a specific context impact local and state stability?

This series of questions is not comprehensive, but it does capture the complexity and multifaceted nature of the study of borders and borderlands.

I chose the border between Afghanistan and Tajikistan in Badakhshan as a means to study these questions. This location provided a natural laboratory in which to observe the impact of border formalization on border stability—it is a porous border in a remote, mountainous region located between two weak states. At the time of the fieldwork in 2009–2014 there were over 30 projects at various stages of implementation along this border. Additionally, there is a high level of illicit trade and illegal activity along this border since Afghanistan produces about 80 percent or more of the world's opiates, and approximately 20 percent of this transits the border between Afghanistan and Tajikistan.[1] Additionally, trafficking of humans, weapons, antiquities, and gemstones is endemic to this border. Therefore, given the saturation of illicit activity, coupled with the high level of attempted formalization in these borderlands, it seemed an ideal laboratory to study how formalization impacts local and state stability. Moreover, this region has been historically, politically, and culturally autonomous, adding another dimension to the study.

This book describes how local organizations and leaders, institutions, and informal networks at the border both deepen informal networks of cooperation and further disconnect the region from the formal state to which the border belongs. How local leaders and organizations on both sides of the border react to outside pressure, whether domestic or international, contributing to both border instability and state instability. This is not to say that autonomy leads to instability; rather, autonomy as an accepted condition of the state increases stability.

Importance of the research

Asserting a country's territorial integrity through border institutions as well as symbols of nationhood has been commonplace for centuries. How well this works within the framework of a more globalized community is becoming less and less clear. In fact, attempting to secure a state through its borders and the institutions that control the border may do more harm than good. Moreover, emphasizing the state over the local community may, in fact, decrease regional security, particularly in a territory that does not match the characteristics of the state linguistically, ethnically, or geographically.

Border crossings are natural points of political, social, and economic development since local groups must work together in order to facilitate transit and to secure passage. Borders associated with economically and socially important routes of exchange such as the Silk Road remain important areas of power-concentration even today. These transit areas dominate politically and economically and often breed conflict. In states where this point of concentrated power is located amid a marginalized population, control over the border becomes a prize for opposition groups and/or a lever for undermining the state.

The assertion that one of the key factors of the stability of the state is a monopoly over power, including its military and security institutions, is widely held in political science. Karen Barkey argues that one source of the Ottoman Empire's early success was its strategy of "negotiation by inclusion" and that "this form of state development was clearly distinct from western models"

(1994: 12–13). She argues that "the process of state development is diverse" and that the Ottoman period is an example that highlights how "bandits and bureaucrats" worked together to consolidate the previously chaotic region that the Ottomans came to control and later lost. Later on, Atatürk killed all of the local warlords and many Armenians, which has created areas of tension in the country ever since.

Writing about resistance to development and state-formation efforts in mountainous and agrarian communities, James Scott (2009) asserts, "Formal schemes of order are untenable without some elements of the practical knowledge they tend to dismiss." This "practical knowledge" as it pertains to the borderlands includes unwritten agreements, local organizational structures, and the context in which the border operates. For most of its history, Badakhshan had a measure of autonomy, and most outsiders remained blind to the inner-workings of the local community. The intrinsic political system, conflict mediation processes, and socio-economic agreements still remain primary to the people in Badakhshan. Dismissing them only makes the informal networks stronger, thereby weakening the state-sanctioned institutions.

Scott (2009) says that trying to subsume local populations into the institutions of the state when they have been operating under distinct and often complex local customs and norms tends to have unknown and often tragic outcomes. Moreover, he says that development often is done under the guise of universal principles and laws that have nothing to do with the local context of the population on which they are being imposed, even if lip-service is paid to the importance of local context. The underlying assumption of progress through science and technology is aggressively enforced and imposed on those who are considered to be backward or needing development within this matrix even if it is detrimental to local stability and security. There is an assumed natural order to things, and whatever is deemed to be outside of—or not in line with—this "rational design of social order" must be brought under control or developed to meet such standards. As Scott asserts, these assumptions of state development do not apply to a place like Badakhshan, where power emanates not from central state institutions but from kinship networks and ruling elites based on familial and economic ties. Clearly, in this type of state, "formation" and formalization of security institutions have greater potential for negative impacts on groups who are not part of the central ruling elite and kinship networks.

According to Peter Andreas, U.S. policy along the Mexico–California border asserts that we need to bring it "under control" through ordered development and technologically advanced equipment. Paradoxically, even with a state as developed as the United States, hardening this border has inspired local marginalized actors to enhance their ability to do business. Namely, the drug cartels of Mexico and the drug gangs in California have expanded and formalized their cooperation. Moreover, they have managed to gain a foothold as far north as Monterey, which is many hundreds of miles from the California–Mexico border.

Water infrastructural development efforts in Tajik Gorno-Badakhshan during Soviet times offers an important case of a failed development scheme that ignored "practical knowledge" and local organizational practices. The same development schemes did not occur on the Afghan side of Badakhshan, which makes comparing the two forms of development rather easy. In Gorno-Badakhshan, which has about 3 percent arable land and relies on glacier and snow melts and a few springs for its main water sources, the Soviets put in pipelines and outdoor faucets and sinks. A few houses acquired indoor sinks and/or plumbing, but even today, this is rare in most of the villages. But, even the limited infrastructure installed during the Soviet times has caused a skewed distribution of water in many villages, and as the glacier and snow melts decrease, water scarcity has increased. A specialist on water who was working for the Deutsche Gesellschaft für Internationale Zusammenarbeit (GIZ) told me that the Soviet-era system funnels all the water into pipes for downstream distribution, which only works if there is an adequate supply of water available. As the overall volume has decreased due to lower melting rates, the households at the top use up all the water, and the ones at the bottom have none. Some villages have crafted water-sharing agreements, but in other areas the shortages have caused tension among villagers and health risks associated with water scarcity.

On the Afghan side, ancient canals still exist throughout the villages, which use complex systems of water division in the open air channels and, while the current drought has depleted crops and caused rock slides, it has not caused local tensions and the community has borne the consequences more evenly. Interestingly, the narrative on both sides of the border is that the Soviet Union developed the region and that the Tajik side is far more "civilized" than the Afghan side. Additionally, the oft-repeated narrative among Tajiks and internationals claims that "if you want to go see Tajikistan 200 years ago, just go to the Afghan side. They are stuck in time." This is a case where development has had a perverse effect on the local resources.[2] Scott argues that universal modernization schemes and technological "advancement" applied to communities while ignoring local knowledge and practices is done at the peril of both those living there and those imposing their practices from outside.

While the international community and the domestic authority work to "develop" the border institutions and provide technical progress, guidance, and "laws," the locals in Badakhshan continue to operate as they have for centuries. The more that these local institutions are disrupted, the more the locals unite against those who are disrupting their status quo. The difference between the rather detrimental water projects during the Soviet period and today's development of the border institutions is that the water projects did not attempt to control the local fabric of everyday political existence, which the development of the security institutions, at least in some measure, are attempting.[3] In contrast to the Soviet water distribution schemes, the security arrangements supported by the international communities have imposed central ruling elites (largely controlled by kinship networks from outside the area—such as from Dangara, Tajikistan), which has delegitimized and in some cases actually eroded or marginalized the very state structures and institutions the international community aims to formalize and institutionalize.

The informal rent seeking throughout state institutions is common knowledge to both internationals and locals, so developing formal state institutions on either side of the border is a bit of an oxymoron at first glance. That being said, institutions do exist at the border, the international community assumes that they need to function, and the various trust networks and international/domestic/local organizations operate within and around these rather dysfunctional but enduring institutions.

The ripple effects of the 2012 and 2014 military actions and conflicts in Gorno-Badakhshan and Afghan Badakhshan are currently unknown. Given the importance of the unwritten agreements and modes of cooperation, the hidden systems and networks of cooperation that have existed throughout the development of the border need to be better understood in order to grasp their effects on development projects and the impact of state assertion of authority at the border.

Methodology

The original goal of my fieldwork in Badakhshan was to understand how increasing border controls in the borderlands of Badakhshan, which spans Tajikistan and Afghanistan, impacted cross-border cooperation. Due to the lack of existing information about the borderlands of Tajik/Afghan Badakhshan in both scholarly materials and international development reports, and following preliminary interviews in the field, it became clear that I would have to do my own fieldwork and gather data from existing sources in Tajikistan and Afghanistan. Thus, I read numerous papers, books, reports and scholarly articles about the people of Gorno-Badakhshan (in Tajikistan) and Badakhshan (in Afghanistan), reports about drug trafficking in the region, drug policy debates, and the historical lineages and narratives of the region. I also interviewed specialists; academics; US, Afghan, and Tajik government officials; and NGO/IGO workers to gather recommendations about how I might best conduct my research.

I participated in customs and border guard training with the Organization for Security and Co-operation in Europe (OSCE) and the International Organization for Migration (IOM). OSCE conducted the customs officer and agent training, while IOM and the United States Department of State implemented the border guard workshop and training. I also assessed the European Union's Border Management Program for Badakhshan, Afghanistan, (EUBOMBAF) for the United Nations Development Programme (UNDP). Working with the Aga Khan Foundation, I assessed and suggested revisions to their drug demand reduction program (DDRP) for Badakhshan,

Afghanistan. Both of these assessments entailed interviewing officials and locals as well as ethnographic fieldwork. I worked alongside and interviewed border guards, customs agents, government officials, and gemstone and drug traffickers. I asked about legal and illegal trade, border institutions, the bazaars, healthcare, women's issues, human trafficking, government accountability (or lack thereof), state and individual security, economic development, and addiction. Additionally, I interviewed numerous officials on both sides of the border, local stakeholders, illicit traders, and local, domestic, and international formal and informal leaders.

My fieldwork would not have been possible without the generous support of numerous individuals and organizations. The Aga Khan Foundation (AKF), a religious organization that helps Ismaili Shi'a worldwide, provided some logistical support on the Afghan side of the border in the districts of Shugnan and Ishkashem. They are the main organization working in Badakhshan at this time and, without their support, it is difficult to accomplish anything in the area. The United Nations (UN) and OSCE provided some support on the Tajik side. Apart from the assistance from these three organizations, I conducted the majority of my research independently. I lived in and around the area on both sides of the border on and off for five years. I primarily focused on ethnographic methods, including political ethnography and auto-ethnography and participant observation, but I also supplemented this with unstructured interviews and one short survey. The complexity of Tajik/Afghan Badakhshan and its linguistic, cultural, and historical diversity deserve many books in and of themselves, but I will provide only a brief discussion here.

Badakhshan: past and present

A pivotal location along the Silk Road and during the nineteenth-century Great Game, Badakhshan's multi-faceted history mixes languages, cultures, and religions. The traditional Pamiri dwellings combine Zoroastrian symbols with Shi'a Ismailism—an interweaving of two foundational belief systems for the area, which I will describe in more detail in later chapters. Many of the people are quick to share their history, culture, and religion, which are key unifying factors in the community. However, people also identify themselves by smaller units, such as districts, sub-districts, neighborhoods, family networks, village clusters, and even streets—meaning the physical territory as opposed to the cultural practices and ethno-linguistic groups. Despite these self-professed divisions, there is still an overarching and cohesive sense of community within the Ismaili areas and a shared desire to protect the Pamiri culture, language, and traditions.

Trafficking in illegal goods is a primary source of income generation and addiction a growing problem due to the increasing availability of drugs. The border guards and border institutions, the traffickers and networks of cooperation, and local leaders and organizations are all part of the complex interplay among power, money, and identity. First, power goes to whomever controls the drugs or other parts of the illicit economy. Second, the local economy (legal and illegal) intersects with regional illicit trade, offering great potential for generating money. Third, identity, where you locate yourself, is key because there is competition between local and state networks for control over the illicit trade.

How does one study how these border areas either maintain stability and/or increase security? Can these areas be places of cooperation among stakeholders, not zones of shadowy networks controlled by the state and locals alike? One way is to analyze the mechanisms of influence at the border through the formal institutions of the state, local organizations, and local leaders. Since many of these mechanisms are hidden behind walls erected by various local, domestic, and international groups or other forms of "trust networks," my book works to uncover these mechanisms.

Preliminary findings

Three key issues highlight how border security affects cross-border cooperation within the context of local leaders and organizations and licit and illicit trade. First, increased border controls and the increased presence of the state in their respective autonomous region have not only frustrated many of the people living along the border, but also have made them increasingly willing to work with local leaders and organizations. This is also true of the border guards and customs officers, who take orders from the person with the most authority (whether a central government official or informal local leader). This can be authority in the form of money or group allegiances.

Second, since trafficking functions through different local groups and cross-border networks of cooperation, the increasing local presence of state security raises the cost of doing business, which deepens already established illicit networks. Moreover, the increased presence of outsiders heightens the perception that the "rights" of the individuals living and working in these areas are being violated by the increased presence of outsiders—including Tajiks who are not from Badakhshan. This deepens the desire to empower and/or cooperate with both local and/or illicit networks. Since these networks deepen when threatened either socially or economically, thereby decreasing security in the region, and it will become more difficult for development schemes to take hold.

Third, increasing border security increases the price differentials across the border, which increases the potential gains from smuggling. Lastly, I found that actual respect for the nation-state on either side of the border, including a willingness to obey a centralized authority, decreases as outside interventions at the border increase. This decreases territorial integrity in terms of stability and security in general.

Framework of the book

The following chapters highlight the importance of local leaders and their organizational ties to border stability and, ultimately, state security along the borderlands of Badakhshan. In Chapter 2, I provide the conceptual framework. Chapter 3 outlines the historical background that influences group dynamics in Badakhshan. I do this through a synthesis of locals' perceptions and narratives about their history, scholarly materials, and other primary sources. Chapter 4 discusses local foundational myths through my fieldwork and other materials. Chapter 5 studies the social organization of Khorog, Tajikistan, through the lens of local leaders and organizations. Chapter 6 focuses specifically on the institutions at the border, including the cross-border bazaars, customs, and the border infrastructure. In Chapter 7 I detail how addiction and trafficking impact local security and stability in Shughnan, Ishkashem, and the Wakhan Corridor in Afghanistan. In the concluding chapter I recap the book and provide implications, findings, and suggestions for future avenues of research on border stability within the context of the local leaders and organizations.

Notes

1 www.unodc.org/documents/data-and-analysis/WDR2011/The_opium-heroin_market.pdf; www.unodc.org/documents/crop-monitoring/Afghanistan/ORAS_report_2012.pdf.
2 Data regarding the water infrastructure came from an official of GIZ who had worked on water infrastructure and management in Badakhshan for three years.
3 Elinor Ostrom's research on development (1990, 2005, 2006; and Poteete, Jansen & Ostrom, 2010), for which she won the Nobel Peace prize in 2009, is pertinent here.

2 Conceptualization, theoretical framework, and methodology

Conceptualization

The concepts of borders, institutions, and identity[1] all play key roles in my book. All of them have extensive, interdisciplinary, and well-established bodies of research. Given space limitations, I will highlight each concept in this chapter and explain how I am using them for my research. Specifically, I define all of my concepts through their relationship to local leadership.

What are borders?

Borders create boundaries both symbolically and physically. They manifest themselves to state leaders, mapmakers, and local residents in quite different ways, depending on what institutions are used to reinforce borders and how people see themselves in relation to the border.

I first conceptualize borders and how the regional context and local versus state authority influences border stability. I discuss this difference and then conceptualize how these two ideas intersect my analysis. Second, I define the formal/informal institutions, organizations, and networks that operate at the border. Third, I provide an overview of identity in relation to Tajik Badakhshan and Afghan Badakhshan. In Badakhshan, religious, territorial, national, and ethnic/sub-ethnic identities, as asserted by the locals, are key categories of identity and a primary influence on the way informal institutions and organizations operate.

Each of my concepts informs the next. Namely, I study the borderlands of Badakhshan. These borders are institutions of the state. Informal institutions and organizations co-exist with the state (formal) institutions. Citizens work in these institutions and participate in the non-state organizations and institutions. Therefore, what is a border? What kind of institutions? What is an informal versus formal institution and organization? Who are the citizens? How do they function within the myriad of local and state institutions and organizations at the border? What is their role within the local (and informal) institutions? Who are the leaders of these informal and formal (state/non-state) institutions and organizations? All of these questions need defining and refining.

Places

I conceptualize borders as places that are important in two ways: symbolically and physically. Symbolically, because for a state to exist the local population must accept that it is part of the state in conjunction with the state apparatus that rhetorically asserts the importance of the border including through the narratives of the state and national identity. Physically, because the institutional formalization process at the border has an impact on the local community and therefore plays an important role in border and state stability. Formalizing state-run institutions along the border has the potential to increase cooperation among local cross-border non-state networks and thereby decreases state authority at the border.

Contests for control

Borders are declarations of control over a particular territory. One of the most common assertions by scholars and policymakers is that borders are more stable when they are either controlled or hardened through formalization or clear delineation such as by walls, fences, or infrastructure. The design and implementation of numerous border control/security projects throughout the globe based on this assumption provides further evidence for the prevalence of this view.[2]

Border infrastructural development and institutional formalization may increase security at the periphery in countries with a well-established rule-of-law, although even that is questionable, but not in borderlands that have marginalized groups who do not self-identify ethnically, culturally, religiously, or linguistically with the state. In fact, physically tightening a border may not be the most important aspect of border control.

Peter Andreas emphasizes that, "The popularity of the border as a political stage is based as much on the 'expressive role' of law enforcement (reaffirming moral boundaries) as it is on the 'instrumental goal' of law enforcement (effective defense of physical boundaries)" (2000: 11).[3] Essentially, enforcement is two-fold: symbolic and physical. The inability to control a physical border creates a legitimacy problem on the actual, geographical territory; it forces policymakers to increase rhetoric about the symbolic border (Andreas, 2000).[4] It also forces lawmakers to increase the criminal costs for violations that at the same time deepen criminal networks by forcing them to be more innovative.[5] If people don't buy into the idea of "their" border, and at the same time the state is rhetorically and physically increasing its institutional presence at the border, there will be perverse effects. Increased cooperation among illicit networks capitalizing on the lack of support for the institutionalized border is an example of just one of them. This hinders positive cooperation, causing even further discounting of the border by locals.

Points of cooperation

Borders also provide opportunities for cooperation, either state/local to enforce the border or local/local to bypass it. Border stability could increase if state and local actors partnered on cross-border security (Gavrilis, 2008: 8–11). According to this logic, local institutional actors controlling and patrolling the border should be granted considerable autonomy. Gavrilis adds that local institutions should be developed based on the particular state's institutional, geographic, and security characteristics,[6] arguing that "no paths of state formation are exactly alike. As work on state formation demonstrates, state leaders practice a wide array of combinations of extraction, co-option, coercion, and legitimization to enable rule and ensure compliance" (2008: 11).[7]

It is clear that local institutions at the border should play an important role in border security, but the local institutions need autonomy, and depending on the context, they also serve as independent arbiters of local safety measures at the periphery. In fact, when the state-constructed institutions ignore the local context in which they operate, there is potential for local organizations to cooperate across the border and outside of the state's purview, thus destabilizing the borderlands and deteriorating the legitimacy of the state. This limits perceived legitimacy as well as degrades symbolic acceptance of the border.

This is applicable particularly in borderlands that divide ethnically, religiously, or linguistic connected territories, as is the case with the borderlands of Tajik/Afghan Badakhshan. In fact, the assumption that the institutions of the state should be the only unit of political authority and legitimate institution for territorial control deserves further interrogation. My work aligns closely with noted scholar James Scott's research on resistance to state interventions among mountainous and often autonomous regions. But, I am suggesting something slightly different. Namely, cooperating with local organizations at the periphery and allowing for partial autonomy may create legitimacy for the state *as a whole* and provide deeper buy-in from local groups.

John Williams supports the idea of a partnership between local groups and the state. He adds to Gavrilis's argument asserting that local communities are an important component of border and state security.[8] Williams's study overlooks the role of local leaders and organizations in border stability.[9] In his work he says that in the past borders were places to be controlled or built up, but in the increasingly globalized community, borders now assert or reflect a state's "social cohesion" (Williams, 2006: 125). This is due to transnational communication, global trade networks, and other ways in which borders are more easily transcended than they could be in the past. Additionally,

Williams (2006) asserts that the exclusion or marginalization of the local communities occurs at the peril of the state in such areas as they could become breeding grounds for transnational terrorism.

While Badakhshan is not an area that has the potential for suicide or Islamic terrorism, it does have the potential for instability. This is largely due to the fact that the central authorities on both sides of the border have different ethnic affiliations than the locals and marginalize the indigenous Pamiri (non-Tajik) population. Moreover, the majority of the state officials are Sunni as opposed to Ismaili Shi'a, which is the primary religious identity along much of borderlands in Tajik/Afghan Badakhshan.

Similar cases of a border that divides an ethnically cohesive territory, a marginalized population, and increased assertion of state authority, are seen in some of the hottest and most insecure places in the world such as Kurdistan, Baluchistan, Kashmir, the Federally Administered Tribal Areas (FATA), Fergana Valley, and the North Caucasus. Research on border control often overlooks the impact of local leaders and local organizations on the stability of the border, which is particularly important in cases such as these.

Trade zones

Borders and what crosses them inherently includes trade, and where there is legal trade, illegal trade is not far behind. Many states currently include in their border development schemes plans to increase cross-border cooperation and trade. The goal is to provide easier means of exchanging goods for both local populations as well as international traders. There is no doubt the dilemma of increasing state reach through border security, while simultaneously decreasing state control through trade openness, provides a rather challenging puzzle, particularly if illicit networks are endemic.[10]

Andreas points out that illicit trade networks in post-war economies, which have had several years of war to cement these networks, make them almost impossible to change. If this is true, Afghanistan, which has had 30 years of almost non-stop war, must have almost no other networks in place. Moreover, increasing physical infrastructure while potentially decreasing symbolic buy-in clearly allows for illicit networks to find more fluid pathways (and rhetorical legitimacy) over the border. If locals do not view the state border institutions as including them, they find other means to operate locally.[11] Moreover, if the basis for political authority is the territorial division comprising the state, while separate but equally legitimate political authority exists along different geographic delimitations, denouncing one (local) while asserting the other (state), will clearly increase discord between an already dissonant geographical framework.

The question then becomes—who controls what economically at the periphery of the state? This is where local leaders and organizations become really important. While the state may hold a monopoly over state institutions and security at the border (although not in any way completely), alternative localized forms of political and economic authority control and influence many of the non-state networks that are often marginalized and socio-economically disadvantaged. This provides additional incentive to find alternative forms of livelihoods that are outside of the state's control.

Along most of the borders I have studied (some in the field and some strictly through scholarly materials) including Pakistan/Afghanistan, Afghanistan/Tajikistan, Tajikistan/Kyrgyzstan, Iran/Azerbaijan, and the Baluch and Kurdish areas, economic inequality is not present. Unlike, for example, North and South Korea, they all have socio-economically disadvantaged communities on both sides of the border. These areas also have numerous border development projects in process. As border infrastructure projects and more formalized access points are being implemented and designed, the geographically hostile terrain makes barriers along the border impossible to erect (due to ongoing erosion, landslides, avalanches, and high mountains). In many of these areas, substantial physical barriers would have been erected long ago if the geography and/or financial means had permitted it. Currently, this appears to be the case in the borderlands of Badakhshan, particularly on the Tajik side, where state and international forces increasingly are working to assert authority coupled with the central governments taking more and more control over the illicit trade wherever possible. The question is why? Why is it assumed that increasing physical infrastructure along a border will either increase security or stability?

Paradoxically, tightening a border through infrastructural development or building barriers between two states that are either economically unequal or both weak economies, does not improve stability.[12] While the physical border is being built up, local acceptance of the state institutions enforcing the borders decreases. Moreover, due to corrupt security institutions that lack local legitimacy, the central authority of the state lessens in the border regions and the symbolic significance of the state erodes and even is perceived as an oppressive arm of state officials and elites.

Along with the negative impact of increased state institutional infrastructure on border (and state) stability, there is the issue of two neighboring countries that lack an entrenched rule of law and have porous borders due to harsh terrain. In these cases increasing the institutional infrastructure has the potential for causing even more instability. This is particularly true when new regulations and non-local law enforcement personnel put laws into effect. In this context, "securing" a border may accomplish just the opposite. By further marginalizing the people who live at the border, the central authorities cause an increased disconnect from the state. In fact, formal institutionalization at the border without local buy-in inspires increased cooperation among informal, non-state networks.

When it is clear to the citizens living at the border that the state institutions meant to provide security are doing anything but making them secure, they look elsewhere for protection and justice such as local leaders and their associated organizations. More importantly, in much of the world the rule of law as asserted by the state is anything but entrenched. Unwritten agreements are the norm and are enforced by a multitude of individuals and organizations such as family and kinship networks, neighborhoods, and religious affiliation. These networks often include ethnic and sub-ethnic identity as a key factor for inclusion. Often people living at the periphery belong to different ethnic and sub-ethnic groups. Therefore, when local groups along the border are marginalized by the state, since they do not belong to the same networks (for the most part), they will partner with their own kinship networks, particularly if their income comes in large part from illicit activity.

For example, if the national organizations and institutions supported by the international community are in competition for resources, control, or authority with the local leaders, and (formal or informal) organizations, located at the border, each of these outside groups projects different roles for the border and border personnel. Additionally, local leadership and their associated networks perceive a presence by outsiders as a threat to their local community. These local leaders and their groups then deepen their networks in opposition to the domestic and international organizations implementing border development projects or other security projects. It is not difficult to ascertain that this will cause tension at the border and in the surrounding region.

This is even truer in a territory with a distinct and insular community (ethnically, religiously, and/or culturally) but with border institutions imposed by outsiders. In this case, isolating local organizations and leaders might indeed have a deleterious effect on both the stability of that border as well as the state. While some of these areas have territorial disputes and others do not, they all have populations that are marginal from the point of view of the central state authority, borders that cut between distinct social, cultural, and/or religious groups, and are subject to either domestic and/or international intervention and/or assertion of control.

As Williams, Andreas, and others highlight in various ways, even if the border is "controlled" by legitimate state institutions, cross-border cooperation among local non-state groups is present. Thus, a community that is coherent and cohesive across a border and within its own territory but different from the state authority is vulnerable to recruitment by trafficking groups involved in criminal activities and subversion of the state, particularly if that group of people is marginalized by the state. Furthermore, if that "border" area is regarded as an outcast by the state and the security forces operating along the border, its residents will not envisage the state as representing them.[13]

Some cross-border cooperation projects recently have included joint-security training for border commanders, guards, and troops, and customs official and agents. This is true along the border of Tajikistan and Afghanistan. This type of development assumes that cooperation: (1) among state security apparatuses at the border will decrease border disputes; (2) will decrease trafficking because the local institutions will be empowered through development of the rule of law within these "regimes" as trans-border teams of security institutions. These assumptions exclude the role and context of the local population along the borderlands and their relationship to and with the central authority as well as the symbolic importance of the border (or in some cases, lack of importance) for the communities along the periphery of each state.

I conceptualize the borderlands as a place not only at the edge or periphery of a well-developed state center, but a place in and of itself; a thriving territory both belonging to the state as well as an autonomous region. This autonomy extends through the physical and in the symbolic. Borders are a key institution of the state as they define where the actual state resides. For Badakhshan/Gorno-Badakhshan in particular, the physical, geographic importance and symbolic depth of the local culture, language and identity define its *Boundaries and Belonging*, as Joel Migdal (2004) fully explores in his noted book of the same name. The territory simultaneously acknowledges its relationship within the state and its status as a historically self-governing region. Since the border both belongs to the state but also at the same time has its own autonomous identity, the same is true of the institutions, formal and informal. This leads me to my next set of concepts: institutions, organizations, and networks.

Who controls the border? Institutions and organizations

In Tajikistan and Afghanistan, informal networks, groups, and non-state-run institutions including clans,[14] sub-ethnic groups,[15] and even neighborhoods, often trump state-run institutions.[16] Moreover, these unwritten rules and informal constraints make up the majority of locally accepted and legitimate interactions at the border. This makes these non-state-sanctioned institutions the more legitimate institutions even though they are unrecognized and in some cases (but not all) illegal, according to the state.

What I mean by legitimate here is that the unwritten agreements are forms of accepted behavior as understood by the people actually living, working, and crossing the border. Additionally, when these unwritten rules are broken there are negative consequences for the people breaking them. In some cases, members of different groups and networks operating along the borderlands administer justice based on consensus within the group. The adherents/members of these local organizations and institutions often must operate within, around, and outside of the state run institutions and organizations.[17]

Formal and informal local organizations differ from formal and informal institutions (Helmke and Levitsky, 2004: 724–727; Collins, 2004: 231).[18] Helmke and Levitsky define informal institutions as "enforced outside of officially sanctioned channels" whereas formal ones are "enforced through channels widely accepted as official" (2004: 726).[19] Moreover, informal institutions operate within a given set of accepted norms, customs, and/or rules including any group or collective behavior such as hospitality, family life, and extrajudicial practices (Barth, 1969: 120).[20]

Organizations are structured differently. Collins (2004: 231) says that informal organizations are "social (non-state-created) groups that have a corporate character; specific informal unwritten agreements shape individuals' expectations and behavior within the group." Essentially, organizations are the groups operating around a set of written or unwritten constraints. Organizations sustain themselves around a set of common goals, beliefs, or other self/group identified categories, traits, or features. Informal/local organizations mediate through, and are constrained by, the unwritten agreements, customary norms of the informal institutions.

There are other forms of informal groups or "umbrella"[21] groups, which transcend the boundaries of ethnic, sub-ethnic groups and networks on each side of the border as well as spanning the border.[22] Some of these networks engage in drug, weapons, human, and gemstone trafficking, medical and agricultural exchanges, and other forms of legal and illegal trade. These "networks of cooperation"[23] transcend formal institutions the state works to maintain.

For example, illicit trade groups often cooperate as a network even though they may have other tensions, such as clan or tribe-based rivalries, spatial/territorial disagreements, or ethnically derived conflicts. Some local leaders and their associated organizations may cooperate with some state officials and institutions. Moreover, not only might these networks operate within intra-state boundaries, but also inter-state and internationally. This forms a larger network of cooperation such as the gray market economy, which is a mix of legal and illegal transactions as well as licit and illicit trade groups.[24] How they cooperate and to what degree this impacts stability at the border and/or the state is unclear. Local power brokers' relationships with the central authorities shift according to state intervention schemes or convenient alliances with local leaders and groups across the border. Informal institutions operate within the formal institutions at the border—both spanning the border and on each side of the border.

The question then becomes, from where do these unwritten rules, constraints, norms, customs, and practices come? How did they become widely accepted? Who buys in and why? One way to explain this is through a study of identity. Identity is the aspect of informal institutions and organizations I explore most. Particularly, how do different identity groups interact with the institutions at the border and how do they determine what delineates their group from others. Therefore, it is important to understand how the different groups define their own identity. For example, are they based on territory, religion, descent/kinship, or fictive descent/kinship? How are the boundaries for their identity maintained and/or transcended? In all cases a self-defined boundary plays a central role. People have to identify with something in order to create a boundary and define what constitutes what is outside of that boundary. Or, sometimes they change which boundary they belong to based upon what is most beneficial to them in the moment. In order to understand how these boundaries are maintained and/or created I must first conceptualize identity.

Identity

Decades ago Frederik Barth wandered into the Swat Valley in the newly formed country of Pakistan.[25] During his fieldwork he spent eight months living in Swat, observing the region's people, and participating in their lives. This ended up being his dissertation on the Swat Pathans (known today more commonly as Pakhtuns or Pashtuns) in which he re-conceptualized the study of ethnicity and identity. Once thought of as primordial, he asserted that instead identity is based on groups defining themselves based on who they aren't as opposed to who they are. He also suggested that ethnicity is not fixed; it is more what the groups define themselves to be at any given moment.[26] This was a radical notion at the time since the assumption had been that identity, and ethnic identity in particular, was based on "discrete groups of people" and should be studied as a single unit of analysis. Barth's definition suggested something quite different: ethnic identity is what people make of it.

Many scholars consider him the founding father of constructivism because he suggested that identity was anything but immutable.[27] Instead, according to Barth, it was mutable and based on "boundary maintenance" meaning "ethnic groups are categories of ascription and identification by the actors themselves, and thus have the characteristic of organizing interaction between people." He also suggested studying ethnic identity through the "different processes that seem to be involved in generating and maintaining ethnic groups" (Barth, 1969: 10–11).[28]

In Barth's later work, he made an important addition to his original conceptualization of identity. He asserted that there is an overall "social system" with many nested groups within the larger social organization and that each group may have a different identity (even ethnic) (1973). This is similar to my own conceptualization. As with the case of my local research partner Sher, he asserted the parts of his identity he needed to within a given situation. Barth analyzed the "process of boundary maintenance in different sectors of Pashtun/Pakhtun territory" (1969: 117). [29] People belong to various self-identified ethnic identities within the social organization and they use different identities strategically. In one social setting belonging to one segment of an identity might provide more status in a given circumstance.

For example, Barth describes how the Pakhtunwali (or non-written ethical and traditional code of behavior) is quite different among the Pakhtuns of Afghanistan and the Pakistani Pakhtuns. One of the ways these groups self-identify is through how their names are pronounced in local dialects. In Southern Afghanistan and Kabul the "sh" is used whereas in the Tribal regions along the border of Afghanistan and Pakistan the "kh" is used. Additionally, in the Afghan tribal areas a soft "kh" is used and on the

Pakistan side a hard "kh" is used. People writing about them subsume them all under one name but the rivalries between these groups are long and bloody (Marsden and Hopkins, 2012).[30] In Afghanistan these battles still are a recurring theme in the streets and the newspapers.

Similar to the way FATA has both long-standing divisions between geo-located groups as well as an over-arching ethnic affiliation in the region, Badakhshan maintains boundaries in segments as well. Within each asserted boundary there are sub-groups that belong to the bigger social organization as well as different informal institutions that belong to each segment as well as the whole. Who belongs, and more importantly, does not belong to each group, is frequently debated in the area.[31] As Jo-Ann Gross puts it, "The sifting of cultural symbols and meaning is part of the dialectal process of untangling the threads of identity" (1992: 1). This is as much a process for the local as it is the non-local researcher. Building on Keyes (1981), Gross points out that, "the subjective perceptions of ethnic identity and the historical dimensions of how such identities are formed, changed, adapted, utilized, or manipulated" is key to understanding "the social and political uses of ethnic identities" in Central Asia (1992: 9).

According to Kanchan Chandra (2012), ethnic identity is based on descent constraints or rules.[32] Both the locals and others impose such constraints. Barth also asserts that identity is maintained through constraints and/or rules and offers a very broad definition of descent groups. As Barth says, "We are faced with an increasing number of types of descent systems in which the very concept of descent can imply a range of different things" (1969: 4).[33] Chandra is somewhat more utilitarian in her application of constraints, focusing primarily on the rules as opposed to the context of those rules and how they change depending on the circumstances. What Barth and Gross assert, which differs from Chandra, is important here. If different groups conceptualize descent in different ways, then the rules depend on the context within which they are asserted.

Chandra and Barth (in some of his work) focus on the individual choices and thus treat identity as a resource to be used strategically and under-play identity as a set of constraints that limit individual choice. All of these authors focus less on the ways in which norms and other unwritten agreements inform identity and group identification. Both constraints (or fixed aspects of identity) and changing or more fluid aspects of identity are equally important to my study. In order to understand the combination of fixed or external constraints of identity as well as the changing or more individual or internal aspects, it is critical to study empirically the reasons why certain aspects of identity are mutable and others immutable (Brubaker and Cooper, 2000). Identity clearly is a complex intertwining of the two.

Not only are there varying degrees of assertion of identity but also different identities that people might choose to assert. Moreover, some aspects of identity are immutable and some are not. As Jan Kubik once said to me, "If I am a large Polish man, I certainly can't suddenly change into a small Chinese woman no matter how much I say it is so."[34] Immutable as that might be, this same Polish (now American) man might assert his being Polish over Catholic or a scholar or a part of Solidarity or an American or any combination therein depending on the circumstance he is in at the time and what serves his purposes. Of course, different degrees of change and assertion are highly individual and depend on the context the person lives.

In some borderlands a broadly accepted self-defined identity (ethnic, religious or a combination of native-described traits) is present. Importantly, it is often different from the identity promoted by the state apparatuses and centers of power. Much of the local population might self-identify differently from the center of the state and therefore, see itself not only as existing at the periphery of the state geographically, but also being different religiously, ethnically, socially, and/or linguistically. If people do not perceive the nation that the state demarcates as being important to their well-being or as a community to which they belong, a state's borders will be more difficult to control and this will weaken the legitimacy of the state. As Andreas and Wallman say, "State power is based on physical capabilities and coercion, but is also fundamentally based on legitimacy and its symbolic representation" (2009: 143).

When different forms of pressure from "outsiders" occur, the boundary maintenance assertions may go up or down depending on the situation but certain aspects of the boundary are fixed, such as the territory, the place of birth, or the socio-economic status. In the case of Badakhshan, boundary maintenance of identities depends on how groups decide to adopt different categorizations. Essentially, many in Badakhshan assert identity partially as an individual and partially because of norms, customs, and unwritten rules. For example, in public they may profess to be a nationalist and a Tajik, but in private they may assert that they dislike Tajiks and are completely different from them. In either forum, they may be doing it because they have decided to strategically assert their identity for a practical purpose or because they simply are following the accepted norms of behavior in a given place.

For example, when the state threatens local identity groups or attempts to control the border without local input, local identity groups become more hidden out of fears of repercussion from the state but in private the assertions of belonging to certain groups become more intense and even involve discussions of separatism and mobilization. When pressure occurs certain identity groups and their self-ascribed boundaries are "activated," which can cause mobilization (Tilly, 2005: 134–135; Chandra, 2012: 18). Some use other segments of their identity as a resource, for example as a means of protest.

Douglass North conceived institutions as "the rules of the game" or, in other words, as a set of constraints. If one defines institutions as North does, as mutable within a set of constraints (immutability), then informal institutions become performed in ways similar to identity. In fact, informal institutions often are associated with identities. To rephrase this: *an informal institution can become a vehicle for identities to be asserted.* Moreover, boundary-maintenance and transcendence by groups inside and outside the boundaries make up the common rules/customs/norms of both the identities and the informal institutions (Chilton, 2004). I categorize four types of identity as important to my analysis: ethnic, religious, territorial, and national. Gross (1992a) highlights three of these groups in her edited volume: ethnic, religious, and national. Both Muriel Atkin and Olivier Roy build on these forms of identity in their contributions to this book, respectively, on Tajikistan and Afghanistan. They both argue that all forms of these local identity groups are used in different ways at different times. As Atkin points out:

> The setting of particular interactions determines which affiliations meet a person's needs in that situation or are pushed to the fore in reaction to the behavior of others. Many forms of group identity, whether of long-standing or transient significance, do not have well-established names to distinguish them from such familiar categories as "nationality" and "religion". Thus, terms like "Tajik" and "Muslim" tend to subsume, and at times conceal, a complex assortment of other loyalties that also exist among the members of those broadly defined communities.
>
> (Atkin, 1992: 65–66)

My research encompasses a similar conception to Gross, Atkin, and Roy's understanding of identity groups in Central Asia and Afghanistan, but I add territorial identity. Territory, as a defining feature of local identity, plays a key role in many forms of group assertion along the borderlands. While each identity is not mutually exclusive, each has its own role within the community, depending on the situation, and territorial affiliation is no exception.

Different forms of people's identities empower, or constrain, or some combination of the two, how they change under different pressures, and how this impacts stability at the border. Namely, what are the key mechanisms through which local identity groups impact formal institutions and their interactions? According to Schatz, "group cohesion does not survive merely by definition; rather it survives (if and when it does) because of identifiable mechanisms of identity reproduction. Consequently, if such mechanisms are disrupted or changed, we can expect concurrent changes in the shape and meaning, and salience of group identities" (2004: xx). I am concerned with the relationship between local identity groups and their associated informal institutions and organizations and how these organizations impact the formal institutions. These interactions highlight the key mechanisms for stability and instability along the border.

Now that I have defined my three main concepts, I will discuss my methodology and methods. After that, the rest of my research focuses on answering my questions through providing a historical context and a brief discussion of the foundational myths (compiled from a combination of the fieldwork and other primary sources as well as scholarly materials and other secondary sources), and then provide three extended case-analyses from my ethnographic fieldwork in the context of my concepts and questions. In conclusion I provide findings and offer some recommendations.

Methodology and methods

What I mean by methodology is the way in which I analyze my research. As for methods, these are the way in which I collected my data. This is a subtle distinction but an important one. How I collected my data, the methods in which I chose to observe the phenomena I was studying aligns with the way in which I analyzed the data after I returned home or was working at my desk overseas.

Ethnography

Ethnography is both a methodology and a method. Ethnographic fieldwork often is based on "deep hanging out" and "situated knowledge." Moreover, at least as it pertains to my research, I am as much a part of the research as my research participants. I constantly evaluate my own role within my lived experiences and in the lives of those I am living with. Data from the area I chose to conduct my fieldwork was not only difficult to collect but also sometimes dangerous even to observe. Therefore, participant observation and lived experience were the most effective, and in fact, the only ways to gather data in the area. Additionally, since my subject of study is focused on hidden mechanisms of identity production and reproduction, I observed interactions, not to find the "truth" but to uncover the ways in which people assert belonging and, conversely, not belonging to different groups, organizations, and networks. This requires living and observing in situ, which is at the heart of what it means to do ethnography.

My analysis derived from extended case-studies which includes three main components:

1   Situational analysis.
2   An "approach to social change that takes actors' own cultural perspectives seriously".
3   Sensitivity "to the fact that data fathering via ethnography is based on a dialogue between the 'researcher' and 'respondent'".

(Aronoff and Kubik, 2012: 57)

Extended case analysis uses a variety of ethnographic methods. This analytic approach provided me with the means to study my data and then interpret what I experienced and observed on the border and how those experiences aided in answering my research questions. I also consulted historical materials, other open source data, museums, and literature. This was either to further understand what was told to me by the locals or to understand whether the way they framed their narratives was a form of protest against the central government or outside forces or to assert their own local political legitimacy.

In my analysis and research, I am guided by the principle that I am not separate from my research subjects and they are not separate from each other. "'Objects' of study do not exist out there, in an 'objective reality,' ready to be 'discovered'; rather, they are co-constituted by the two (or more) participants in a research interaction" (Aronoff and Kubik, 2012: 26). We are all mutually interacting, reacting, and acting, which all combine together to co-constitute the context and data I am gathering from the field.[35]

The way different actors formulate, transmit, or define the group they belong to and their identities is more important than any "true" definition of what that identity might or might not be. Instead it is how and why their identity(ies) are talked about and asserted or contested. My fieldwork and resultant analysis focuses on various forms of identity production in a challenging location.

I aim to uncover hidden mechanisms of identity production and the ways in which various networks of cooperation contest, produce, and reproduce identity. Moreover, I follow in the footsteps of those who believe that the line between signifier and signified is blurred. As Kubik says:

> If we agree with an (anti-naturalist) assumption that the signifying process through which people build models of the world, has political relevance, then the study of how such models are constructed, transmitted, maintained, and received becomes of interest to us. The study of such issues is inconceivable without interpretation.
>
> (Kubik, 2009: 11)

Hence it is referred to as an interpretive methodology. Therefore, after I returned to the field and finalized the conceptual framework and research design, I used an interpretive methodology for the analysis. Schwartz-Shea and Yanow refer to the three components of an interpretive research design as "fieldwork, deskwork, and textwork" (2012: 7).

Allowing key concepts to emerge from the fieldwork is also integral to interpretive research.[36] As opposed to having defined my concepts before my fieldwork, I formulated and reformulated them during each trip to Badakhshan and afterwards during my deskwork. Peregrine Schwartz-Shea and Dvora Yanow say that:

> Concepts [emerging] from the field in a bottom-up fashion—concept development, rather than a priori concept formation [which] clearly demarcates interpretive from positivist research designs. [And that] at a more philosophical level, this discussion points to the interrelationships among "facts," "concepts," and "theories." Whereas "theory" is often understood as conjectural, 'fact' is taken to have the opposite meaning—as

certain, real, truthful, proven. But "facts" can be understood as crystallized concepts—areas of lived experience that have produced widespread intersubjective agreement such that only a historical [or ethnographic] excavation can reveal their constructedness.

(Schwartz-Shea and Yanow, 2012: 39–40)

This type of excavation was the goal in my fieldwork, but due to time and resource limitations, I dedicated only five years. Given the complexity of the topic, it deserved many more years. The point here is that in order to study a complex issue in an area that is difficult to gain access to, it takes time spent living in the area and close observation through participation.

Ed Schatz (2004) says that in order to study the "mechanisms by which identities are produced" one must observe them in the field since most of them are performed in situations that require close observations.[37] In Badakhshan this is particularly true in that some aspects of the local self-identified ethnic identity are hidden and even against the law and dangerous for the locals to admit or show. These include some civil society groups, local neighborhood organizations and groups, and locally elected leaders.[38] By observing all of these groups, living with the people participating in them, and engaging in their lives, I was able to develop a picture of how increasing border infrastructure and security impacts people's lives. Moreover, the importance of local leaders to the stability of the border emerged as a key issue during my time in the field.

When I made my first trip to the Tajikistan in 2009, my initial fieldwork revealed certain critical aspects of how development of the border was impacting border and state stability. Early in this first round of fieldwork I decided to study the border between Tajikistan and Afghanistan and in particular, in Badakhshan. Three main factors compelled me to study the borderlands in this remote mountainous region. (1) Due to the military interventions in Afghanistan and the tribal areas of Pakistan, hundreds of millions of dollars poured (and continue to be invested) into border development between Afghanistan and Tajikistan. (2) In Afghan and Tajik Badakhshan, the border cuts through an area that had common religious and self-identified ethnic and sub-ethnic groups, which differ from the ethnic and religious groups of the central authorities of the state on both sides of the border. (3) These particularities were similar to the Tribal Areas on the border of Afghanistan and Pakistan. The difference being that the Af/Pak border was more deeply entrenched in violent conflicts, is largely inaccessible to outsiders (due to government control) and is too dangerous to conduct fieldwork in. The border between Afghanistan and Tajikistan was calm enough for fieldwork. Therefore, I picked my locality based on issues of access and safety as well as on the central idea that this was an important border that cut through a group that spanned a border but which had little power at the state level on both sides of that border.

My preliminary research on the topic of border security and cooperation made it clear that there was a paucity of reliable data. This made it difficult for me to gather statistical data and/or other forms of available data about cross-border activity either before or during the subsequent trips to the field. Even gathering data through surveys or structured interviews proved unreliable (more on this later). Given the lack of available data, I went to the field unsure whether my first question—*What happens to legal and illegal cross-border cooperation when border security increases?*—would be answerable. In the end, in order to understand the impact of increasing border security on the stability of the border and the state, I had to go and see for myself what was going on at the border.[39]

Each of my cases involves the borderlands in Badakhshan and explores to what degree the particular case answers my questions and supports my hypotheses. I provide descriptive vignettes as emblematic of what I observed. Then, I discuss how it is relevant to my questions. In order to develop my case-studies, the ethnographic methods I employ are three-fold. I use ethnography for my "data-collection, modeling of social reality, and genre of writing" (Aronoff and Kubik, 2012: 28). These methods support an interpretive methodological approach. For the data collection I primarily used the ethnographic method of participant-observation although I supplemented with unstructured interviewing and focus discussion groups (FDGs).

Using these methods while I was in the field meant that I ended up gathering a myriad of data from living and working in and around the border on and off from 2009–2014.

Fieldwork

As a means for data collection, I chose primarily participant-observation, because it allowed me to stay close to the empirical material and the subject. The research for my dissertation took place in Tajikistan and Afghanistan. In Tajikistan, the fieldwork focused on the cities of Dushanbe, Khorog, Ishkashim, and Murghab. Dushanbe is the capital city of Tajikistan, and it is where both the government as well as the majority of the international organizations are located. Khorog, Ishkashim, and Murghab are located along the borders and in the autonomous region of Gorno-Badakhshan. Khorog is the capital of the province of Gorno-Badakhshan. In Afghanistan, the fieldwork was conducted in three districts of Badakhshan, Afghanistan—Shughnan, Ishkashim, and the upper, middle, and lower Wakhan Corridor. I also visited Faizabad and Kabul. Faizabad is the capital of Badakhshan province in Afghanistan, and Kabul is the capital of the country. I spent as much of my time on the border of Badakhshan as possible.

The original goal of the fieldwork conducted in Badakhshan was to understand how increasing border controls in the borderlands of Badakhshan

(Tajikistan/Afghanistan) impacted cross-border cooperation. As I spent time in the field, I came to understand that how I answered that question involved understanding the way ethnic identity was asserted within the formal and informal institutions. I spent time participating and observing both inter-governmental organizations (IGOs) and non-governmental organizations (NGOs) operating at the border. This included the United Nations Development Programme (UNDP), European Union (EU), the Organization for Security and Cooperation in Europe (OSCE), and the Aga Khan Foundation (AKF), the Aga Khan Development Network (AKDN), the Aga Health Services Program (AKHS), the Mountain Societies Development Support Program (MSDSP), and Khorog State English Preparatory Program (KEPP). The fieldwork included participation in customs and border guard training with the OSCE, Tajik and Afghan border guard training with International Organization for Migration (IOM). For UNDP I assessed the EU Border Management Program in Badakhshan, Afghanistan (EUBOMBAF). I also assessed AKF's Drug Demand Reduction Program (DDRP) in three districts in Badakhshan, Afghanistan. The research from this assessment is only used as residual knowledge as I already had done research in this area for two years before I was hired by AKF.[40]

I also spent time in the villages doing ethnographic fieldwork in addition to interviewing throughout the time in the field. Being involved with all of these NGOs and IGOs helped me to gain access to the border as an institution and into sensitive locations I would not have been able to if I had been alone during the entirety of my fieldwork. Additionally, many of these institutions provided some logistical and financial support for my independent fieldwork.

Over the course of my research, I lived in and around the area on both sides of the border on and off for 24 months over the course of five years. This part of the fieldwork based on participant-observation was by far the most valuable in that it allowed me to live in the community and observe the daily lives of those living there. The rest of the book analyzes this fieldwork in the context of local leadership, identity, and the border institutions and provides a brief historiography of the formation of the borders in Badakhshan and an overview of some of the key foundational myths.

Notes

1 My concepts were borne out of my fieldwork, as is the case with interpretive methodologies. That being said, I agree that the ensuing extended case-analysis, derived from my ethnographic fieldwork, would be inefficient without first developing my conceptual framework. Chandra (2012) says that one might be able to do research without first defining the concepts, but it would be much less efficient. I disagree as explained above. For detailed discussions on concept-formation, see: Chandra (2012); Goertz (2005); Sartori (1970). Goertz's pioneering examination of the layers within a proper conceptualization of a research project (which builds on Sartori's earlier ground-breaking scholarship) provided the clearest foundation on which I could build my own concept-formation. As I defined my concepts I kept

Goertz's explanation of the levels of abstraction, along with my Adviser, Jan Kubik's constant reminders about the importance of clearly defined concepts, constantly in the front of my mind.

2 See UNDP, AKDN, OSCE, IOM, US Customs Agency, EU border management program, *et al.*

3 Joel Migdal (2004) says that borderlands are rarely clear and rather, the actual territorial demarcation embodies accepted norms of practice and symbolic delineation as opposed to an official, delimited physical boundary.

4 Benedict Anderson's influential treatise, *Imagined Communities* (Anderson, 1983) while primarily a study of nationalism, bears some importance for my project in that, without some sort of buy-in, or accepted understanding of a coherent semblance of a group, asserting institutional rules, laws, and even, state boundaries of the state, is at best, difficult, at worst, impossible. Specifically, according to Anderson, nations gain legitimacy through imagined or socially constructed ideas of the state or a collective national imagination of what constitutes belonging to that nation. According to Anderson, the nation "is an imagined political community—as imagined as both limited and sovereign" as opposed to the physical and delimited boundaries demarcated on the land or in a map. Anderson goes on to say, "communities are to be distinguished, not by their falsity/genuineness, but by the style in which they are imagined." Anderson argues that Gellner takes this idea too far in that he asserts that nations are not only imagined but the product of "'falsity' and 'fabrication' rather than [sic] 'imagining' and 'creation'" (1983: 6).

5 According to Peter Andreas (2000), "Criminalizing activities for which high market demand exists inflates their profitability and encourages new market entrants ... Indeed, the illicit global economy is defined by and depends on the state exercising meta-political authority to criminalize without the full capacity to effectively enforce its criminal laws."

6 "This variation in state-building strategies, consequently, should explain the variation in how states perceive their borders and intervene in them" (Gavrilis, 2008: 6).

7 Gavrilis (2008: 6) supports this assertion.

8 Peter Andreas says that borders are essentially political stages and the symbolic assertion of their importance trumps the actual border itself. Many borders, as they exist geographically, are uncontrollable and sometimes attempts at control actually cause negative elements to increase cooperation and thereby decrease state stability (Andreas, 2000; see also Andreas and Nadelmann, 2006; Andreas and Wallman, 2009).

9 Midgal also says that the seeking of local power both at the border or boundaries of a state at the central authority by "strongmen" causes and increases the fragmentation of the state (1988: 256–7). The question is—what happens when a strongman is the head of the state and other strongmen who consider themselves as belonging to a different ethnic and religious group, are trying to control their territory?

10 Andreas explains that "The dynamics of the illicit global economy provide a new and powerful, if rather unconventional, lens through which to examine core issues of concern to international relations scholars: the changing nature of states and the sources of cooperation and conflict between and among states and non-state actors" (Andreas, 1999: 17).

11 The types and nature of various illicit trade networks provide another puzzle. There exist pragmatic and ideological networks in the forms of criminals and terrorists. Usually, criminal networks do not like partnering with terrorist networks. As Moises Naim (2006) puts it, "Terrorists are driven by God; illicit traders are driven by greed." Many of the illicit (criminal) traders shy away from the potential complications the terrorists might bring to their businesses as well as the fact that

they often have diverging goals. This appears not to be the case in Northern Afghanistan where pragmatism often trumps ideology when it comes to illicit trade. Uzbek traders partner with Tajiks who partner with Ismailis who partner with others. These diverse groups of traders not only control much of the illicit trade, they also have a hand in the legal trade. Increased instability in the area, given the common interest of the monetary rewards from the drug, gemstone, endangered animals, and antiquities trafficking, is more likely if the local leaders and organizations begin to feel they are being locked out of their own illicit businesses.

12 Economic inequality between bordering states also has been found to cause border instability. In a cross-sectional statistical analysis, David Carter and Paul Poast (2015) used the "erection of a barrier" as their key indicator of border instability. They focused on the physical aspect of the border as opposed to the symbolic. In their research they found that barriers were constructed most often along borders of states with economic inequality. Andreas (2000, 2009) points out that at the border of Mexico and California, a strong and a weak state, strengthening measures have caused even more instability.

13 The question that deserves further research is whether or not total buy-in to the state is necessary. Perhaps more of a loosely bound group of principalities or a decentralized partnership system would be more effective over the long-term, both for the local civil society and the overall project of state stability.

14 I will define what I mean by clan in Chapter 6.

15 In the next section I define ethnic identity and assert that sub-ethnic groups and clans belong within this concept.

16 North noted that informal institutions "defy, for the most part, neat specification, and it is extremely difficult to develop unambiguous tests of their significance, they are important ... formal rules in even the most developed economy, make up a small (although very important) part of the sum of constraints that shape choices; a moment's reflection should suggest to us the pervasiveness of informal constraints" (1990: 36–7). (See also Hughes and Sasse, 2002: 29; Collins, 2004; Schatz, 2004; Giustozzi, 2009, 2011; Braithwaite, 2011).

17 Based on interviews with border guards and Customs agents from 2010–2011 and observed while participating in workshops with OSCE and IOM.

18 Extensive scholarship exists on institutions and organizations not only in comparative politics but also in international relations, sociology, anthropology, economics, and other fields. This section highlights key threads in the literature relevant to my study.

19 I also build on Douglas North's definition. North says that institutions are "any form of constraint on human action" (Hughes and Gwendolyn, 2002: 25; North, 1990: 4).

20 North (1990: 4); Helmke and Levitsky (2004: 726); see also Kubik (1994); Collins (2004); Luong (2008). Additionally, Helmke and Levitsky suggest this conception of informal institutions: "We employ a fourth approach. We define informal institutions as *socially shared rules, usually unwritten, that are created, communicated, and enforced outside of officially sanctioned channels*" (2004: 56). By contrast, *formal* institutions are rules and procedures that are created, communicated, and enforced through channels widely accepted as official. This includes state institutions (courts, legislatures, bureaucracies) and state-enforced rules (constitutions, laws, regulations), but also what Robert C. Ellickson calls 'organization rules,' the rules that govern organizations such as corporations, political parties, and interest groups. "We treat informal institutions and norms synonymously. However, norms have been defined in a variety of ways, and some conceptualizations do not include external enforcement" (Helmke and Levitsky, 2004: 726).

21 This term is used by Collins (2004) to describe clans that are linked together to form larger networks. She calls these groups "umbrella clans."

22 For example—Shughni to Wakhi to Ishkashem both encompass territorial districts on each side of the border as well as spanning the border. The networks are the same. Additionally, Sunni/Ismaili networks exist in the same way—on each side of the border but, more so, spanning the border.

23 This concept builds on Charles Tilly's (2005a: 41) formative work on "trust networks." As he explains, "trust networks [are] strong ties within which people set valued, consequential, long-term resources and enterprises at risk to the malfeasance, mistakes, and failures of other."

24 Moises Naim (2006: 2) refers to this as the "gray market".

25 Swat Valley had been off-limits under the British Protectorate from 1947–1954, and before this period as far back as the early 1800s when the British were using it as a buffer zone. (Tomsen, 2011). It was 1954 and Barth was the first person allowed into the area to conduct research.

26 Barth defined ethnic-group as having "a membership which identifies itself, and is identified by others, as constituting a category distinguishable from other categories of the same order" (1969: 10–11).

27 Some people contend that "Barth pioneered what later became known as 'constructivism': the claim that ethnicity is the product of a social process rather than a cultural given, made and remade rather than taken for granted, chosen depending on circumstances rather than ascribed through birth" (Wimmer, 2008: 971). See also: Green (2005); Bjorn (2005); Yeros (1999).

28 Barth (1969: 10) also added, that in order, "To observe these processes we shift the focus of the investigation from internal constitution and history of separate groups to ethnic boundaries and boundary maintenance."

29 In an earlier work Barth (1969: 12) referred to this as "frameworks of organization". He defines this type of social organization as segmented identity. Specifically, he says that "Pathans (Pashtuns, Pakhtuns, Afghans) constitute a large, highly self-aware ethnic group inhabiting adjoining areas of Afghanistan and West Pakistan, generally organized in a segmentary, replicating social system without centralized institutions" (1969: 117).

30 Marsden and Hopkins, both noted scholars of FATA and Swat, explain that "naming has come to be central to the ways in which states have sought to map the Frontier...and that such processes reflect the power disparities between different actors; the power to name is indeed a considerable one" (2012: 9). They include in their analysis, linguistic differences, ethnic names, and pronunciations.

31 It was my experience, that in every household I entered and lived in on both sides of the border, the discussion of who belonged and who did not belong came up without prompting. Perhaps because I am an outsider and therefore this inspired certain discussions, but it was even the topic of many discussions I had with people who were from Badakhshan in London, the U.S., India, and Kyrgyzstan.

32 Chandra says, "All individuals have a 'repertoire' of nominal ethnic-identity categories. This consists of all the meaningful membership rules that can be fashioned from an individual's given set of descent-based attributes, with each rule corresponding to a nominal category. The ethnic identity an individual actually activates is chosen from this repertoire" (2012: 11). Additionally, "The existence of this baseline constraint on change in activated ethnic identities is the fundamental distinction between ethnic and non-ethnic identities, on average." (Chandra, 2012: 17). Although, as I show later in this book, I do not agree that the baseline constraint is descent, at least as it pertains to my research which includes ethno-religious identification, spatial identification, and ethno linguistic self-identification.

33 See also Barth (1971); Collins (2004); Schatz (2004); Adams (2009).

34 Kubik provides a solution for studying boundary maintenance and the mutability and immutability of identity although in his research he focuses on traditions as opposed to identity. I take his idea and translate it into a useful approach for studying identity boundary maintenance. Kubik refers to traditions as invented, saying that, "In general, I have come to share Hobsbawm and Ranger's view that all traditions and values are constantly 'invented.' [But], there exist perceptible differences of intensity, of degree or, perhaps even of kind, between various types of 'inventions and they are all worth noting'" (1994: 259). This idea of differences of intensity applies to boundary maintenance of both individual and group identity. This idea is similar to Chilton's (2004) discussion of the impact of language on how we shape reality. He says that while many things change depending on perception, there is also something to the effect of that a red chair is a red chair (even though there are many different types) and as much as we might rename it, it is still a chair. Some aspects of identity are simply what they are and other aspects are in the eye of the beholder. Identity is an intertwining of degrees of assertion of mutable aspects of identity and unconscious acceptance and daily practices defined by the immutable factors.

35 Constructivism has a long history in a number of fields and many of the underlying assumptions span a wide array of disciplines. "The ontology of constructivism is antinaturalist (the social world is different from the natural world); thus the methodology consistent with this position requires interpretation. Scholars who agree with an (antinaturalist) assumption that the signifying process through which people build models of the world, particularly of the social and political world, has political relevance, proceed to study how such models are constructed, transmitted, maintained, and received, and how this whole machinery of cultural construction influences, and is influenced by, political and economic transformations. While the utility of interpretivist approaches is taken for granted in anthropology, sociology, cultural studies, or feminism, it is far from obvious to many practitioners of political science. The reasons for this may be complex, but they seem to be rooted in the predominantly naturalistic tenor of the discipline" (Kubik, 2013: 54).

36 Schwartz-Shea and Yanow (2012).

37 See also Aronoff and Kubik (2012); Schatz (2009); Greenhouse, Mertz, and Warren (2002); Joseph, Mahler, and Auyero (2007).

38 I use elected loosely here. Most local leaders are chosen by the men in a neighborhood, street, or district through consensus during a gathering or several gatherings of men.

39 For any ethnographer, particularly one doing research in a sensitive or dangerous location, or both in my case, getting approval is challenging. Before I left for the second round of fieldwork, I had to submit my proposal to the Institutional Review Board (IRB) for approval. Due to the sensitive nature of my subject and challenging location, I knew it might be difficult. In the end, in order to get my research proposal approved by the IRB in 2010, due to the potential dangers to my research participants, it was agreed upon that both people and precise locations would remain anonymous. After getting approval from the IRB, I went to the field with two case studies in mind using extended case-analysis as my approach.

40 For the assessment I visited seven village clusters and within each village interviewed community members, local and regional leaders, government officials, and healthcare workers regarding the DDRP. I conducted 37 unstructured and semi-structured FDGs and 67 unstructured interviews of community, district, other leaders, villagers, and healthcare workers. While in the field, others came forward who were willing to be interviewed and were given the opportunity to share their experiences on an ad hoc basis. This was the same for their families and extended relatives.

3 Border development in Badakhshan

History is an essential starting point for understanding any place and the people who populate it. History, of course, is what one makes of it. Groups use history to assert identities and boundaries in the present (Barth, 1981; Schatz, 2004, 2009). Groups produce historical narratives about themselves, others, and in this way they influence identity (Marsden and Hopkins, 2012). Sometimes, the history as explained by those who lived it, whether "true" or not, is more important than what actually happened. The recounting of history—or historical memory—highlights the narratives people have chosen to let rise to the top of the local perceptions of the past, and what they have culled from collective memories as their past.

Table 3.1 Overview of provinces and districts

Countries	Afghanistan	Tajikistan	Languages—Afghan side	Languages—Tajik side
Province	Badakhshan	Gorno-Badakhshan	Pamiri	
Key districts in my research	Darvaz	Darwaz	Dari	Tajik
	Ishkashem	Iskhashim	Dari Ishkashemi	Tajik Reni
	Shughnan	Shughnan (Khorog is the capital city of this district)	Shughni	Shughni
	Rushan	Rushan	Rushani	Rushani
	Wakhan Corridor	Wakhan	Wakhi	Wakhi
	Zebok	Roshtqala/Shokhdara	Dari Zeboki	Shughni dialect

Note: Please see map provided in the Introduction.

This chapter is the result of countless conversations among my research subjects, analysis of scholarly materials, and my own interpretation of how the current political administration (formal and informal) came to Badakhshan. I have had ongoing discussions with several local historians for a number of years, and they made important contributions to this chapter.[1] Rather than seeking some kind of deep, historical "truth" from outside sources, I simply wanted to understand where some of the ideas about local identity might have originated. History, in the context I am using it, is not for telling a true or definitive history. It is presented as a guide for understanding how competing histories have been used to shape identities (Lustick, 1996). One well-known historian, who is also a mentor of mine, told me that historians will "bridle" at my "histories." So, in honor of him, I want to clearly state: this is not a history! It is an ethnography of historical sources—both oral and written.

The construction and reconstruction of history and identity is an ongoing war of legitimacy. The informal networks of cooperation, formal delimitation and demarcation agreements imposed by outsiders, and infrastructure as it developed over time define the continuity and transformation of local organizations and their associated leaders at this border. "Delimitation" refers to written agreements and "demarcation" refers to written agreements that also include decisions or actions to construct or somehow physically mark the territory. Borders constructed by outsiders only increase the perceived need to assert insider (local) identities in order to maintain and clarify what constituted local understandings of their own lands and organizations and to resist control by outsiders.

Soviet historians of Central Asia realized that:

> In order to provide historical legitimization to their new nations, it was not enough to project into the past the modern borders of their territories; since a nation was defined first of all in terms of ethnicity, it became necessary to provide the ethnic continuity of the titular nation.
>
> (Bregel, 1996: 15)

Other scholars from the time claimed that this form of nationalism was a victory for the complex feuds among ethnic groups, which had been going on for centuries.[2] A 1922 treaty by the British Foreign Office and a subsequent one by Stalin in 1924 designated the area as a free land. Both the British and the Soviets asserted that they were the arbiters of freedom in Badakhshan. A Soviet geographer said:

> This act has had no parallel in history, and has been made possible only in the land of the Soviets, where all nationalities have equal rights and where in perfect conformity with the great principles of the Soviet Government each people is allowed to determine its own destiny.
>
> (Kunitz, 1935: 165)

The various narratives are hardly free of political viewpoints. In fact, the residents and rulers alike used the kaleidoscope of stories spawned from a confluence of narratives to influence local dynamics and politics. Nor is there any way for me to be free from some biases, whether conscious or unconscious. Institutionalization, in the post-Soviet context, is a complex mix of past institutions, present conditions, and future goals related to the border. Thus, I offer the next sections with the caveat that I am providing no "real" history, just narratives upon narratives from which I draw and attempt to construct a picture, as imperfect as that may be. Groups inside and outside of the region use four competing narratives to assert or control identity on both sides of the border: (1) Pre-Islamic (pre-Colonial), (2) colonial, (3) Soviet, and (4) post-Communist.

Pre-colonial development of the borderlands of Badakhshan

Badakhshan and the Pamirs—as defined and recognized territories with administrative centers—predate the formation of the countries of Tajikistan and Afghanistan by many centuries. Khans, emirs, empires, statelets, and rivaling local groups all laid claim to the area long before the Russians or the British. Within the matrix of local boundary negotiations among local leaders, a complex array of local institutions developed. The formal and local border institutions also are older than the externally created states that they delineate. The boundaries formed by the ongoing agreements among these local leaders remain the underpinning of informal agreements today.

As early as 500BC, empires based near the southern border of what is now Iran referred to the people in the north as dangerous, wild nomads who must to be kept out. Documents from that time show that there was a ring of local leaders deployed along the border of the mountains, possibly to keep the nomadic groups from the mountainous areas, including Badakhshan, from entering the more "civilized" areas.[3] Artifacts, texts, poetry and historical analysis highlight that these perceptions including sources from Afghans (from the south), Tajiks, Soviets/Russians, British, Americans, Chinese, Indians/British Indians, Iranians/Persians, and Moghuls all held similar beliefs. The veracity of this statement is less relevant here than the fact that this narrative of "wild northerners" has been perpetuated over centuries.[4] Moreover, the importance of local leaders, how they gained and negotiated power, and how they dealt with rivals and disputes over territory—essentially local border disputes—are common debates throughout the literature.

Religion and religious identity throughout this period also played an important role in the development of both leadership and indigenous institutions in the region. Zoroastrianism and its kin—Mithraism and Mazdianism—were the primary religions in the region. Some of the literature and within local narratives, Mazdianism (and Mithraism) trace their origins to the region and preceded Zoroastrianism. Additionally, Zardusht, the founder of Zoroastrianism, came from the region of Badakhshan. Ancient Buddhist culture and religion, which came to the region through Buddhist missionaries during the early Kushanid Empire (late 300s AD) also absorbed Mazdianism and elements of Zoroastrianism.

The area began to convert to Islam in the seventh century AD. The influence of the Shi'a branch known as the Nizaris quickly spread through-out the area through the Fatimid Empire in the ninth century. In the tenth century, Nasiri Khusrow claimed much of the remaining Zoroastrian areas under the Ismaili-Shi'a religion. Locally this branch of Shi'a Ismailism was called Panj-Tani (five bodies) (Hunsberger, 2000; DeWeese, 2001; Gross, 2013). The latter name refers to the "five bodies" of the Prophet Muhammad's family.[5] Additionally, Panj-Tani acknowledges the spiritual connection to nature, an important aspect of Zoroastrianism and Buddhism. This clearly is shown through the Pamiri houses, which are decorated with the four symbols of nature (fire, wind, earth, and air) as well as the five members of the prophet's family. The conceptualization of nature, as an integral part of their spiritual traditions and practices, is a commonly offered narrative in regular conversation (Gross, 2013).[6]

During the pre-Islamic and Islamic period (Post-Kushanid to c. 500–800 AD), *dehqans*, meaning village leaders (Persian origin: دهقان), ruled the lands delineated through agreements with other *dehqans* (Bartold, 1918: 41). Later, mirs and khans (Turkic origin for a leader of a territory) delineated their emirates and khanates in much the same way.[7] However, all had vague segments of their borders where conflicts often occurred. Moreover, when khans wanted to expand, they did so by absorbing neighboring khanates, often beginning in the borderlands usually through force or marriage.[8] As a khan absorbed more and more land, eventually he would control enough for his realm to be considered a larger administrative unit—the top level being an empire of some form.[9]

Local leaders mediated all issues related to trade and security. Their leadership styles were influenced by the local terrain (mountains, plains, water/no water), religious practices, lifestyle (nomadic or sedentary), and economics (rural/bazaar/city centers). Also, since the region had both set-tled communities and nomads, separate currencies were necessary for trade. In the thirteenth century, for example, stamped coins began to be made in two metals. Brass coins were used within the boundaries of a khanate or emirate, and the silver ones for trans-boundary trade (Bartold, 1918: 58). Moreover, territorial agreements also functioned in multiple ways. They had to accommodate settled groups in urban and rural areas and nomads moving from north to south and west to east. Later, during the Soviet period, a concerted effort was made to erase these well-developed local institutions, organizations, and systems of governance and their associated leaders.

Part of contemporary Afghan Badakhshan had a highly structured society composed of a multilevel nobility. One level was comprised of the shahs, local leaders of Persian origin (in the local language of Shughni shah is pronounced *khah*). Second, were the Shahs (which differ from the khahs/shahs) who were the top religious caste within the Ismaili religion. They were connected with the Ismaili Imam, and religious legitimacy gave them more power than the khahs. If there were any conflicts the khahs would consult the religious Shahs. Third were the Syeds, who claimed to be the progeny of the Prophet Muhammad and Hazrat Ali. The Syeds also were a religious caste but had highly institutionalized leadership structures. Under the Syeds were the *pirs* (elders or wise ones) and under them the *khalifes* (local religions leaders). The *mirs* and *akobirs* were courtesans and had equal status. *Mirs* were governors, representatives of the kings (Haqnazarov, 1998; Maysky, 1935; Monogarova, 1972). Some scholars refer to them as the military aristocracy. *Akobirs* accompanied the *khahs* and enforced security when the king was in trouble. They also were responsible for preventing invasions. Many folk tales recount their missions, and they are well documented within the scholarly literature.

The *beks* occupied the next level in the leadership hierarchy. They were often wealthy individuals and/or people with both wealth and influence through strong clan networks. They paid taxes to the khah and dues to the Imam. This money created revenue for the local treasuries and helped to form a basis of institutional legitimacy for the local administrations. (Maysky, 1935; Monogarova, 1972). Lastly, at the bottom of the social pyramid, came the *faqir*. They were a combination of citizens, peasants, and the poor. All of these groups mentioned above formed the basis for the local statelets in the Pamiri governments/administrations. The *faqir* essentially were landless peasants who rented agricultural and grazing lands from the local Beks/landowners. In some cases, they became servants or slaves (*nuwkar*)[10] of the local leaders/beks. Armed with whips, *faqirs* served other leaders within the hierarchy, functioning as security forces, governmental bureaucrats, and tax collectors. According to a number of local historians, and contrary to more popular histories, there was not a class of *fedayi* (martyrs) or mercenaries (similar to Samurais of Japan).[11] The *Siapusht* (black robes) were Zoroastrians, not assassins, as commonly thought. During the early Islamic period they were referred to as "unbelievers" (*kafirs*) because they did not convert to Islam. This local hierarchical structure survived until the Soviet era (Interview with Soultan Khojaniyozov in 2015).

Clans, political parties, religious and language groups, territorial affiliations, and local cultural and social organizations all make up the civil society along the border. Numerous border experts, local scholars, and elders assert that formal institutions and outside systems of governance, including proxy-leaders and partnerships, never fully replaced the traditional local systems of governance and their associated leaders.[12] Living under constant oppression and/or outside interference, the clans, tribes, and other local informal governance structures have been forced to operate in hidden forms, disguised as religious and civil society organizations.

Colonial period

The Russians and Chinese began to actively colonize the region as early as the 1600s and the British since the early 1700s. They all cultivated allies and stoked divisions causing various bloody conflicts (Curzon, 1896).

During the so-called Great Game and the colonial conquests in the nineteenth century, potential colonizers often identified the most powerful local leaders—amirs, khans, shahs—and forced them to accept arms and money and to assist them in their colonial projects or be attacked. Accepting the arms and money also forced these local leaders to relinquish their autonomy. The local populations living under the local leaders' spheres of influence had little input in the decision-making process and the ongoing strategic military partnerships with various outsiders.[13]

By the 1800s the area had consolidated into a mixture of nomadic groups and settled villages with power dispersed throughout the region. Loosely affiliated, self-identified ethnic groups intermixed, including the Tajiks, Uzbeks, Kyrgyz (all with many groups and sub-groups). These groups, which later became key designations for the Soviet Central Asian countries, had hundreds of other ethnic groups and sub-ethnic groups.[14]

The British and Russians used their proxy states to extend their spheres of influence in the area. The British staked their claim on the Amir of Afghanistan and provided him with military and political support as diplomatic leverage in the demarcation of borders, while the Russians acted on behalf of the Amir of Bokhara. According to scholars in Khorog and numerous scholarly materials, the Amir (Islamic leader) of Afghanistan, Aburahmon Khan, controlled the northern border of what is now Afghanistan, including part of Darwaz now referred to as Roshan, (his great grandfather originating from Samarqand). However, the Amir of Bokhara had jurisdiction over Darwaz and the area to the West of Darwaz, and the Khan of Kokand controlled territories to the East of what is now called Murghab District in Gorno-Badakhshan (populated by primarily Kyrgyz tribes and Sunnis). The Amirs of Afghanistan and Bokhara considered the statelets along the periphery of their territories as remote areas inhabited by nomads and kafirs (unbelievers); the neighboring statelets of Shughnan *et al.* were even more unknown and undefined.

Locally, the leaders of the statelets of Shughnan, Wakhan, and Goron, did not consider themselves as belonging to Badakhshan.[15] The harsh terrain limited outside incursions, allowing the khahs and shahs (religious leaders) to exercise authority in most matters (although they did fight intense battles amongst themselves and neighboring emirates/khanates at times).[16] Moreover, the people had developed in distinct sections—often around a charismatic Shah, khah, mir, pir, or clan. Each principality had its own practices, customs, local laws, and economic systems. Local institutions were loosely held arrangements among the clans, emirates, khanates, and elites (Fredholm, 2014; Barry, 2010).[17] The territories encompassing Shughnan, the Wakhan, and Goron had more structured, and some might say, more developed local governance systems and institutions. In these statelets the indigenous political systems were largely accepted as legitimate systems of governance and had become fairly formalized and were divided into at least seven ethno-linguistic groupings. These groups organized physical space, cultural norms, security, and pooled economic resources.

The languages included Shughni, Sanglechi, Ishkashimi Reni, Zeboki,[18] Munji (now mostly in Chitral, Pakistan), Wakhi (which subdivides into three dialects—upper, mid, and lower Wakhi), Yazgholami, Roshani, Vanji, Darwazi, Khowari, and Balti. Most are still spoken today.[19] Moreover, there were related groups within what is now China's Xinjiang province. There is an Ismaili subdivision within Sare Kul that belongs to the same ethno-linguistic groups as the rest of the Pamiris in Tajikistan and Afghanistan.[20] There are multiple competing histories about how and why these many groups formed in the ways they did. I discuss this a little more in my chapter on foundational myths. Linguistic, places of origin, and ethnic affiliations often are used interchangeably.[21]

By the mid-nineteenth century, the Emir of Afghanistan had consolidated power and controlled much of what is today's Afghanistan. In an attempt to integrate the many warring ethnic groups and tribes, he moved part of the Pashtun Ghilzais to various districts in the North: Qunduz, Jalalabad, Parwan, Loghar, (the same areas that are the most unstable today). He also divided land evenly among families in Afghanistan.[22]

In 1873 the Bokharan Emirate formally became a Russian protectorate, with St. Petersburg controlling local trade.[23] A decade before this, the Emir of Bokhara became a vassal of the Russian state but the mullahs, merchants, and other local leaders organized against him. They formed the Bokharan War (or Revolutionary) Party, forcing the Emir to temporarily flee the area. After his return in 1867 and reconciliation with the Bokharans, the Emir refused to work with the Russians.[24] Consequently, Tsar Alexander II dispatched soldiers who seized most of the land surrounding Bokhara in 1868. Soon thereafter, the British and the Russians drafted a demarcation agreement ceding certain parts of Badakhshan (which was loosely under the Bokharan Emirate but had eluded control) to the Afghans and British and other portions to the Russians and Turkestanis. While formalizing the border between what was Turkestan and Afghanistan, the Russians and the British declined to delimit the eastern areas, leaving the statelets of Wakhan, Shughnan, Darwaz, and Ishkashim vague and an unofficial buffer zone.

During this period, the statelets surrounding Shughnan were autonomous territories administered according to fluid unwritten agreements between the local leaders. Discussions of this area referred to the "Pamiri question" due to the vagueness of the territorial divisions. Some say the Russians and the British viewed the area as sacred, as a sort of cradle of the human race. As one local put it, they did not want to "mar the grave of our ancestors with blood," so they allowed the area to remain autonomous to avoid a bloody conflict over who controlled what.[25] Additionally, while many of the northern areas of what became Afghanistan were subsumed into the Pashtun South during the Durrani period in the 1800s, Shughnan area escaped control by the Pashtun-controlled Afghan South (Noelle-Karimi, 1997: 271; see also Barry, 2010; Dalrymple, 2013).

In 1891 the Russians arrested Lieutenant-Colonel Francis Young-husband, a British intelligence officer, in the Wakhan Corridor. This created a rift in the détente between the British and Russians because the British officer was in the official Russian sphere of influence (Habberton, 1937). It also provided the impetus for clear delimitation and demarcation of the entire region.[26] The Russians sought to control Southern and South-eastern Tajikistan, part of which was still part of the so-called buffer zone.

Shortly thereafter, Russia formally annexed Bokhara in 1895, calling the area Eastern Bokhara and officially designated it as part of their territory. They also brought the Bokhari military units with them to the statelets of the Shughnan area to justify Bokhari jurisdiction over the area to the British. They created garrisons of both Russians and Bokharis in Shughnan, wMurghab, Darwaz, and the Wakhan. The Bokharis were Sunni Muslim Uzbeks who had authority over the Shi'a Ismailis and ethnic Pamiri groups, and the locals regarded them as invaders. Heavily armed by the Russians, the Bokharis out-powered and oppressed the local communities, including religious and cultural oppression and sexual exploitation of the local population. The locals rebelled, riots ensued, and the Russians replaced the Bokharan troops with Russian and Cossack soldiers (Interview with Soultan Khoja-niyozov in 2015) in order to diffuse the clashes between the Bokharans and Pamiris.

Eventually, as a result of the border delimitation and demarcation, the local statelets of the Shughnan area were subsumed and split by the Russians and British. The Russians formally annexed their side of the Pamirs (what they had termed Eastern Bokhara). This ended the so-called Pamiri question, meaning the formal delimitation of the border and the end of the informal buffer zone. The Russians then began swiftly consolidating territories, which would become part of the Union of Soviet Socialist Republics (USSR).

The newly devised border divided the people of Badakhshan between the Russian empire and Afghanistan despite their long history together and common identity. What had been functioning statelets, structured around centralized rule within each state, and agreements between statelets about borders and local resources, became Soviet district units. In the local language the principalities that were formed during this period were called Mulk (meaning—kingship, domain, or dominion) (Habberton, 1937: 58–67). The Soviet ethnographers magnified the local ethnic and cultural differences down to the village level in order to divide, and ultimately weaken, the local statelets. The result of the divisions was an incoherent tangle of new geographic and administrative divisions for the local citizens.

Soviet period along the borderlands in Badakhshan

Soviet period in Tajik Gorno-Badakhshan Autonomous Oblast

The Soviet regime redrew the map of Central Asia according to ethnic majorities, a process that involved the meticulous work of Soviet ethnographers. Researchers went out among the people, counting and categorizing each person. They separated them into Tajiks, Uzbeks, Kazakhs, Kyrgyz, and Turkmen and divided the land according to which ethnic group had the largest number of inhabitants in that area. They named the new administrative units in this same way, so that the land with the most "Tajiks" became Tajikistan (Tajik-land); the area with the largest number of Uzbeks became Uzbekistan, and so on (Bregel, 1996; Bergne, 2007). Additionally, they rewrote histories and foundational myths for each of the newly created Central Asian republics, basing them on "autochthonous" and ethnically based narratives (Bregel, 1996: 8).

In 1921 the USSR officially created Turkestan as an Autonomous Soviet Socialist Republic (ASSR); Tajikistan was a component of Turkestan. The Bokharan Revolutionary Movement, which had rallied early on with the Soviets against the Tsarist Russians and the Bokharan Amir, became the center of power (Togan, 2011). Bokhara had a diverse population of many ethnic groups including Uzbeks, Tajiks, Pamiris (whom the Soviets referred to as "Mountain Tajiks"), Sunni Muslims, Jews, and Hindus (Monogarova, 1972).

Next, Moscow developed plans to further partition the region into Soviet Socialist Republics (SSRs) based on majority ethnic affiliations (Bergne, 2007). The Uzbek SSR was created in 1924, with Tajikistan an ASSR of the new Uzbekistan until it was formally elevated to union-republic status in 1926. The Pamiri communities, which had virtually no ethnic Tajiks, were designated an autonomous province of Tajikistan (Gorno-Badakhshan Autonomous Oblast—GBAO).

Although the Soviet regime stopped referring to the region as Turkestan in 1924, the word continued to be used in publications related to the region as late as the mid-1960s including maps, books, and ethnographies (albeit by British researchers). In this sense, the area, even with the incoherent borders cut through it, was still being studied by the majority of Western academics in ways that recognized the informal and clan-based groupings and power structures that had been there and, in various ways continued to exist in the region, long after the USSR divided Turkestan and stopped referring to the area as such.

Russian ethnographers asserted that the Tajiks were closely linked to the Persians and the Uzbeks to the Moguls (or Turks). In reality, these groups were intermixed throughout the region as a result of the intermingling of nomadic and sedentary populations over many centuries (Golden, 2011; Atkin, 1992; Roy, 1992). Moreover, while clan conflicts, resource competition, and poverty existed, conflicts among the nomadic people, the villagers, and other groups occurred for reasons other than simply being Uzbek or Tajik (Bregel, 1996: 4–8). Ethnicity was more "fictive" or the product of family assertions than actual lineage or blood line.[27]

One narrative that I often heard in the field asserted that the Soviets deliberately cut Tajikistan off from its intellectual centers, Samarqand and Bokhara. As a result, it has been difficult for Tajikistan to realize its full potential as a nation. Some locals (either in jest or seriously) suggested that these two important cities should be reassigned from Uzbekistan to Tajikistan. Moreover, they pointed out that the majority of residents in these two cities speak Tajik, not Uzbek, and that this separation of the people from their intellectual centers has created lasting strife throughout Central Asia.[28]

The Soviets did the same on a smaller level in Shughnan and the Wakhan, splitting them into administrative units based on ethnic group names. Many of the administrative designations, such as Roshan, Vanj, and Ishkashem, are still being used today. In Ishkashem, which was known as Goron prior to Soviet rule, the Soviets concentrated power within the Persian-speaking population and marginalized the Wakhi-speaking people who had been the dominant group in that area. Moscow installed the local administration in Ishkashem, which was home to the minority group.[29]

During discussions about the region a local scholar told me:

> When the Soviets came into power, they stripped these leaders of their status. They designated the hierarchy naming different leaders in terms of their ideology in order to stratify the society. The labels were called *kulak* [fist] in Russian and *mushtzur* in Tajik. This translates, literally, to "power of the fist" or "people who used fist." The Russian word also translates roughly as meaning someone who uses force for his own enrichment and as a danger to Soviets and therefore the *kulaks* were stripped of their power and belongings. The Soviets said they "neutralized" them or in Tajik—*Asudahal* (quieted them) and Russian—*sredniak* (rendered harmless to the Soviet authorities). The *batrak* (meaning poor or destitute or in Tajik—*faqir*) became the allies of the Soviets. My mother spoke about this—saying that my uncle was made *Asudahal*. They didn't leave people anything at all. They even took their grievances by appropriating the terms, the very words we used. There was no room for grievances or mourning our losses. The Soviets were not even mean to us, they just took everything and took control. They confiscated all of our land, animals, and other belongings.
>
> Prior to the Soviet period, the Russian Tsars actually collaborated with the local leaders—pirs, khahs, shahs, etc., in order to spread their influence and maintain control over the region. The Soviet strategy had a

different ideology. They wanted to control the area by dethroning the leaders and replacing them with the new Soviet intelligentsia. These new leaders were trained and schooled by the Russian garrisons. Most of the people trained by the Russians were orphans and marginalized groups. *Nuwkor* now is used in the pejorative about people who serve and are enslaved by others. They were called *Nuwkor* by other people because they served the rich. It is still used today—as in—someone might say—I'm not your slave and they will say—I'm not your *nuwkor*.

Another local scholar told me that *"kulak"* is a:

Derisive name for a peasant well enough off to lend money at high interest or just to be relatively well off. Applied as a class category by the Soviet regime during collectivization to all opponents of collectivization, which was accompanied by 'liquidation of the *kulaks* as a class'—murder or deportation of anyone the collectivizers didn't like or whose possessions they coveted.

This issue has been well-researched, most prominently by Lynne Viola (2000, 2007) in her work on Soviet farm collectivization and "de-kulakization," particularly during the time of Stalin.

In Gorno-Badakhshan, it ended the local forms of governance and created tensions among local groups that are still being played out today. For example, the district of Roshtqala (locally known as Shokhdara) was created by chopping up the statelet of Shughnan. According to a local historian:

The Soviets manipulated identity using it for elections and other political purposes. The Soviets divided the whole of Shughnan because they didn't want any trace of pre-Soviet identity. It was also used for administrative rule. The locals would be more likely to compete for access to the central authorities. This would allow them to push out resistance/traditional Shughni rulers and authorities (such as *pirs*). This was the case with the Roshanis making them the Soviet elite and using them to push out the traditional leaders. The same with the Wakhan—moving central administration to Ishkashim so that the traditional Wakhi leaders and elite would be delegitimized and neutralized.

(Interview, February, 2015)[30]

Soviet leaders also adhered to a strict ideology that assumed Soviet citizens had no sub-ethnic, religious, or cultural attachments. The goal was to turn all of the Central Asians into citizens of the Soviet Union with a carefully planned strategy of homogenized identity, the same strategy used for Slavs, Balts, and Caucasians as well. Moscow would divide the people up into groups based on ethnicity but detach these groups from their intellectual centers and create borders that were neither logical nor coherent in terms of the long-standing local social frameworks.[31]

According to Yuri Bregel (1996), the project of the Soviets to re-make the history and myths of origin and identity, particularly ethnic, was a purposeful and planned method of nation-building. The goal was to build a nation by asserting how certain groups belonged together due to their history and ethnic origin.[32] The indigenous communities of Central Asia did not accept their remade histories and soon began to question them. For example, many of the Tajiks did not want to be connected to the Persians, as Soviet scholars had proposed. They wanted their own ethnic identity and even separate and distinct identities from the different groups with the Tajiks such as Pamiris.[33] The reconstruction of this identity encompasses many local debates about pre-Soviet, Soviet, and post-Soviet historiographies, as well as oral histories (Bregel, 1996: 14–15). Schatz says that history informs continuity and/or persistence of identity (2004: *xx*). A complex mix of attempts at remaking identity by outsiders and insiders debating how, why, or if it was made and remade has created a myriad of histories for the area and the development of the border.

Border delimitation during the mid-Soviet period

Border agreements signed by the USSR and Afghanistan in 1946, 1948, and 1950 all defined the demarcation much more thoroughly and clarified the role of the border guards on either side of the border. The 1950 agreement included annual joint trainings and "monitoring of border marks."[34] The border tightened significantly after the 1950 agreement; illegal crossings were often punishable by death. After the early 1950s, Soviet border troops shot anyone caught swimming in the Panj River, according to locals.

A number of elders, local leaders, and scholars who currently live in Shughnan, Khorog, the Wakhan, and Ishkashim, recall that before World War II the border between Tajikistan and Afghanistan remained somewhat open to the relatives living on either side of the border, as well as for medical, agricultural, and other types of humanitarian assistance. According to a local historian:

> During the mid-Soviet period the local leaders and religious authorities had their own influence and legitimacy of authority within the population but, for the most part, were hidden from the Soviet party leaders. Additionally, these informal networks of religious authority survived despite the marginalization by the Soviet power. The Soviets attempted to control the religion through creating a network of religious institutions in the form of official Islam. The khalifas represented the local population officially and the Soviets received information from them (similar to their relationship with the Tajik government today) but, hidden from view, were informal religious leaders. These local

religious authorities were unnamed and very secret. They were similar to a book club and exchanged religious materials and smuggled some materials from outside into the area. It was through this network that the picture of His Highness the Aga Khan was smuggled into the area in 1970.[35] The informal religious leaders kept pictures of him locked up in hidden cabinets and hidden compartments.

In 1992 the Aga Khan sent his representatives to the area to replace the old prayers with new ones that had the new Imams' names. The new prayers were the ones some of the informal religious leaders already possessed since they had been smuggled in since the 1970s but as of yet were unknown to the network of khalifes who were part of the Soviet Union's "official Islam" program and reported to the Soviet *apparatchiks*. At this time there was a split between the formal and informal religious authorities: the Soviet-backed khalifas who had not had information from outside and who were much more traditionalist due to a lack of religious sources from the Aga Khan, and the informal religious leaders who had access to ongoing changes to religious practices from the smuggling of information into the area.

Numerous families told me about the creative ways they used to trade goods and help the needy on either side of the border. Residents of two extremely isolated and vulnerable districts, Shughnan, on the Afghan side of the border, and Roshan, on the Tajik side, could not survive without outside help. Opium addiction was commonplace both because it was the most accessible pain-killer, used for everything from stomach ailments to childbirth, and offered to guests at weddings and funerals. It is still used in many places and addiction to opiates remains high and a contributing factor to instability in the region.

Given the common usage of opiates, clearly the business involved sellers and buyers—meaning trafficking thrived during (and after) the Soviet period. While illegal drug use was punished harshly in the Tajik SSR, Soviet border troops reportedly were heavily involved in the illicit flow of opiates and other commodities until the fall of the Soviet Union. Some locals also assert that Soviet intelligence officers were involved in the opium trade along the border areas as early as the 1940s. They certainly had a hand in the complex and endemic Soviet black market economy.

Essentially, while the border was controlled by the Soviets and within the "iron curtain" for social and legal exchanges and trade, the Soviets had a rather open policy when it came to illegal trade and illicit flows as long as they controlled them. The networks of cooperation during the Soviet period included Soviet troops, Tajik SSR *apparatchiks* (party functionaries), Tajik clan leaders, and Afghan drug lords, clan leaders, shahs, and khans.

It is important to note here that the Russian troops did not leave Tajikistan until 2005. The agreement between the Tajik and Russian governments was that the Russians troops would stay until 2005 when it was assumed that the

Tajik government would have developed enough capacity to control the border. After the Tajiks took over, the bounty from this illicit market was split among several local war/drug lords and is largely controlled by a small group of official elites in Tajikistan who partner with certain local leaders at the border.[36]

Soviet period in Afghan-Badakhshan—Soviet intelligence, Mujahedin, and party politics

Elders and local scholars told me that Moscow moved in Soviet border troops (guards), appointed local leaders as functionaries (*apparatchiks*) of the USSR on the Afghan side of the border and the Soviets increased their intelligence network along the borderlands. They had loyal informants in all of Badakhshan. Some of the local scholars assert that this network even infiltrated the official government institutions and informal leadership on both sides of the border. My fieldwork also uncovered networks of this kind still operating today but, due to their murky nature, this evidence is largely anecdotal.

This snapshot of the northeastern border area describes intelligence networks and Tajik informants that Russian and Soviet leaders spent over a century cultivating. Dating to the first formal alliance formed in the 1880s, this area still has the most entrenched networks of communist parties in Afghanistan today. Because these groups had such deep roots, they garnered considerable influence in Kabul before the Soviet invasion of Afghanistan and for a short period afterward (Gardizi and Theuss, 2006).

An important principle of Marxist ideology, as interpreted by the USSR, was the need to control the boundary of a state *and integrate* the population of the borderlands as much as possible into the state (Gellner, 1980: 66). Specifically, for a state to pass through the proper "stages of historical development" and achieve utopian peace, it had to first properly demarcate its territory and institute cultural homogeneity and economic hegemony within that territory (Gellner, 1980; Semenov, 1980). Once the border and state were properly controlled, then expansion of that territory became possible. Expansion required gaining popular support and control of the borderlands around a territory. With this ideology in mind, Soviet intelligence spread propaganda about how great life was for the Tajiks on the Tajik SSR side of the border. They paid informants and created networks of cooperation prior to the highly planned invasion of Afghanistan in 1979.[37] Some say the propaganda about the Tajiks living the good life with the Soviets had been circulating since prior to the Shughnan Rebellion of 1925. The residents on the Afghan side of the mountains formally petitioned the Soviet leaders in Khorog and Dushanbe to join the newly formed Tajikistan, citing the harsh treatment of the Ismailis by the Sunni Afghans.[38] Ultimately, their petition was rejected, and they were assigned to Afghan territory that had been formally demarcated in agreements with the British and the Afghan government.[39]

In the mid-1950s, as the Cold War heated up, the Soviet Union began to more aggressively control its border with Afghanistan. Moscow had cultivated a complex intelligence network on the Afghan side of the border after the Afghans achieved independence from Great Britain in 1919. They intensified this network in the 1960s and supported underground political parties under Zahir Shah.

Communist parties began to form in Afghanistan around 1968, when the constitutional ban on political parties was abolished. Many remained underground, however, until the constitution formally recognized this change in 1973 (Braithwaite, 2011). After Daud Khan overthrew the monarchy in 1974 and declared Afghanistan a republic with a multi-party system, this underground party network emerged and took an active role in politics with the support of the Soviet Union.

Initially, there were two or three leading pro-communist parties, seven Mujahedin parties, and several Afghan Taliban-linked parties, including parties allied with Pakistan and a few Arab countries. The main parties operating in Shughnan, Ishkashem, and the Wakhan were the Khalqi, Parchami, and Jamayati parties. The Khalqi and Parchami parties were the most prevalent in these border regions. Both of these parties were factions within the People's Democratic Party of Afghanistan (PDPA). China backed another pro-communist party, Shu'lai Javid (Eternal Flame), whose members were disparaged as the Shu'lai or Maoists. Moscow threw its support with the Khalqis and the Parchamis, who consequently garnered the most control and power for a period in Kabul.

During the 1970s, the various parties sought Moscow's backing as they competed for control of the government. In 1977–1978, Nur Mohammad Taraki, leader of the Khalqis and the General Secretary of the PDPA, essentially the Soviet-backed leader of Afghanistan, along with other Khalqi members, killed part of the Parchami leadership and attempted to assassinate Hafizullah Amin, Taraki's deputy, with the blessing of Moscow. Amin escaped and, also with the blessing of Moscow, assassinated Taraki.[40] At the time there was a growing rebellion against the Leninist property and education policies that Taraki had implemented and enforced. Many Afghans objected, thinking that their customs and religious practices were being disrespected and violated.

The Soviets hoped that Amin would slow the pace of implementation and calm the situation. But Taraki's assassination only intensified the fighting between the Khalqis and Parchamis.[41] Consequently, Moscow supported exiling the majority of the Parchamis and increased the Khalqi's influence in the army and the government. As pockets of rebellion increased, Soviet troops invaded Afghanistan in December 1979 with orders to stabilize the country. Moscow ordered the assassination of Amin and returned Babrak

Karmal, the exiled leader of the Parchamis, from Moscow, installing him as the new General Secretary of the PDPA in Kabul.

The Soviets used this network and through both the intelligence and the party networks, laid the groundwork for their invasion of Afghanistan in 1979. After the British decolonization and then the Iranian Revolution in 1978–1979, Moscow saw an opportunity to expand the USSR's borders beyond Central Asia. Many *residents* along the border in the Ismaili-dominated districts in Afghan Badakhshan said that they agreed with the Soviet ideology as described by Soviet agents at the time. They said it was in line with what they believed and, moreover, they had heard about the rapid economic development across the border and wanted the same for themselves.[42] Shughnan, Ishkashim, and the Wakhan embraced some precepts of communism (as they interpreted it), and still do today[43] although the interpretation of the communist ideology caused rifts, sometimes violent ones, among communist party members in the area (Braithwaite, 2011). Some were Marxists, some Maoists, and still others adhered to other formative communist thinkers.

Clearly the Soviet Union's information operations had been effective. Even the Mujahedin espoused communist ideology before the Soviet invasion in 1979, which also caused many to reject anything associated with the Soviet regime ever since. By 1988, even many of the Soviet soldiers stationed in Afghanistan disagreed with Soviet political ideology (as did many Soviet citizens).[44] The bloody battle between the Mujahedin (backed by the U.S., Pakistan, Saudi Arabia and other Western countries) and the Soviet troops lasted until 1989 and the end of the Soviet Union. In the 1990s the networks that had fought the Soviet troops devolved into factional, clan, ethnic, and territorial-based battles with enormous costs and bloodshed for Afghanistan. These networks, formed during the Soviet and post-Soviet periods are still in place today, although the leadership and structure have evolved.[45]

The PDPA remained in power until President Mohammed Najibullah was overthrown by the Mujahedin and hanged in 1992. Najibullah is still considered a hero in parts of Badakhshan, especially in Shughnan, the Wakhan, and Ishkashem. His framed portrait adorns the walls of many homes in the area. Many people asked me why the United States had assassinated him (which was what they had been told) and angrily said it was a big mistake that led to the ruin of Afghanistan. In the end, the Mujahedin and Jamayat-i Islami, led by Ahmed Shah Massoud and Gulbuddin Hekmatyar, respectively, waged a successful asymmetrical war against the Soviets with the help of the United States until the Soviet withdrawal in 1989 (Dupee, 2012).

The alliance between Massoud and Hekmatyar proved to be short-lived. As the Taliban movement gathered strength and seized control of the government in 1996, anti-Taliban militias united under the auspices of Massoud's Jamayat-I Islami. Massoud's fighters trafficked emeralds and other precious stones, reportedly netting US$60–200 million annually. Eventually they collaborated with infamous arms dealer Viktor Bout, trading precious stones for weapons, ammunition, and helicopters (Dupee, 2012).

Many of the political parties formed during the Soviet period still exist in Afghanistan although many have lost considerable influence such as Khalqis of which the majority of supporters are located in northeastern Badakhshan. In Shughnan and Ishkashem, I met a few Khalqi party members and spent time talking to them about their education, allegiances, and political beliefs. I also met a few elites in the area who expressed deep support for Iran and/ or Russia, and some had spent time in one of those countries while others had simply heard about Iran, the people, and the linkages to their own culture. These allegiances to past invaders and empires are interesting, particularly since people in the region discuss the historical linkages to outsiders frequently in both negative and positive ways. The alliances contribute to ideological divisions based on threads of agreement and disagreement with different forms of outside influence. In this way, the informal institutionalization, local organizations, and arrangements developed as a result of both overt and covert forms of resistance to various political impositions over centuries of invasions.

The divisions run deeply throughout Shughnan, the Wakhan, and Ishkashem, and parallel already established rifts between clans, religious beliefs, and even trade networks. The continuous nation-building, development, political reformation, alliance formation, and outside control/influence, have created a complex and often stultifying array of factions that overlay the clan and trade networks as ready-made tools for local power-brokers. Consequently, whether one is asserting or resisting control, the narratives of protest and legitimacy from various eras of outside disruption influence the discussion.

Post-Communist period: the Tajik civil war and the Afghan Taliban

According to locals, residents on both sides of the border in Badakhshan had high hopes for the freedoms they might gain after the fall of the Soviet Union. On the Afghan side of eastern Badakhshan, they thought the Mujahedin would be quelled and Najibullah would begin to rebuild the Afghan nation in accordance with the goals of some of the kings of the past. His assassination shattered this hope, leaving the area with extreme, unrelenting poverty, religious and cultural oppression, increased addiction to opiates, forced enslavement of their children, property loss, and, in the case of Shughnan, a short but extremely violent civil insurrection by the Mujahedin fighters (Gardizi and Theuss, 2006). After this period of fighting in Shughnan, an odd alliance was formed among some of the Mujahedin fighters and the Afghan Shughnis and Tajik Khorogis.

On the Tajik side of the border, a number of safe-havens for the Mujahedin fighters were installed in Khorog and Porzhnuff in support of the ethnic Gharmis, who had fled the city of Qurghonteppa due to sexually and ethnically motivated violence during the first years of the Tajik civil war (1992–1995). They escaped into Afghanistan and through Afghan Shughnan and Darwaz and joined with the opposition groups in Gorno-Badakhshan (Mullajonov, 2015).

During the Tajik civil war the Afghan Mujahedin took over a former Soviet military installation in Porzhnuff and used it for weapons storage and training. In exchange for the encampment, they provided the people in Khorog with much-needed supplies and weapons to prevent rival Tajik groups from entering their territory. The Tajiks from Dushanbe were never able to get past Darwaz, the threshold of Gorno-Badakhshan, and the Pamiri war-lords made it clear that they would be slaughtered if they tried to enter their territory.

On the Tajik side of the border, the poverty, violence, and oppression that began in early 1992 lasted until 1997, when the bloody civil war ended. Many local residents and local scholars said that the Tajik civil war and violence was spawned from clan divisions, religious and ethnic identities that had been simmering for years during the Soviet period as well as a fight for power over the newly independent country as a whole.

The main groups struggling for power included the Kulobis (largely from Danghara) in the south, the Khujandis from the north, and the Gharmi/Pamiris, although these groups are far from monolithic entities. These sub-ethnic groups get their names from the actual territory to which they belong as opposed to their ethnicity or familial grouping. During the Soviet period, each group controlled a certain aspect of the government or economy (although it changed over time—who controlled what). Generally, the Gharmis controlled domestic trade, the Soviet Union controlled international trade with the Lenina-badis (Khujandis), the Kulobis controlled the police, and the Pamiris con-trolled the KGB (after 1979) (Roy, 2000). At the district level, the leaders in most areas were Khujandis with the second-in-command in most districts being ethnic Russian.[46] Since the Soviet times there has been a saying about Tajikistan: "The Leninabadis (Soghdis) rule, the Kulobis guard [police], and the Pamiris dance." In the end, the Kulobis pitted the Khujandis against the Pamiris and took control of the country. They are still in control today.

Both the Gharmis and the Pamiris insist that genocide occurred during the civil war but was covered up by the central authorities in Dushanbe. A number of Pamiris gave me locations of mass graves filled with the bodies of Ismailis who they believe were executed because of their religious beliefs (Ismaili-Shi'ism) and ethnicity (Pamiri, not Tajik). They urged me to investigate the mass killings and bring what they considered to be ethnic cleansing to the attention of the international community. Other locals told me that the killing during the Tajik civil war was no worse than other ethnic massacres during struggles for power in civil war and that the number of casualties was not as high as other locals contended. OSCE repre-sentatives said that they had looked into it and did not believe that the number of deaths (under 10,000) warranted the genocide designation.[47]

What is clear is that, whether a genocide or not, the battle has left scars in the country felt decades after the civil war ended. The animosity remaining today, while less intense, closely parallels the factions strategically formed during the early Soviet period.

The OSCE commissioned numerous oral histories from this time in order to gain a better understanding of what occurred and to potentially establish truth and reconciliation processes between groups in the country. A local scholar let me listen to recordings of some of the many women from Gorno-Badakhshan and the Gharmi women who had been raped during the civil war.[48] Much of the violence occurred in southwest Tajikistan in Qurghonteppa and in and around the capital, Dushanbe.

In addition to the sexual violence, hunger spread throughout Gorno-Badakhshan due to its isolated location, organized economic blockades by rival groups (the Khujandis and the Kulobis) and hostile terrain. It was not until the Aga Khan sent food and medical supplies in 1994 that the people found some relief from the famine. A friend of mine told me a story one day. We sat in the Chorboq—the main park in Khorog. I said that I loved the park and the people of Khorog were so lucky to have it as a place to gather. She, rather unexpectedly, started talking about the civil war:

> It is amazing how this place has transformed. During the civil war, I remember I was so hungry and cold. I found a potato and asked my father if I could eat it. He started crying and told me he couldn't give it to me since it was the last one in the house (and the only food we had left). He said he needed to save it since spring was coming soon and he needed it for planting.

My friend started crying and said that in her house they did not even have shoes to leave the house in the winter. This is one of dozens of stories of misery recounted to me during my time in Khorog. The civil war remains fresh in people's memories even two decades after its end.

A local historian provided the following section about the civil war. I thought, rather than paraphrasing, it was important to keep his words and thoughts in full since he was worried about being portrayed negatively or misrepresented. He wanted to remain anonymous, as there have been ongoing human rights violations against various marginalized groups in the Tajikistan. He served as a Soviet intelligence officer in Afghanistan for over a decade prior to the fall of the Soviet Union. What he told me is not a comprehensive history but it does capture the intensity of the crisis in Tajikistan, and in particular from the perspective of Gorno-Badakhshan, during the Civil War 1992–1997:

> The first signs of trouble and social unrest in Tajikistan surfaced in 1990 under the then First Secretary of the Communist Party of Tajikistan, Kahhar Mahkamov, being the last Soviet leader of Tajikistan. Having

ruled the country for about a decade, he was considered by some to be a fairly decent leader, except that he could never overcome his clan and regionalist mindset. Mahkamov was deposed in 1990 by pro-democracy forces, in all appearances, supported by a pro-Gorbachev faction from the Kremlin in Moscow. It is often alleged that Gorbachev intended to unseat the entrenched Soviet era Communist leaders of the cotton-producing Central Asian republics, whose career track and reputation was marred by allegations of corruption in the cotton industry. With the downfall of Kahhar Mahkamov, Rahmon Nabiev, the Chairman of the Council of Ministries [similar to a Prime Minister] and the second in command at the time, automatically replaced him. Nabiev (from Khujand and Uzbek by ethnicity), was the First Secretary of the Communist Party of Tajikistan for years before Mahkamov. This time, he was elected primarily by the Kulobis and Leninabadis [Khujandis]. Having controlled the government for the past forty years since the beginning of the Second World War, the Leninabadis were not ready to share power with the representatives of southern or mountainous regions. Since the early decades of the Soviet rule, the Leninabadis perceived the southerners as "uneducated" and "uncultured" mountain-dwellers, who did not have the political wisdom to rule the country along with them. The nature of rule in Tajikistan since the time of the Soviet rule has always been clan-based, where the point of reference was regionalist or clan-based structure rather than a nationalist framework. Political rivalry has always revolved around clans and regions.

In 1991, Rahmon Nabiev was promoted to the presidency by the Leninabadi clan in the first democratic elections ever held in Tajikistan, since the very beginning of the Soviet rule. Nabiev won a landslide victory with the votes of the majority of Khujandis, Kulobis (including the large Uzbek population of Tajikistan) and five hundred thousand Russians and Russian-speaking populations of the capital. He ran against Davlat Khodanazarov, the pro-democracy candidate. Being the Chairman of All-Union Committee of Cinematographers and a Member of the Parliament of the USSR, Khudonazarov had the support of the Tajik and Russian intellectual and cultural elites, but not that of the Russian army and state security, who overtly or covertly stood against Michail Gorbachev. In this fashion, about seventy percent—majority of Turkic-Tajik, Uzbeks and Russian population of Tajikistan voted for Nabiev.

The political opposition questioned the outcome of the votes on grounds that, during the elections, various local and regional groups promoted proxy presidential candidates, who subsequently gave their votes to Nabiev, thus ensuring his victory by unconstitutional means. Although the political opposition claimed that the elections were rigged, still, the results were accepted on the stipulations that for dispensation of justice, the rival pro-democracy parties and movements should be represented in the Parliament. At the time the political atmosphere, influenced by Gorbachev's openness and perestroika, was that there was and would be a multi-party system. Initially, Nabiev agreed, but very soon after the Khujandis, who held the majority in Parliament, put the opposition parties under pressure in order to oust them from the Parliament. Eventually, this manner of rule led to more protests by masses of population from mountainous regions, headed by the prominent representatives of democratic intelligentsia in the center of the capital. The demonstrators aired demands to form a coalition government, in which the members of the political opposition were entitled to positions along with the majority members of Parliament, who came predominantly from the Leninabad Region. In response, the Leninabadi clan, headed by President Nabiev and Speaker of Parliament, Safarali Kenjaev, did not honor this truce and threatened war with help from the ethnic Uzbeks of Tajikistan and the Kulobis. They also had support from the sizeable Russian Diaspora community of Dushanbe who were linked to the Russian military and state security network. Despite the mounting pressure and public uproar, Nabiev and Leninabadi strongman, Kenjaev, were staunchly against sharing power with others in the country.

Meanwhile, the Russian media and press successfully spread the propaganda, blared in mass media and press to the effect that the Gharmis and Pamiris were, in fact, radical Islamists, engaged in political moorings to overthrow the constitutional government, and establish an Islamic state in Tajikistan. Visiting Tajikistan, around this time, the American diplomat, James Baker, was told by the Communist leader, Rahmon Nabiev, that Tajikistan needed U.S. support for his government against Islamic fundamentalists. The fundamentalists, quite interestingly, appeared to be the Gharmis and Pamiris, which were in fact, the rival regional groups. Following skirmishes between pro-Government and pro-Opposition demonstrators, and involvement of the Russian 201 Motor Rifle Division in the street brawls through a show of force with arms on tanks and APCs in the streets of Dushanbe, the Russian military escorted the American Embassy and the Ambassador out of Dushanbe. They did so on those same tanks and APCs on the pretext of worsening security situation, and involvement of "anti-Western" Islamic movements in the political ongoing conflict in Tajikistan.

After six months of popular demonstrations of pro-Government and pro-Opposition supporters, President Rahmon Nabiev attempted to flee to his native region, Khujand. He was caught by the pro-democracy youth of the capital and the Pamiris and Gharmis at the airport. They wanted to force him to return to his position, but the Russian military intervened and let Nabiev go. Following Nabiev's flight from Dushanbe, Russia and Uzbekistan organized the ethnic Uzbeks of Tajikistan and the Kulobis along paramilitary lines and conducted military training in Termez, Uzbekistan. A few months later, they were sent back to the southern region of Tajikistan, Qurghonteppa, where they attacked the civilian Gharmis and Pamiris [who, due to forced migration in the 1930s and 1960s, had settled in this region]. The unrest and violence in this region coincided with the alliance among the Gharmis and Pamiris who consolidated around the Islamic democratic alliance in Dushanbe, and formed provisional government.

In the meantime, the former Speaker of Parliament, Soviet-trained lawyer, Safarali Kenjaev and President Nabiev started collecting funds and making secret sleazy deals with 201 Motor Rifle Division for the overthrow of the provisional government in Dushanbe. Subsequently, the Leninabadis created paramilitary forces, recruited from among the ethnic Uzbeks of Tajikistan and the Kulobis, and attempted to storm Dushanbe. This incursion from Hissor district in the vicinity of Dushanbe resulted in hundreds of deaths of the assaulting Uzbeks and Kulobis. There were allegations that it was in fact the 201 Motor Rifle Division that turned the attacks from Hissor into a bloodbath by mistaking them for unidentified groups of armed ethnic marauders, targeting the civilian population of Dushanbe including the sizeable five-hundred-thousand-strong Russian and Russian-speaking diaspora of the capital.

In the aftermath of this bloody incident, the Leninabadi and Kulobi clan leaders continued organizing paramilitary groups in Qurghonteppa, and trained the militia, now called the Popular Front, with the help of Russian officers in Termez. By the beginning of the summer of 1992, the armed Uzbek and Kulobi militia returned to the places of their traditional residence, Kulob, Hissor, and Qurghonteppa and, subsequently, engaged in an active war against the administration and supporters of the provisional government of Dushanbe. The paramilitary Kulobis and Uzbeks specifically targeted the civilian Pamiris and Gharmis as the carriers of rival ideology in Kulob, Qurghonteppa and Hissor. Gradually, by the end of summer 1992, they managed to block Dushanbe. They cut railways and other supply routes, the lifeline of the capital to such an extent that the population started living on bread rations.

Having effectively isolated the capital, the Kulobis and Leninabadis were in a good position to bargain for political power and control of the government. Throughout this time, Akbarsho Iskandarov, the Speaker of Parliament of the provisional Government went back and forth between Dushanbe and Moscow, asking the Russians for help. The promised military aid was sent through Uzbekistan, but it was, in fact, intended for other beneficiaries. Arms and ammunitions were unloaded there and redirected to Termez for the Uzbek and Kulobi militias from the Popular Front, and in fact, the rival faction of the Government. To delegitimize the provisional Government, the leaders of the paramilitary wing of Khujandi-Kulobi clans alleged that the provisional government was unconstitutional, and the head of the Government, that is, the Speaker of the Parliament, Akbarsho Iskandarov, was not elected. In reality however the real reason for disqualifying the then Head of the Provisional Government, Akbarsho Iskandarov, was that he originally came from Darwaz, GBAO. Prior to his appointment as the Speaker of Parliament, he was Vice-President under President Nabiev in the Coalition Government of the Old Communist Guard and Islamic Democratic Alliance. As soon as President Nabiev fled to Khujand, Iskandarov automatically replaced him as the Head of the State. He was promoted to this position by the political opposition from GBAO, representing both the Ismailis and Sunnis of the Region, on the assumption that being a Sunni, he would be acceptable to their allies, the Gharmis and to rest of Tajikistan. Despite these precautions, however, the Khujandi and Kulobi clans rejected Iskandarov, since the political and ideological divide reflected the traditional fault lines of the age-old division between the populations of the mountains and plains. In this geographically defined political context, the Islamic democratic opposition was perceived as the political organization of mountain-dwellers as opposed to plain-dwellers. For this reason, indeed, Iskandorov, as representing the mountain-dwellers, was deligitimized as a not legitimately elected Speaker of the Parliament.

Towards the end of 1992 the armed confrontation intensified. Fierce infightings between the supporters of political and ideological factions came to a head in the southern regions of Tajikistan. The Khujandi and Kulobi clans managed to purge a large part of the country with the help of the Russian and Uzbek troops and were in the position to dictate the rules of the game. By the end of 1992, Uzbeks and Kulobi paramilitary groups blocked Dushanbe from the rest of the country, and invited the members of provisional government of Dushanbe to attend the Sixteenth Session of the Communist Party of Tajikistan. This political event was ostensibly motivated as "national reconciliation" called "oshi oshti", loosely translated as the breaking of bread between the Tajiks. During the proceedings of the session, organized on a heavily guarded collective farm in the vicinity of Khujand city, they forced Iskandorov to step down. To all intents and purposes, the collective farm was chosen as a venue for degrading the unworthy opposition, as the French and Germans did to each other during the First and Second World Wars. The Members of Parliament, coming from a Region that had grown several generations of "politicians" on its soil, treated the uncouth mountain-dweller, as "illegitimate" acting head of the state and not having been elected as such. While "approving" his "legitimate" abdication, the members of parliament voted for Rahmon Nabiev, the preceding "legitimately" elected President to be replaced by Emomali Rahmon from Kulob, who, quite interestingly, was to substitute Akbarsho Iskandarov as the Speaker of Parliament rather than Nabiev as the President. Emomali Rahmon was a Chairman of a *Kolkhoz* (collective farm) from Kulob. Rahmon was one of hundreds of unknown provincial members of Parliament prior to his involvement in military operations in Qurghonteppa and Kulob. He then became one of the "political" deputy commanders in the paramilitary Popular Front along with Sangak Safarov. So, Rahmon was appointed as the Speaker of Parliament and by implication as the new head of state.

In this fashion, by the end of 1992, the Kulobis and Leninabadis were able to organize the "Sixteenth" Session of Parliament in order to form a constitutional government, by totally excluding members of the provisional government, the Pamiris and Gharmis, from participation in the ongoing political processes. Russian President, Boris Yeltsin and the provincial Russians of Tajikistan supported the new constitutionally elected government of Tajikistan and Western countries followed suit. This was the so-called national reconciliation among the Tajiks to signal the birth of a country in the country of nations. At this time, Nabiev abdicated in favor of Emomali Rahmon, the Speaker of Parliament, and current President of Tajikistan. Rahmon promised to end the war and re-establish the status quo among the groups and start rehabilitating the country. The representatives of the Gharmis and Pamiris accepted the conditions and formally recognized the new President, but even this capitulation did not end the war.

As soon as the constitutionally elected government moved to Dushanbe, targeted killing of Gharmis and Pamiris started in the capital and throughout the flatlands of Tajikistan. The Pamiris and Gharmis, who were living in the flatlands, began fleeing to the mountainous areas from where they came prior to forced relocation by the Soviets in 1950s. The Gharmis, who were living in the southern region of Qurghonteppa, could not access their original homeland through Dushanbe. So, they crossed the river into Afghanistan. The Pamiris (under the Opposition commander named Majnun) also went south to Afghanistan and re-entered Badakhshan through Porshinev [located at the western edge of the city of Khorog]. Others fled along the Dushanbe-Khorog route, and arrived in GBAO by the beginning of the winter, in December 1992. Throughout 1993, a vicious war continued in the eastern region of the Gharm Valley and Tawil-dara terrain. The Popular Front, which was the Kulobi paramilitary, supported with arms and ammunitions by the 201 Motor-Rifle Russian Division stationed in Dushanbe, followed air bombardments, carried out by Russian air force in the Gharm Valley. Mass killings, violence and rape in villages continued against the Gharmis, forcing the remaining Gharmi civilian population to flee to the Afghan side.

With the end of armed resistance in Gharm and Tawil-dara mountainous areas by the end of 1993, the Kulobi and Uzbek Popular Front with air cover, provided by Russian air force, moved closer to the foot of the Pamir Mountains. Incursions began into Gorno-Badakhshan through Tawil-dara in the direction of Darwaz. Two attempts to break through the defenses of GBAO self-defense forces [militias] and invade Gorno-Badakhshan failed, after long fierce battles in Tawil-dara and Dashte-Sher (before Darwaz) in the summer of 1994. The outcome of these battles led to a stalemate, whereupon Tajikistan fell apart across valleys and mountains. The third military campaign was organized under the cover of "humanitarian assistance" for Gorno-Badakhshan by the Russian military alone, but it stopped in a short determined stand-off after the attempts to enter into the territory of the region were blocked by Opposition forces. Following long negotiations, only an elderly Russian General and his guards on three APCs were allowed to enter Khorog. As a military strategist, the General imparted wisdom in an interview to the local TV program to the effect that "It is difficult here, for every inch of this mountainous land must be fought from nature." In their way out of the region shortly after, the convoy got stuck for several days on the road along a narrow terrain, blocked by mudflow.

By the end of 1994, the Russian-backed Popular Front resorted to different tactics to infiltrate Gorno-Badakhshan. The armed units of the Kulobi Popular Front were flown to Darwaz under the cover of Tajik border guards on board Russian military helicopters. This became possible only after a considerable amount of "counter-insurgency" activities were carried out by Russian border guards. Some Sunni Opposition military commanders like Sallam and Nazaramon from Vanj Valley were co-opted by the Russian counter-intelligence unit of Khorog-based Russian border guard garrison, and stopped resistance to the intrusion of Popular Front in the areas of their control. During this period, self-defense forces of GBAO remained the only fighting force under the command of the United Tajik Opposition on the territory of Tajikistan. The Gharmis continued fighting from across the Afghan border in the area of Panj with the help of the Mujahedin and their leader Ahmed Shah Massoud as well as other groups in Afghanistan. There were also unconfirmed allegations that the opposition Gharmi fighters were supported by the Arabs and al-Qaeda terrorist groups under Usama bin Laden.

The Gharmi opposition fighters could cross to Tajikistan only via Gorno-Badakhshan, where border crossings were partially controlled by GBAO self-defense forces. Taking advantage of this corridor, guarded by GBAO self-defense forces, large numbers of Gharmi combatants crossed back into Tajik territory, and moved along the border to Tawildara terrain and to Gharm valley to regain the territories, earlier lost to Kulobi Popular Front. Russian border guards claimed neutrality in the inter-Tajik conflict, but continued erecting checkpoints on the roads, and sometimes shot individuals from among the civilian population. Often, these killings were blamed on "mercenaries", hired by the Tajik Government, and not connected with the Russian border guard garrisons. Eventually, in separate incidents, these so-called "mercenaries" were cornered by GBAO self-defense forces and driven to mountains. They were allowed to come down from the mountains through the mediation of Russian border guards and instantly flown to Dushanbe.

The behavior of the border guards resulted in a change of attitude among the population towards the Russians, who had been seen as "liberators" until then. Now, the benign Russians showed a different face to the local civilian population. The drunken "mercenary" border guards threatened civilian youth and juveniles, held at gunpoint and detained them, and sometimes even shot some of them. In retaliation, the Pamiri self-defense forces took Russian soldiers hostage at checkpoints and sent them to Afghanistan. The Russians bargained with the self-defense forces, who alone, could bring the soldiers back to Tajikistan. Whenever they were brought back, the border guards boasted in the Russian media that the hostages were released thanks to "energetic" actions of the Khorog border guard garrison. One of those incidents with Russian hostages, brought back with the help of self-defense forces, resulted in a bloody incident, in which fourteen civilians, riding on a truck along with the Russian prisoners, were shot dead by the "mercenary" personnel of a Russian checkpoint, who managed to overdo the "rescue operation" in a zeal to "release the captive by using force."

One of the many incidents of crossing the border by the Opposition forces involved that of "Minister of Defense of Tajik Government in Exile," General Rizwan, into Gorno-Badakhshan, Moving to Darwaz, his combatants, including himself, began "marrying" the local girls and harassing their fathers and brothers. After allegations about the misconduct of the Tajik Opposition spread far and wide, the commander of the Khorog-based GBAO self-defense forces, Majnun, went to Darwaz, and asked Rizwan to leave Majnun, and saw Rizwan off across the border. Taking advantage of the incident, the Russian counter-intelligence unit drafted a letter of appeal on behalf of the population of Darwaz to the Tajik Government. Apparently, the incident was used as a pretext for flying the Kulobi and Uzbek Popular Front fighters, now called Tajik border guards, to Darwaz on Russian aircrafts. It happened, when Opposition Commander of Vanj Valley, now retired General Sallam, was invited to Dushanbe for "negotiations." Sallam was a world champion in eastern martial arts after "defeating" several Russian champions. The Russian border guards, winning over the population, began purging the political opposition in Darwaz. The murder of a local opposition commander by Russian commando, resulted in clashes along the border that occurred in the Darwaz area between the Russian soldiers and the Gharmi opposition and crossing the river to the Tajik side. During this armed conflict, several dozen soldiers on both sides lost their lives. A civilian truck, carrying wounded Russian officers and soldiers was caught by Gharmi combatants on the road. The wounded military personnel survived only thanks to the intervention of UNMOT [United Nations Mission of Observers in Tajikistan] officers on the spot.

The presence of the Popular Front in Darwaz, who were under the protection of ostensibly "neutral" Russian border guards, resulted in a heightened security situation. Around the beginning of 1995, Russian border guards blocked the mouth of Yazghulam valley. A few days later, the Gharmi Opposition fighters appeared across the border on the Afghan side. They took control of the main road and engaged in fighting with the Russians. The Khorog Border guard garrison sent additional forces, but they were stopped in Kalat, at the intersection of the road between Rushan and Vanj by GBAO self-defense forces. After a few hours of exchange of gun fire, the border guards came with a white flag to make peace, and returned to Khorog. In the meantime, fierce fighting between the Russians and Gharmi and Yazghulami combatants continued on the border near the mouth of Yazghulam valley. The war resulted in dozens of deaths of Russian officers and soldiers and Gharmi Opposition fighters until a truce was reached through the mediation of UNMOT. The intrusion of Russian border guards into Vanj also left dozens of dead among the border guards and Vanji self-defense forces, and remained inconclusive.

Following these failed attempts to impose the control of ethnically different Kulobi and Uzbek fighters of Popular Front on areas formerly under Opposition, security arrangements on the Tajik–Afghan border became even more fragile. A number of Afghan and other foreign fighters were spotted on the check-points, controlled by the Opposition and even deep in the valleys of Yazghulam and Porshinev. The Afghans moved freely back and forth across the border. One of the Russian checkpoints, manned with 300 border guards in Panj area was wiped out by the Tajik Opposition in a matter of hours, leaving no more than a dozen of survivors. Following this incident, the Organization of Collective Defense of the CIS countries, including Russia and Uzbekistan launched military exercises along the Tajik–Afghan border.

For the Kulobi Government of Tajikistan, the only way out of the impasse remained pressing for peace and national reconciliation. President Rahmon went to Afghanistan to meet Ahmed Shah Massoud and Burhaniddin Rabbani to arrange the repatriation of the Tajik refugees from Afghanistan. They agreed to a meeting with President Rahmon. Rabbani and Massoud were seasoned warriors and had considerable influence with the Tajik Opposition and refugees. President Rahmon promised amnesty and immunity from persecution to the Gharmi refugees provided that they returned and cooperated in rebuilding the country as a common home and included both political factions. Lots of tears were shed, and refugees naively believed in the sincerity of rustic-looking President. While crossing the border, the UN officers together with the "neutral" Russian 201 Motor Rifle Division disarmed the refugees. Once they returned, the national security officers of Tajikistan put many of the refugees in prison within a few months, and killed many more through extra-judicial executions in the course of a methodical and systematic witch-hunt. Even before that back in 1993, the Kulobi authorities in

Dushanbe settled the score with the Pamiris in an undignified manner by humiliating their women. The central authorities ordered the local government in GBAO to repatriate the internally displaced people back to their places of residence in Dushanbe and other cities in the flatlands of Tajikistan. These groups of women and young girls faced more violence after their return to DushanbeThe majority of the women and female children, who were relocated, were forced into cohabitation with Kulobi and Uzbek intruders, some of them became the second or third wives, meaning as sex-slaves for the Kulobis. Even now some three hundred former refugees are still in prison, although larger numbers of refugees were released due to old age and infirmity. Kabiri—former head of the Islamic Revival Party of Tajikistan—appealed to the President to release the rest of the former refugees and by implication political prisoners.[49]

The war against the mountain-dwellers continued long after the national reconciliation in the areas of their traditional residence. In 2008, the Tajik national army again launched military operations in Gharm and killed what the government alleged were supporters of the former Islamic opposition. After quelling armed resistance of a handful of fighters, the Tajik national army turned to barbaric violence against the civilian population. Based on eye-witness accounts of the residents of the valley, in one incident in a remote village, they killed seventy young men and male teenagers on the riverbed and drowned their dead bodies in the river. This manner of execution has been called "fishing" since the civil war. It is alleged that they raped the women in the area—after they killed Mullah Abdullah, a local leader of the former opposition from that area. During the second, military operations in 2010 in Gharm, the Tajik National Army and personnel of other "power ministries" closed the terrain, and conducted systematic mass rape of women for three months. They also attempted a military intervention into GBAO in 2008 in order to kill the local leaders in the area. They threatened the population with mass rape and some allege this included young girls. The army and other power ministries repeated the same threats, through informal channels, when they planned the invasion of Gorno-Badakhshan in 2012. Mass rape of women was planned after the end of the successful military operation on the pretext of house-to-house searches for the confiscation of weapons. This continued for several days. Such threats resulted in determined resistance to the Tajik army, and caused many deaths both among the military and civilian population. Despite this, during the infamous operations of the Tajik Army and other "power ministries" in the Pamirs, a Russian political analyst said that while it was a disgrace for Russia to support a government like that in Tajikistan, but given a choice between bearded fundamentalists or a secular government, she would most certainly support the secular government, even if was despicable.

This historian's focus on the tensions between the "mountain dwellers" and the plains inhabitants has deep roots in the historical memory of the region and underpins both the current tensions as well as the reason for the bloodletting during the Tajik Civil War. Unlike Uzbekistan or Kyrgyzstan, which had larger majority populations controlling the ruling ethnic group/elites, Tajikistan had at the time of the Civil War much less of a majority of one group. Additionally, the Soviet Union's planned economy and administrative system put a lot of focus on homogenizing ethnic groups through power-sharing arrangements along ministerial lines. This strategy had the opposite effect in Tajikistan. It entrenched the differences and made them the pivotal point for competition between ethnic/sub-ethnic groups.

Today

The last sentence of the historian's narrative about the Russian analyst's comments about a secular versus "bearded Islamist" government is important. The fact is there is not a dichotomous choice between secular and Islamic militant control in Tajikistan. The Russian strategy embodies their overarching goal, which is to come back to the border and have a central role in the politics, economy, and security of Central Asia. They use Islam as a tool to prop up their strategic narrative in this gambit. But, on the ground this is only creating new and imposed divisions along lines of religions that were not at the forefront of debates. The Islamic Revival Party of Tajikistan has a diverse array of groups who belong to the party. They include Sunnis of various Islamic sects and Ismaili-Shi'ites. They are not pushing for a strict Shari'a agenda or to overthrow the current authoritarian leader. They have been pushing for a more balanced set of voices within the political arena and with very little success. In fact, the President of Tajikistan has increasingly marginalized any opposition to his dictatorship and administration through a complex array of co-opting authority within every opposing party. Moreover, if co-optation failed, he made sure the opposition was silenced through imprisonment, threats to families, mysterious deaths, and other means. Most of the opposition groups in Tajikistan are pushing for more democratic elections and access to government. None are a threat due to their beliefs in imposing strict Shari'a in the country.

What is interesting is that the informal leaders in Khorog and Gorno-Badakhshan dislike the Islamic "militants" and extremists as much as the Tajik, or the U.S. Government for that matter. Moreover, the Islamic militants such as the Taliban, Islamic State in Iraq and Syria (ISIS), and Islamic Militants of Uzbekistan (IMU) dislike the Ismailis as much as the Ismailis dislike ISIS and IMU. To many Sunnis who belong to conservative sects of Islam, (not only extremists) Ismailis are Kafirs (non-believers). So the narrative the Russians have been putting forth about the "militants" along the border of Gorno-Badakhshan is just a ploy to gain legitimacy within various local powerbrokers and foreign governments for coming back to the border.

Apparently, it has worked to some extent. In 2014, Russian UAVs (unmanned aerial vehicles—non-lethal) flew alongside the Russian 201st Regiment (the one located in Tajikistan) conducting a training exercise from Khatlon over the most challenging mountainous terrain into Gorno-Badakhshan. They also have signed new agreements with the government of Tajikistan, increasing their presence along the border. While I was in GBAO just after violent clashes between locals and the Tajik Government in May of 2014, two women walked through several neighborhoods in Khorog collecting signatures for seceding from Tajikistan and having Gorno-Badakhshan join Russia. They used the ongoing conflict in the Ukraine and the annexation of Crimea as a model for why they should secede. Some of the local warlords allegedly threatened to kill them if they continued. I was told they did stop soon after they started.

Today, in Gorno-Badakhshan, narratives of difference abound. Whether they focus on religion, ethnicity, territory, or visions of the nation-state, they are the frequent topic of scholarly debates, living room discussions, and in public spaces such as shared taxi rides and bazaars. While the international community and the domestic authority work to "develop" the border institutions and provide technical progress, guidance, and "laws," the locals continue to operate in the way they have been for generations. The more that is disrupted, the more the locals unite against those who are disrupting their status quo. The similarities between the rather detrimental administrative projects during the Soviet period and today's development of the border institutions is that both attempted to control the local fabric of everyday political existence. The security arrangements supported by the international communities have imposed central ruling elites (largely controlled by kinship networks from outside the area—such as from Dangara) that have delegitimized and in some cases actually eroded or marginalized the very state structures and institutions the international community aims to formalize and institutionalize.

Notes

1 For various reasons, they prefer to remain anonymous for now.
2 See Kunitz's 1935 book, *Dawn Over Samarqand.*
3 See, for example, the tablets, coins, stamps, and other objects held within the "Oxus River Collection" at the British Museum in London.
4 There were warlike tribes which culminated in the Kushanid Empire, the rulers/ army of which are allegedly descendent from the territory throughout the Pamir mountains.
5 According to Khojaniyozov: "While more recent scholarly research more comprehensively linked Zoroastrianism with Ismailism, the footprints for these connections were laid by Nasiri 'Khussraw, who allegedly said that he Islamized many of the indigenous Zoroastrians cults through incorporating the symbols of the Ismaili faith with the customs and symbols of the indigenous people and Zoroastrianism. An example of this merging of faiths is the Cheroghroshan, the funeral ceremony which uses Zoroastrian symbols but also uses religious rituals from the Ismaili-

Shi'a tradition and faith. Both the family of the prophet and the symbols of nature are an intrinsic part of local traditions and customs and expressed in the local vernacular and architecture" (during discussions in 2014–2015).

6 I also heard this repeatedly in my fieldwork from many people on both sides of the border.

7 My use of Khan is not to be confused with the bloodline links to Genghis Khan (which some still assert today) or a khan in the sense of a supreme leader. Khan in the Turkic sense and khan in the sense I am using it are two different words. In Badakhshan khan is similar to the older Persian meaning of Dihqan: "Dihqan and khan are two very different words. As noted earlier, dihqan is Iranian and referred to a class of landowning nobles (the extent of their power varied). Khan, old Turkic qaghan, and qan, both terms for supreme leader, emperor, appear to have had a slight distinction between the two in the earliest Turkic inscriptions—but that is still in dispute. Qaghan is not of Turkic origin. Indeed, its etymology is unknown. Recent attempts have been made to construct an etymology for it in Kettic (a Yeniseic language, spoken now by a handful of people). It is first attested in 265 CE as the title used by a Xianbei ruler. The Xianbei, successors of the Xiongnu (Asian Huns) as the nomadic power in Mongolia, were a tribal union that seems to have largely consisted of speakers of early Mongolic, along with Xiongnu (whose language affiliation is still uncertain) and some Turkic peoples. Qaghan becomes the standard term in Old Turkic. Also used in Mongol in which it undergoes the sound changes Qaghan > Qa'an > khan. I would guess that in Shughnan and Wakhan they are using Khan as a title of high respect and standing. In the aftermath of the Mongol Empire, only Chinggisids (descendants of Genghis Khan) could take this title. Among Turkic peoples this remained true. Chinggisids (I know some) may still use it. Among the Pamir Iranian peoples *et al.* it does not have this sense, but simply indicates higher social/political status. Just as your research has shown. Be careful not to confuse it with dihqan, which has, as I noted, undergone a certain devaluation in some parts of the Iranian world." Email discussion with Peter Golden (January 30, 2013).

8 Vasily V. Bartold, Lord Elphinstone, Magnus Marsden, Akbar Ahmed.

9 From primary research at the British Museum that outlines the maps and wars waged over the area during this time period. It also highlights the development of trade routes and associated agreements with local Khans, traders, and local groups. See also: Cobbold (1900); Maysky (1935); Habberton (1937); Philips (1951); Schurmann (1962); Mangarova (1972); Vogelsang (2002); Barry (2010); Golden (2011); Interviews with Soultan Khojaniyozov (2010–2015).

10 According to Peter Golden (email communication June 15, 2015): Nuwkar is from Mongol nökür, pl. nököd—originally, there were the boon companions of Chinggis khan, men who had left their previous source of loyalty (clan or tribe) and transferred it to the person of Chinggis khan. The word is borrowed into Turkic (nöker/nöger and variants of it, also into Hungarian nyögér) with the meaning of "comrade, companion," "bodyguard to ruler," "servitor" etc. Also borrowed into Persian نوکر nukar, naukar, "servant, dependent."

11 More commonly known as the Hasheshi, as made famous by Bernard Lewis (2002).

12 The history of the tensions between local leaders and outsiders is important; their power has ebbed and flowed but always remained essential to security and stability in the area given the nature of the terrain. Even the Amir of Bukhara had difficulty asserting influence or governing the area.

13 Alexei V. Postnikov, Bronislav Grombchevsky, and archives (inaccessible to me) in the Russian military headquarters held in Uzbekistan provide important insights into the history of the Great Game.

14 Badakhshan was always subject to bigger powers, like the different Persianate Empires, Genghis Khan Tamerlane, and others. The Mughals were considered a Persian dynasty that moved to Kabul in the early sixteenth century when Babur lost his parental land in Central Asia.

15 At the time, Badakhshan was the area from Faizabad up to Shiwa in Afghanistan. Starting from Shiwa and north and east, there were four autonomous principalities (with shifting loyalties and allied partnerships with the neighbors in the area such as Bokhara (later under Russian influence), Qashqar (now China), Kokand (now Fergana—influenced by Uzbeks) and Badakhshan (under British influence) as well as the statelets of Shughnan, Wakhan, Ghoran and Darwaz (under British and Russian influence.)

16 This is true today, although it is not formally recognized by the central authorities and at various times threats of either retribution or outright invasion by the central authority in Dushanbe are made.

17 Michael Barry's (2010) four volume set of primary documents from these period which have nearly every border agreement from the time period has been an invaluable resource underpinning some of the narratives told to me in the field.

18 Bartold (1918, 1920); Grierson (1920).

19 This is a complex and often contested subject which I am only touching on briefly. The best research on the ethno-religious division of the region is by Kushkeki (1926) and Abaeva (1964). Also, see Grierson (1920).

20 "When the British helped the Afghans to take over this area there were clashes between the Russians and the Afghans. The Wakhi leader, Pir Shahzodalais, was in contact with the headquarters of the Imam in Bombay. The Russians accused him of conspiring with the British and with the coming of the Sunni-Afghans to the area, he found it too dangerous to stay in the Wakhan and moved all of his followers to Hunza in order protect them" (Interview with Khojanizayov, 2015). They have remained there ever since. The Afghan Amir wrote him a letter saying that he could safely return to the Wakhan to which Shahzodlais replied he would only return when the British controlled the area. Russian intelligence continued tracking him and expected him to return and to arrest him, but he never returned." Interviews with Khojanizayov (2013–2015). Also in compilation of articles, "Pamir"; see also Shokhumurov (2008).

21 "The Khanates also were referred to as Mirgari or Shahigari—translated as Princedom and principality. The titles of Mirs versus Amirs, versus Khans versus Shahs are one that deserves more discussion, but in the interest of space, I will refer to them as Khans, Mirs, and/or Amirs for the rest of the chapter. In some areas they were referred to as one and other places another name" (Interview with Nurmahmadsho Nurmahmadshoev in 2013). Noted scholar, Peter Golden explained that, "Historically, these are different terms: dihqân in medieval Persian meant 'local nobleman/landholder.' Today in Tajikistan it means 'peasant.' Khan is from Turkic (I won't go into all the philological details). It originally denoted the supreme ruler. It continued to have this sense into the nineteenth century. But, it was also subject to a certain devaluation, especially in Tajik or other non-Turkic-speaking areas. It just became a polite term, 'mister,' if you like. Amîr is Arabic for 'commander' originally. Then, was used for higher-ranking officials and in more modern times has even been (mis-)translated as 'prince.' In the areas you are working in (not overly familiar to me in their modern setting—I am a medievalist), Amir would be well above dihqân" (Golden, 2013). What is unknown to most, is that Mir was used to denote a local leader, like a prince, in Shughnan, Ishkashim, and the Wakhan and, today there are still two khans in the area who are considered important leaders and to be from important bloodlines. Villagers have to kiss their hands when they encounter them (observed during my fieldwork in 2011).

22 During my fieldwork, I observed families in Shughnan, Ishkashim, and the Wakhan who use these long-standing agreements to settle disputes and to recognize legitimate land ownership.

23 See Habberton (1937: 60–62; 64–67). Also, the British had created a loose border delimitation between Afghanistan and Central Asia along the river Panj, meaning five (referring to the connection to "five waterways"), which outsiders referred to as the Oxus River or the Amu Darya (great river or uncle river). The locals referred to the Panj and believed it to be a spawn of the Amu Darya. The Russians called it *Piandzh* which is the Russified version of the Dari name. "This body of water bisects the two areas and flows [from] East to West with the glacier melts contributing to its ebb and flow. The Oxus was a historical name used by the Greeks. During the Islamic conquest it was referred to as Mowara-al-Nahr (land beyond the river). The Arabs came from the south. Transoxiana means the same thing—land beyond the river. This name traces back to the time of Alexander the Great and is often used to indicate the historical significance of the river. The Arabs also called it Jayhoon (meaning crazy – always on the move)." (Museum literature from the mosque of Sufi Abu Abdullah Mohammed ibn Ali al Termezi in Termez, Uzbekistan).

24 The following text is written by Evelyn Roy, a scholar/Marxist in 1924. It has obvious biases but still shows how outsiders sought to control local leaders. "The Bokharan Revolutionary movement had existed since the end of the nineteenth century, as a natural result of the intolerable conditions which prevailed under the combined oppression of the Russian and Bokharan autocracies. Open rebellion had been prevented by the armies of the Tsar, which were placed at the disposal of the Amir. The government of the latter, nominally independent, was in reality a protectorate of Russia, which kept a Resident Agent there to exercise control. Railways and telegraphs, built by the Tsar's government, were entirely controlled by the latter and Russian garrisons maintained respect for the real power behind the Amir's throne. This theocratic potentate, regarded by the Moslems of Central Asia and neighboring countries as the embodiment of powers not only earthly, but divine, was held in superstitious veneration by the Moslem world, and the fame of Bokhara el Sharif as a center of Islamic culture attracted pilgrims and students from all the Mussulman countries. Such international prestige in no way lightened the burden which official robbery, corruption and vice imposed upon the Amir's immediate subjects. This despot regarded Bokhara as his own personal estate, and the government income, wrung from the labor of the people, as his pocket-money. Over one-half the national income was given over forthwith to himself and the Mullahs and Begs (clergy and nobles). The wealth extracted from the miserable populace was squandered in the licentious pleasures of the court and harem, and in maintaining the dignity of the Amir in neighboring capitals. One of his pleasure-palaces in the Russian Caucasus has now been turned into a rest-house for convalescent workers, who to-day enjoy the luxury which was wrung from the sweat and blood of the Bokharan peasant and handicraftsman. It is one of the minor conquests of the Russian Revolution" (Roy, 1924: 404–404; from the archives of Evelyn Roy).

25 Elnazarov and Aksaqolov (2011: Ch. 3); Postnikov (2000); Shokhumorov (2008); Habberton (1937).

26 Prior to this, as a number of scholars of the time make reference to, that area of Afghanistan and Turkestan was considered so remote and unruly, it seemed like "a natural border" and "barrier" to encroachment (Schurmann, 1962).

27 For example, Ustad Atta, a prominent leader in the North of Afghanistan, ethnically identifies as Tajik but his mother is actually Uzbek as is one of his wives. Moreover, President Rahmon of Tajikistan is alleged to be ethnically Uzbek while the President of Uzbekistan is Tajik.

28 There were others from the area who disputed this but they were younger. The elders were fairly consistent in their assertion of the border hardening over time and not right away.

29 See also Atkin (1992). This was similar to what occurred in Uzbekistan, Kazakhstan, and other parts of Central Asia. The Soviets often took a less dominant group and created the nation—including the national language, mythology, and history of the people with the goal of creating homogeneity among the citizens and decreasing ties to ethnicity and culture. This history is well-cited in the scholarly literature (Golden, 2011; Bregel, 1996; DeWeese, 2001).

30 The incoherent and undesired division of the territory is a common topic of conversation and even the source of an important but somewhat secret/hidden project supported by AKDN called the Badakhshan-Badakhshan Project (BBP). The BBP came up in numerous interviews with locals who worked for AKF/AKDN as well as local leaders. This is controversial in that some assert that the project is one of secession but, in reality, it is not. The BBP is primarily humanitarian with the goal of cooperative development of the region which spans the border areas.

31 Tajiks fought in the early stages to become a full republic instead of an annex of Uzbekistan and finally were granted SSR status. This began a long history of resource competition between Uzbekistan and Tajikistan which still is present today (Bergne, 2007). These borders are still being negotiated today. Since 2012, the Kazakh/Kyrgyz, Tajik/Chinese, Kyrgyz/Tajik, Tajik/Uzbek, and Uzbek/Kyrgyz have all been negotiated and/or re-negotiated or have been once again in contention. I know this from my fieldwork, work with OSCE, UNDP, and daily reading of the press.

32 Bregel explains "the most important concern of Central Asian historians (from the former Soviet Union): it was clear to them that, in order to provide historical legitimization to their new nations, it was not enough to project into the past the modern borders of their territories; since a nation was defined first of all in terms of ethnicity, it became necessary to provide the ethnic continuity of the titular nation on the territory of its republic during the entire period covered by their newly written histories—that is, since the Paleolithic times. There is an interesting similarity between the approach of 'modern' Central Asian historians and that of their 'pre-modern' predecessors: the latter created genealogical myths to provide legitimacy to their royal patrons, while the 'modern' ones created historical myths in order to provide legitimacy to their nations" (1996: 12).

33 "The concern of the Tajik historians was somewhat different: they had no problem with proving the uninterrupted presence of the Tajiks on the same territory throughout the Islamic period, but they did not want them to be counted, as Persian scholars and writers tend to do, as just another group of Persians with a language that was a dialect of Persian and a culture that was a dialect of Persian and a culture that was an extension of the great Persian culture. To counter this, the Tajik scholars not only stressed linguistic and cultural distinctiveness and separateness of the Tajiks from the Persians, but also promoted a theory, which held that the modern Persian language originated in Mavarannahr and from there spread to Persia, not vice versa. In another respect the Tajiks did the same as the Uzbeks; they did not admit the existence of other Iranian ethnic groups in Tajikistan, with separate histories and separate identities, namely, the small peoples of the Pamirs, who are quite distinct from the Tajiks both linguistically and historically, and classified as 'Pamir Tajiks'" (Bregel, 1996: 15).

34 Protocol Number 354 and Agreement Number 855: "Agreement between the Government of USSR and Royal Government of Afghanistan on the Status of the Soviet-Afghan State Border," original Protocol (1921), revised Protocol (1950), and Re-Demarcation Agreement (1946, 1948) obtained from the Organization of Security and Cooperation in Europe in September, 2009.

35　A local friend told me about a story from his childhood. It was the mid-1980s and his father had never told him that they were Ismaili because he was a hidden religious leader. His father took him to a back room, opened a safe—which he had always known about, and he finally got to see what was in the safe. It was a picture of the Aga Khan.

36　Information obtained from informal interviews with officials in Dushanbe and Khorog between March 2010 and October 2011. Moreover, this appeared to be common knowledge in that every person I spoke with, in an informal setting or after they decided I could be trusted, confirmed this.

37　A number of informants/elders in Badakhshan on both sides of this border talked about this in casual conversations and in interviews.

38　Bregel (1996). According to Bregel, this had been the Russian plan/strategy since the early 1600s when the Russians were negotiating borders in the region with the Chinese, albeit in different forms due to different political ideologies (Tsarist versus Communist). The Russians just had to wait until the right moment in history.

39　"The Shiahite massacre of 1909, directed against the Bokharan Government for giving the biggest posts to the Shiah sect of Moslems, and repressed by the Tsarist troops, was organised by another priest, Mullah Bachi. But the real centre of discontent lay in the exploited peasant masses, whom exorbitant taxation has reduced to the direst poverty. Not a year passed by without its peasant riot or rebellion, put down with the utmost cruelty" (Roy, 1924). Also see: "Shughnan Rebellion of 1925 and Verdict," The Russian Center of Preservation and Exploration of Documents in Recent History, Collection 62, list 2, file 243 (pp. 53–55; 61). London: Access to this document provided by the Institute for Ismaili Studies.

40　Many Khalqis I spoke with in Shughnan are still bitter about this.

41　Rashid (2000, 2009); Tanner (2002); Hoover Institution paper, 1982; interviews and discussions by the author with local elites in Shughnan, the Wakhan, and Ishkashim, 2010, 2011, 2012.

42　This was brought up in many conversations and debates with locals, leaders, and officials during my fieldwork in 2009–2011. A number of Afghans pointed out that the Afghan Parliament as of 2011 was 70% Communist. One of my informants brought me to numerous houses which belonged to the Sazaye party in Badakhshan. This is a communist-linked party. I spoke to a number of local leaders who also confirmed that there was and still is a strong allegiance to communist ideology.

43　Ibid.

44　Based on two interviews with two Special Forces soldiers in 2012 and 2013, who worked with Hekmatyar and Massoud from 1982–1988 in Afghanistan.

45　In the districts where I conducted my fieldwork, including Shughnan, Ishkashim, and the Wakhan, a number of the local leaders from the Soviet period in Afghanistan were educated in Moscow and spoke to me (in Dari) often about the Soviet Union and their connections to Russia today. The border remained shut until the late 1980s when the war ended. I conducted additional fieldwork in Dushanbe, Darwaz, Murgab, Tajikistan; Kabul, Faizabad, Zebok, Nusai, Afghanistan; Osh and Bishkek, Kyrgystan; and Baku, Lankaran, and the Talysh region of Azerbaijan.

46　Information obtained from several informants in Dushanbe and Khorog from 2010–2014.

47　See Emelianova, 2007.

48　These tapes are held by one German scholar with extremely limited access to outside scholars, which makes it difficult to ascertain the extent of the sexual violence during the Civil War although it can be safely assumed that it was considerable.

49　Kabiri is now living in exile and has to move frequently for safety reasons. His family is under constant attack by the government authorities in Tajikistan, and a number of male members of the family have been detained by the authorities and accused of extremism (Human Rights Watch, 2016).

4 Ancient myths, modern identity

The myths and histories of Badakhshan vary greatly, depending on who is asserting them, and they often overlap and compete with one another. Today, local leaders and groups assert ethnic, territorial, and religious identities to legitimate their own authority and as a means of resistance to the state. At the same time, these same myths and histories may be transcended for strategic or pragmatic purposes to unify groups otherwise mired in discord. For this very reason, scholarship on identity needs to "account equally for stasis and persistence as for fluidity and change" (Schatz 2004: xx).[1] Identities—territorial, ethnic, religious, and national—persist and evolve through the strategic usage of foundational myths and histories.

In the nineteenth century and earlier, ethnicity and culture "were not congruent and neither factor determined broad political affiliations" (Atkin, 1992: 151). Intermarriage and multilingualism were a normal feature of the region partly due to the complex interweaving of nomadic and sedentary populations. Mixing and finding ways to communicate were part of daily life, intrinsic to survival.

During the Soviet period, the opposite was true. Ethnicity became supremely important and was used to divide people where divisions had not previously existed. The Soviet Union built administrative units around ethnicity, categorized people through it, and carved out languages, some which barely existed, to support their political and social project. These divisions administratively based on ethnicity contradicted the Soviet Union's goal of citizen homogeneity. The overarching goal of the Soviet ethnic project was to mix all the people in the Soviet Union and create a single nation. The scholarship on ethnic groups and identities was a means to an end. In order to create a homogenous citizenry they first had to know the existing situation in the region. The early archeological and paleo-anthropological studies, along with the anthropological studies later by scholars such as Managorova (1972), and other Russian orientalists like Semenov (1980), asserted that the assimilation of the Pamirs with the rest of the Tajik population was inevitable.

At varying times, for example, Moscow tried to consolidate Tajikistan under a "Persian" umbrella, to separate the constructed Tajik identity from its Persian culture and language, to leverage its ethnic identity to decrease the

Soviet worry of a pan-Turkic identity, and to link the region to Alexander the Great (Iskandar) and the Macedonians (Atkin, 1992: 150–153).

The paradox, of course, is that once identified and divided into distinct groups, the identities became a means to an end. Namely, the different groups (both ethnically and territorially) lobbied for various resources based on these divisions instead of as a homogenous group of citizens from the region. Religious affiliation, which was largely hidden during the Soviet period, also was important but played a supporting role to the ethnic identities created by the Soviets. Additionally, the nationalist identity was spurned by the Soviet leaders as being counterproductive to the mission of a unified Soviet Union (Atkin, 1992). Therefore, the assertion of identity through these earlier defined ethnic groups (most often linked to territory), became the primary way that people engaged in collective petitioning for resources from Moscow (as opposed to nationality). The undercurrent of different ethnic and sub-ethnic groups competing for resources and power by currying favor with the Soviet party elite, while at the same time proving that they were all part of one USSR, created a black market economy of sub-ethnic rivalry.

Throughout my fieldwork, I frequently heard heated discussions and debates regarding origins, ethno-linguistic identity, and the "real" history of the region. The following discussion of myths highlights how locals assert identity as well as how it is conceived and/or imposed by non-locals.[2] The two perspectives inter-mix to create debates beneath the surface of conversations, the lingering shadows of past outside interference.[3]

Competing foundational myths

There are a number of foundational myths, both in the literature and as described by locals, about how people found their way into the isolated Pamir mountain range. People also debate the origin of the names such as Badakhshan, Khurasan, and Pamir. Which names and myths of origin are the authentic versions and which ones were imposed by outsiders remains an ongoing topic of heated discussion.[4]

The Russians promoted several competing myths based on their changing strategic needs. For example, the Aryan myth links the indigenous people to Zoroastrianism as well as Mithraism and Mazdianism, highlighting that the area was the cradle of the Aryans, the birth place of Zoroastrianism, and the root of Persian identity.[5] Conversely, the legend of Alexander the Great served to weaken the pan-Turkic potential the Soviets regarded as a competing state-formation project. The myths linking the region to the Persians served this same purpose. As a local teacher, whom I will refer to as Alim, told me:

> The Russians created their own myth of Macedonia for political purposes while the Aryan myth/aboriginal myth served Russian academic purposes to compete in Oriental studies. The fact that these myths directly

contradict each other is not important, simply that they countered both the Western and Nazi myths of origin that were being used for political purposes by their foes at the time.

These myths are still used today. I heard the myth of Alexander the Great repeatedly, particularly how he had left his progeny throughout the region.

Alexander the Great

The British, the Russians, the Soviets, and even the Turkic rulers of Badakh-shan promoted the Alexander the Great myth into the nineteenth century. I heard the story on both sides of the globe.

During a few conversations with specialists of Tajikistan and Central Asia both in U.S. government and think tanks in Washington, DC, the myth of the "beautiful people" mixed with the blood of the Persians and the ancient Greeks dominated. I was told that Alexander the Great had conquered the area, left descendants throughout the region, and that the diverse mix of light and dark skin; blond, brown, and black hair; and blue, green, hazel, and brown eyes came from the genes of Alexander mixed with indigenous peoples.

I also heard this myth from non-Pamiri elites in Tajikistan, including officials at the U.S. Embassy in Dushanbe, the UN, OSCE, and Tajik officials and citizens. Sitting at a party in a mansion in Dushanbe (many of the expatriate contractors and embassy officials had enormous houses in upscale areas of Dushanbe), very few people had visited Gorno-Badakhshan, but all seemed to know about the myth of Alexander and the resulting blue/green eyes throughout the Pamirs, such as seen in Steve McCurry's famous photographic portrait of the Afghan girl on the cover of *National Geographic* in June of 1985.[6]

Many Pamiris I spoke with disagreed with the Alexander the Great version of their origins. Two local scholars brought this point up repeatedly, and the more they drank the angrier they would become. They bitterly resented the many outsiders, possibly including myself, who had used their land and people for personal gains. Sitting under the stars on a *Tapchan* (a platform for eating outside) after dinner one night, a local scholar told me that outsiders had tried to co-opt the Pamiri ancestry and heritage with myths such as the Alexander one. He asked me rhetorically, "Do you really think one man could spread himself throughout an entire region? Does that make any sense? Or is it the typical way of colonizing an area: through the wombs of the women?" He told me that his forebears had likely descended from the Turks and the Zoroastrians and that many Zoroastrian ruins and traditions supported that view. He pointed out that he had Turkish features, as do many of his family members, while others had a "more indigenous make up" (although I am not sure what that means.) Nevertheless, the Alexander the Great myth sticks.

Alim told me, "Even when I was a child and visited my Russian grand-mother in Dushanbe, we used to fight physically with my Russian cousins. My grandmother would say, 'These are the descendants of Alexander the Great and that is why they are so violent!'" He added that, according to the Russians:

> The rule of Macedonian and the Greeks continued in Central Asia for 200 years where state-like Bactria and Soghdiana and Marghiana and many other statelets were ruled within Greek influence until they were defeated by the Medians (Iranians) and war-like tribes from the North. The Greek rulers were gradually forced by the indigenous tribes to retreat to the mountainous areas like those of the Pamirs, Gilgit, and Hunza and mixed with the local population (circa 200 BC to 1 AD). This is the reason the Pamiris bear a striking resemblance to the Greeks. In its essence however, this theory was a colonial project advanced by the Russians based on the principle of divide and rule.

Allegedly, the local Turkic rulers conveniently had a letter written by Alexander the Great stating that they were directly related to him.

The Alexander the Great myth, however, fails in one major way: Alexander and his army likely never traveled through Shughnan, Ishkashem, or the Wakhan Corridor. Another local scholar told me:

> Tajik intelligence coopted this pseudo-scientific theory [of Alexander the Great] for their own purposes to buttress the foundation of the so-called ancient Central Asian civilization as a connector of the East and the West. Additionally, for the purposes of political pragmatism, the Russians sought an ally in the face of the Pamiris against the predominantly Sunni Muslim population who were intractable to Russian penetration and modernization efforts. The Pamiris were called jokingly "unlucky Macedonians—[who] got stuck in the mountains."

I also heard a completely opposite myth that declared the region to be the birthplace of the Aryans and the "cradle of civilization."

Zoroastrians and Aryans

This second common myth asserts that groups of Zoroastrians (also referred to as Aryans, often for political purposes), escaping oppression from the south and western regions of Persia, found their way to the Pamir mountains and formed villages in the east.

The project of establishing Badakhshan as the original land of the Aryans started with the Soviets, who wanted to delegitimize the Nazi's claim to Aryan descent. Zoroastrian scholars also have supported claims made by Iranians and Russian/Soviet Oriental scholars that Persian linkages exist throughout the region (Laruelle, 2007: 66). During the Soviet era, Tajik scholars began to study the political implications of the Zoroastrian myth (Shokhumurov, 1997). They built on Iranian scholarship on Zoroastrian history, which was being used at the time as the backdrop for Pahlavi's modernization of Iran in the 1950s. Pamiri Tajik scholars such as Iskandarov, who reconstructed the history of the Pamirs back to antiquity and linked them to the Aryan race, expanded the idea. As the local scholar points out:

> The idea that there somehow is the most pure Aryan race located in the Pamirs is difficult to digest. Although there has been some interesting work on genetic origins of the human race in Central Asia, which is indeed compelling, the assignation of Aryan to this human origination in the area, clearly points to a political manipulation of racial superiority and exceptionalism used by the Russians and Nazis for their own nationalistic purposes.

The Zoroastrian/Aryan myth also was used to support Soviet claims that the Tajiks are Persians and the Pamirs are Zoroastrians. As the local scholar explained:

> For the Russians and the Tajik Oriental studies it was no more than a political instrument to create a distinct republic of Tajikistan as opposed to other Turkic republics in Central Asia. The Pamiris became the best of the Tajiks (or the pure "Aryan") who are supposed to be proud of their origin and stand against the Turkic republics and ethnic groups in the region, which was the goal of the Russians as they created the states in Central Asia during the pre-Soviet/early Soviet period. Despite the incredible mix of the population in Tajikistan who were in no way different from the rest of the population in Central Asia, the roots of the Tajik nation had been established surprisingly by the Russian Oriental Studies in which the Pamiris became the most salient element of what might be termed, "pure" Tajikness within the nation. For pragmatic and political purposes this theory would greatly help the assimilation of the Pamiri ethnic groups with the rest of the population in Tajikistan.

There is much evidence that Zoroastrianism was prevalent in the area, including ancient Zoroastrian fire temples, forts, and other ruins in the Wakhan (on both sides of the border), outside Khorog, and in Ishkashim. Many local scholars contend that Ismaili religious rituals and traditions contain elements from Zoroastrianism (Bekhradnia, 1994: 114).[7] Zoroastrianism spread throughout the region a few centuries before Alexander the Great allegedly explored the area (Dhalla, 1938). Some accounts say that the Zoroastrians who came to the hills were escaping persecution by Muslims, others say by other Zoroastrians. In the latter version, the Mazdaki sect within the Zoroastrian religion was massacred by the Sassanians, who were more orthodox Zoroastrians and who believed that the Mazdakism sect was heretical.

I heard the story of Zoroastrians escaping Muslims far more often. The story told said that due to the forced conversions of Persian Zoroastrians by the Arabs and Muslims, they fled to the hills and created a secret language to hide their Persian Zoroastrian origins. Bakhradnia cites sources from the late nineteenth century that single out the Wakhi "as people whose customs manifest what he believes to be aspects of Zoroastrianism" (1994: 113–114). Still others assert that the Mithraists and Mazdians were precursors to Zoroastrianism in the region, providing further evidence for the region being the "cradle" of the Persians and/or the Aryans. Some recent scholarship asserts that Zoroaster (Zardusht) originated someplace west of Badakhshan in Afghanistan.

Jo-Ann Gross wrote about the links among Zoroastrianism, Ismailism, and the cultural roots of Badakhshan based on her study of the Sufi shrines in the area. She finds many connections among Zoroastrianism, Ismailism, and the people of the area today. I also heard this from many locals.

Alim points out:

> In contrast to the Macedonian myth, the Zoroastrian (or Aryan) myth has a wider currency in academic sources. According to this theory the Pamirs is the birthplace and the cradle of Aryan races who descended from the North and gradually spread to India and Iran and then later, to Europe. Originally, the theory came from the German geographer who identified the Pamiris with the early ancestors of India and Iranians based on documentary evidence from archeological and historical sources. From these sources it was deemed that the Pamiri population are the proto-Aryans who invented the religion, which would later become Zoroastrianism in the form professed by the Iranians and the official ideology of the Sassanid Empire. These early studies played counter the earlier Macedonian myth and the Russians used it to make the Pamirs into their own Tibet (as the most pure place of Aryans) in competition with Nazi Germany. They further advanced the presupposition to the effect that the Pamiris in fact are aboriginal people who are not necessarily mixed with other races.

Similar to the assertion of "authentic" identity through the foundational myths of Badakhshan, names of territories in the region also became politicized. The disagreements over names and naming came from a variety of places, including foreign and local academics, oral histories, politicians, and others. Since outsiders affixed names to various areas during different periods in history and for various political reasons, locals often work hard to assert the "real" indigenous names.

Who names whom? Pamir, Badakhshan, Khurasan, and Afghanistan

Which groups people belonged to and/or did not belong to was a frequent topic of discussion on both sides of the border often focusing on myths of origin and/or "true" histories. There are many histories, both written and oral, and all are as true as the next.[8] Names (and naming) is one of these practices that combine elements of the debates about foundational myths and history(ies).

For example, early scholars of the region separated the Tajiks into "mainland" versus "mountain" Tajiks (Curzon, 1896; Bartold, 1918, 1920; Monogarova, 1972). However, most of the people I came to know on both sides of the border in Badakhshan rejected being "Tajik"; instead, they asserted that they were Pamiri, Khorogi, Shughni, Ishkashimi, Wakhi, Zeboki, and sometimes, on the Afghan side, people "of the land of Khurasan."

Pamir

I was told many times that outsiders contrived the name "Pamir." Locals said that Russians came to the area as early as the 1600s when they were fighting the Chinese. Since they had spent time in the northern area known as the Pamir mountains, the Russians decided to name the area Pamir and the people Pamiri. These local scholars contend that the Soviets appropriated this name as a means to reframe the foundations of their people.

Yet the term does have possible local origins. *Pa* means "foot" in old and modern Persian (Bliss, 2005; Olufson, 1904). Due to the height of the mountains in the region, some locals believed that the people living there were closer to Mithra, the Sun God. Thus pa (foot) and Mithra (sun) likely became Pamir, or "at the foot of the sun." *Mir* also can mean king, chief, leader, or commander, so it could also mean that the high mountains touched the foot of the sun king (Mithra). Others interpret Pamir as the "roof of the world" since it is the closest point on earth to the sun or to god. Still, others say that it means "foot of the mountain." There is some evidence for this latter definition because in geography pamir means a plain or flat land in between mountain peaks.[9]

Local scholars pointed out that prior to the Soviet (and Russian) nation-building projects, the ethnonym Pamir was associated exclusively with the northern areas now called Murghab, a Kyrgyz-Sunni section of Gorno-Badakhshan. Many locals refer to the area as Badakhshan, dismissing the name Pamir altogether.

Badakhshan

The most common name I heard on both sides of the border was Badakhshan. Chinese sources from as early as the seventh century AD refer to the area surrounding today's Xinjiang province in China as Badakhshan.

However, in Shughnan, *Badakhshi* is a pejorative term used to denote any outsider or to describe a person who is dangerous or should be avoided, particularly on the Afghan side of the border. Afghan women told me they were not allowed to go the bazaars because their fathers and husbands feared the Badakhshis would hurt their women. The men and women from Afghan-Shughnan also told me that the "Badakhshis" in the bazaar hung around at night and sold drugs, leading to the increase in addiction and overdoses in the area.

Other than this negative connotation, Badakhshan seemed to be the most unifying name and most accepted locally. In fact, recently the Aga Khan Foundation launched the Badakhshan-Badakhshan Project (BBP) to create cross-border pathways for humanitarian interventions since many of the areas along the border are isolated and have little access to outside resources, particularly food and medicine. The project thus far has helped many residents on both the Afghan and Tajik sides through increased trade, medical, and cultural exchanges. The project there also includes a proposed free customs and trade area spanning both sides of the districts of Ishkashim/Ishkashem.

Medieval Arab and European writers referred to the region as "Balascian," and in medieval Arabic *balas* means "ruby." Marco Polo mentioned a "balas" ruby and the "lale badakhshan" was long considered the finest form of ruby. Today there is still a mountain in the area named *Koh-e Lal* (ruby mountain). Nasiri Khusraw, the famous eleventh-century writer credited with bringing Ismailism to Badakhshan, is called the "Ruby of Badakhshan" in Alice Hunsberger's well-known book (2000).

Khurasan

The name "Khurasan" also came up in many conversations. The first time was on a cold day as my guide and I walked through a village in a remote part of the Wakhan Corridor in Afghanistan. A local man struggling with addiction had just shown us a secret opium den where the locals go to smoke. My assistant explained that the Sunni traders (he was Ismaili) forced the locals to buy opium and oppressed them. He asked me if I had heard of Khurasan. At first I did not understand his pronunciation, so I told him no. He looked hurt and shocked. He asked me how I could be conducting research on Badakhshan without knowing this important part of the history. He said to me that he is not Afghan and that name does not apply to his land. His people belonged to Khurasan, the "land of the sun." He was convinced that as long as the Afghans controlled his land, his people would be in misery. Many Afghans in Badakhshan share similar beliefs. It was unclear to me which era of Khurasan he was referring to.

This name and historical lineage are more prevalent in the foundational myths on the Afghan side of the border.[10] Northerners in Afghanistan used the name Khurasan as a means of resistance against the Pashtun power elite in Kabul. Some groups in the north would prefer to be part of Khurasan or to be detached from southern Afghanistan and remapped into the state of Khurasan, dividing Afghanistan into two states. As of 2011–2013 there were numerous social media groups using the name Khurasan and based throughout northern Afghanistan. Three different scholars from Gorno-Badakhshan repeatedly asked me to write about Khurasan with them in order to outline the true origin of the people in the region.

The name Khurasan likely dates to the time of the Zoroastrians. Mithra, as mentioned above, is the name for the Sun God, which is of great importance in the Zoroastrian religion.[11] *Khur* means "sun" and *asan* means "to come from"; essentially, "the place of the sun-worshippers," which is a pseudonym for Zoroastrians. The challenge, of course, is that Khurasan was an area in the region over two thousand years ago as well as a name being used today. In fact, oddly, also has been coopted by part of the Islamic State, ISIS.

In the third century BC the region that spanned Afghanistan, parts of Central Asia, Pakistan, and Iran also belonged to Khurasan. In this version, Khurasan translates as "land where the sun rises" in middle Persian.[12] According to historical sources and maps, Khurasan also existed during the Safavid Empire in the early Islamic period in 750 AD and is shown on maps as late as the early 1700s. Moreover, there are still three districts in Iran today that are under the umbrella of the province of Khurosan. The language spoken in parts of Chitral in Pakistan is Khowar, which is a holdover from when the region was known as Khurasan. In Middle Persian, sun was rendered as *khur* or *khow* and the area was also referred to as Khowarasan.[13]

Khurasan also was used politically on the Tajik side of the border. The local scholar explained:

> In the late 1990s, when the Tajik government contemplated invading the Pamirs, they needed to create more divisions among the local resistance movement and this could be best done through administrative divisions. By then, the governor of GBAO, Mr. Niaz Mahmadov, started talking on the local television station about the Khurasanis allegedly living in Shokhdara [Roshtqa'la]. After these appearances, there were some villagers in Shokhdara Valley who claimed their ancestors had arrived from Khurasan. These alleged descendants of the Khurasanis and the governor's assertions of the Khurasani descendents within the Pamiris did not make sense to anybody among the locals. But sometime later, it transpired that the Shokhdara District, which was part of Shughnan District until then, all of a sudden was made into a separate district.

This administrative partition, by dividing the local population into smaller and smaller groups, would allow the authorities to more easily manipulate them through creating competition for resources among the groups.

Afghanistan

As already mentioned, many people residing in the northern portion of Afghanistan, including the self-identified Tajiks, Persians, Qizalbash (known for having red hair—qizal means red in Turkish), and Uzbeks, said they do not feel a part of this country named "Afghanistan."[14] If the appellation did not come from the residents, then where did the name "Afghanistan" originate? Numerous scholars have written about the origins of the name Afghan, so I will only summarize here.

The Mughal Empire referred to the Pashtun tribesman's territory as "Yaghestan" or the "the land of insolence" (Barry, 2010: 41). Other stories on its inception date as far back as the Kushanid Empire (c. 30–775 AD), the Sassanian Empire (224–651 AD), or the Ghaznavids (c. 950–1200 AD). The word assumed several meanings during these periods, including: (1) "horse-people"; (2) belonging to a list of Sassanian tributary kings; or (3) the "Limits of the World" (Barry, 2010: 81). The most common story holds that the name "Afghan" and the country of Afghanistan became commonly known under the Afghan King Ahmad Shah Durrani in 1837. At the time the territory of Afghanistan included the combined forces of the Durrani and the Ghilzai tribes both Pashtun from the south of the country (Tanner, 2002). Suffice it to say, the contention over this territory and the names/labels used to designate it has a long and sometimes violent history, and it is clear I am not going to settle it here.

Political implications

I can only speculate as to why the myths and names included here became more entrenched than others. On tablets and other ancient forms of documentation, the people in the south frequently referred to the people in the north as wild and uncontrollable. In the Tajik Wakhan, locals pointed to various caves and Buddhist hideouts that were used by locals during attacks by people "from the south." Some of the older accounts, either from the literature or as documented in museums, are strikingly similar to the contemporary stories I heard, except that I heard *northerners* expressing similar feelings about those from the *south*. Namely, outsiders—whether Afghanistan's north versus south, Ismaili versus Sunni, Tajik's west versus east or Pamiri versus Tajik—are often described as uncivilized or dangerous even today.

After hearing about the wild people from the south and reading about the wild people in the northern mountains repeatedly, I decided to investigate this flexible narrative a bit more. Once again, I am not writing history, I am looking at similar depictions of the past and today. The myths I was told always included some form of differentiation between insiders and outsiders.

Portions of all of these myths can be traced to written documents, historical artifacts, and archeological findings.[15] Numerous ring stamps and stone tablets dating back to circa 2000 BC feature symbols used by the people in the mountainous regions in and around Badakhshan.[16] These include a particular type of endangered mountain yak, a distinctive sun, and ring stamps that belonged to traders and leaders in the mountainous areas. The ring stamps were used to indicate the origin of an item.[17] The symbols on the ring stamps also indicated how the particular geographic area was ruled, such as a khanate or another type of grouping. Even in the limited documentation of the era, the distinction between insiders and outsiders (and Southerners and Northerners) was present.

According to the tablets and findings by archeologists, the southern tribes attempted to build a perimeter to protect themselves from the northerners as well as to delineate which territories belonged to the Persian Empire. Even though the tablets from the time assert that the northern people were nomadic and uncontrollable, it appears that these areas, and Badakhshan in particular, were known to be rich in precious minerals and gemstones.

Many Tajiks in Dushanbe told me about the wild mountain people on the Tajik side of the border. Even Kipling referred to the north in terms of "trouble":

> Listen in the North, my boys, there's trouble in the wind.
> Tramp, O Cossacks, troop in front, grey greatcoats behind.
> Trouble on the Frontier of the most amazin' kind,
> Trouble on the waters o' the Oxus.[18]

Not only do Northerners and Southerners refer to each other as primitive or uncivilized, they view their governments in similarly negative ways. Many of the locals on both sides of the border described their central governments as being occupied by uncivilized, uneducated, and corrupt crooks who have sold themselves and their countries to the highest bidder.[19] Conversely, I heard numerous times while in Dushanbe that "the people of the Pamirs are wild and uncivilized." I also witnessed debates between the two, the Sunni Tajiks and the Ismaili Pamiris, about the country's history, the Hanafi versus Ismaili religious beliefs, and family social practices.

Conclusion

Both insiders and outsiders invoke myths to assert local identity. Perhaps in the process of piecing together their own history, they relied not only on their own oral histories and artifacts but also on accounts by the various colonialists and outsiders—Persian, Greek, Russian and British scholars and explorers. As Marsden and Hopkins (2012) point out, "the many competing histories create a mirage of origin instead of myths of origin—too elusive to grasp yet always within sight." And who is defined an "insider" and "outsider" varies according to which myth is being shared. Both categories define themselves according to what they were not—corrupt and without morals or uncivilized and dangerous. It appears these assertions of identity, embodied in the myths I outline above, have roots in numerous places as well as many fluid permutations.

The insider/outsider debate, and who belongs and who does not, highlights the depth of the dislike of outsiders, whether they are attempting to control, partner, or merely live in the area. Clearly, there are good reasons to be wary—over centuries various foreign entities have attempted to control or manipulate the region for their own gains.

If it is easy to identify who is an outsider, it is much more difficult to determine what constitutes an "insider" locally. If even toponyms such as "Afghanistan" and "Pamir Mountains," much less the myths of origin, are in contention, how does one ever resolve who an insider and outsider really is? The answer is: it depends. Crucially, it depends on what an individual is trying to be inside or outside of.

The issue of the "outsider" as oppressor is important in Badakhshan. Many policymakers, scholars, and nongovernmental organizations believe that developing the formal institutions at the border will increase state stability. But in this context, if the formal institutions are primarily developed and implemented by various "outsiders," the process may be not just difficult but detrimental. Additionally, if these outsiders ignore the networks that are already in place, attempt to enforce their new laws, and erect physical structures in order to force local informal leaders, organizations, and groups to dissolve, they do so at their own peril. These informal/local networks will respond with further institutionalization, become more entrenched, and continue as before beneath the façade imposed from the outside.

Notes

1 "Groupness does not survive merely by definition; rather it survives (if and when it does) because of identifiable mechanisms of identity reproduction. Consequently, if such mechanisms are disrupted or changed, we can expect concurrent changes in the shape and meaning, and salience of group identities" (Schatz, 2004: xx). Charles Tilly was the first to define different forms of "groupness" in 1978.

2 The literature on myths (including their associated symbols, theatrical expressions, folktales, rituals and symbols—both semiotic and hermeneutic) crosses many disciplines. But for myths specifically used as political tools, the main scholars include Erving Goffman, Luis Althusser, John Searle, William Beeman, Bronislaw Malinowsky, Richard Schechner and Victor Turner.

3 Marsden and Hopkin's (2012) provide a useful basis for using a combination of history and ethnography to provide analysis for the assertion of what they term a "fluid identity," which forms and reforms through various historical paradigms and is asserted by local domestic, and international players, which all contribute to a continuous construction and reconstruction of identity.

4 Moreover, the "true" myths of origin also included three "ethnic" groups; the Persians, the Pashtuns, and the Turks were the basis for the people in the region and/or the names.

5 "When, as the outcome of the expedition of Alexander (334–323 BC), the civilization of Greece spread throughout all Hither Asia, it impressed itself upon Mazdaism as far east as Bactriana. Nevertheless, Iranism, if we may employ such a designation, never surrendered to Hellenism. Iran proper soon recovered its moral autonomy, as well as its political independence; and generally speaking, the power of resistance offered by Persian traditions to an assimilation which was elsewhere easily effected is one of the most salient traits of the history of the relations of Greece with the Orient. But the Magi of Asia Minor, being much nearer to the great foci of Occidental culture, were more vividly illumined by their radiation. Without suffering themselves to be absorbed by the religion of the conquering strangers, they combined their cults with it. In order to harmonize their barbaric beliefs with the Hellenic ideas, recourse was had to the ancient practice of identification. They strove to demonstrate that the Mazdean heaven was inhabited by the same denizens as Olympus: Ahura-Mazda as Supreme Being was confounded with Zeus; Verethraghna, the victorious hero, with Heracles; Anâhita, to whom the bull was consecrated, became Artemis Tauropolos, and the identification went so far as to localize in her temples the fable of Orestes. Mithra, already regarded in Babylon as the peer of Shamash, was naturally associated with Helios; but he was not subordinated to him, and his Persian name was never replaced in the liturgy by a translation, as had been the case with the other divinities worshipped in the Mysteries" (Cumot, 1903: 20–24).
6 http://ngm.nationalgeographic.com/2002/04/afghan-girl/index-text.
7 "The Wakhi and Shughni members of the Society hold that many of their local traditions are derived from Zoroastrianism, and are sure indicators of a not-too distant Zoroastrian past. The religion of the Badakhshanis was traditionally Ismaili, and some argue that this sect has a direct connection with Zoroastrianism since the founder Ismail was a descendant of the union of the prophet's great grand-nephew with the Zoroastrian princess Shahrbanu, daughter of the last Zoroastrian king of Iran. This king, Yazdegerd, is known to have fled the Arabs and headed for China, and it is suggested that he may have sought refuge in the region of the Pamirs. A photocopied nineteenth-century manuscript copy of the History of Shughnan by Heydar Shah contains several contemporary references to fire worshippers and infidels, terms usually reserved exclusively for Zoroastrians by Muslim writers in Persian. Informants also say that they have a hazy collective memory, based on oral history, of their forefathers having had a different religion. It is of course possible that much of this may merely be wishful thinking. There are, however, the independent writings of European travelers throughout the nineteenth century in which references are made to the inhabitants of the Pamirs, and in the most widely known of these, *Through the Unknown Pamirs*, written in the late nineteenth century, the author singles out the Wakhis as people whose customs manifest in aspects of Zoroastrianism" (Bakhradnia, 1994: 113–114).
8 "The Frontier's multiple spaces are inhabited by, and nurture the existence of, multiple histories, communities, and lifeworlds: what we refer to as 'fragments'" (Marsden and Hopkins, 2012: 4).
9 Robert Middleton outlines various versions of the etymology of Pamir: "Sanskrit: 'upa'-'mery'—the country behind the bank of the river; 'upa'-'meru'—the country above Mount Meru (legendary holy mountain of Hindu mythology, abode of the gods and centre of the universe) Old Persian: 'poye'-'mehr'—the land at the foot of the sun; 'pa-i-mikhr'—pedestal of Mitra, the sun god; 'bom'-'ir'—land of the Aryans; 'pai'-'mir'—foot of the mountain peaks; 'pa-e-Mir'—foot of the Mir (Hazrat Ali) 'fan'-'mir' or ('famir')—the lake country of the *Fani*, who according to Strabo founded Balkh—here 'mir' is etymologically identical with Indo-European words for sea or lake, as in the name 'Kashmir' and modern German 'Meer'. Turkic: a desert; or a plateau" (Middleton, 2008: 515–519).

Middleton also cites a number of sources (which I also have consulted): see also Shokhumurov (1997: 31–32); Iskandarov (1996: 11); Curzon (1896: 29–30); and Curzon (1896: 34).

10 Map of Tribes and associated leaders in power in Afghanistan since 1747: www. nytimes.com/imagepages/2010/01/31/weekinreview/13rohde-grfk-1.html?ref=weekin review.

11 See also on Khurasan: Bartold (1918, 1920); Shaban (1970); and Noelle-Karimi (2008).

12 From Bowen (1747). See also Bartold (1918, 1920).

13 Ibid.

14 This argument was made by numerous locals while I was in the field from 2009–2011. It also is in current analysis in Dari language newspapers and other web-based materials.

15 Citations include: British Museum, Islamic Collection at the Metropolitan Museum of Art, Dodikhudoeva (2004); unpublished archives of the Institute for Ismaili Studies, Khorog, Tajikistan; interviews and discussions with numerous people living in and originating from the region. Additionally, there have been a number of epigraphic studies published in Russian. These studies as well as detailed ethnographic, cartographic, and geological studies were conducted prior to the formation of the Soviet republics in Central Asia.

16 Oxus collection at the British Museum, including my photographs from my visit to the museum in 2012.

17 This is similar to Cuneiform, which was developed as an accounting system prior to the first written language.

18 Quoted from Cobbold (1900: 251).

19 I had numerous discussions between 2009–2012, on the Tajik and Afghan sides of Badakhshan as well as with people from Dushanbe and Kabul (in government positions, working for IGOs and NGOs, and local traders).

5 The social organization of the borderlands of Badakhshan

Social organization defines how a community organizes itself socially. In any area, stability is maintained through complex interactions among informal organizations, networks, and leaders. "Informal organizations are social (non-state-created) groups that have a corporate character; specific informal unwritten agreements shape individuals' expectations and behavior within the group" (Collins, 2004: 231). In his study of Swat Pakhtuns, Barth conceptualized the make-up of daily life in Swat by revealing the population's "underlying frameworks of organization" (1959: 13). He describes identities as "nested" and/or "segmented" and then articulates how people strategically use their different sub-identities to strengthen their position in a given situation.

Local conditions and the overall social organization underpin the mechanisms that allow identity to shape an individual's behavior. Individuals assert identity in Badakhshan through networks. The mechanisms used to produce ethnic, religious, and territorial identities all influence how local networks react to outside pressure. I build on Barth's conceptualization to reveal how different informal organizations and their leaders influence border stability, both geographically and socially. At the same time, I highlight some of the pressures that constrain the daily life of people living in the borderlands. Understanding the boundaries of different identity groups, local organizations, and the varying modes of inter-group cooperation sheds light on the ways that the institutional development of the border shapes local identity groups.

I made my first trip to Badakhshan with little prior research on the region in order to minimize any preconceived notions about what I might or might not find there. As Barth so aptly puts it, while in the field, I "looked to the social life that surrounded me as my only reality and authority" (1993: 25). Once there, I discovered multiple overlapping borders of identity, informal organizations, and leadership. These different borders and informal organizations make up a larger social framework that includes familial/sub-ethnic, local, domestic, regional, and international borders.

As I explained in Chapter 3, I took the stories I found in the field back to the United States and only then tried to interpret them using scholarly materials. After that, I returned to the region three more times to continue the conversation between the fieldwork and the literature about the area. I selected my case studies to reflect what I had experienced, observed, and heard through my interaction with the local communities, events, and organizations, including international governmental organizations (IGOs) and nongovernmental organizations (NGOs). As I uncovered the networks of cooperation and the mechanisms influencing these networks, I adjusted my research focus.

Sub-ethnic identity, familial ties, and clan affiliation are particularly important to the social organization in Badakhshan. Divisions go as far down (micro) as the street level (and family rivalries) but can be also be found at the (macro) state and regional levels. People transcend and assert these borders as part of their daily practices. This chapter offers several case studies about how residents of Badakhshan solve problems ignored—or caused—by state officials. Time and again, locals mobilize their own networks—based on ethnic, religious, professional, family, or regional ties—to provide security when the state has failed to act. These vignettes reveal the underlying frameworks of social organization, including: (1) borders between different parts of the larger community; (2) how people identify with a group they assert they belong to; and (3) how they understand who belongs to what group and who does not.

It cannot be overstated how controversial the terms "ethnic identity" and "sub-ethnic identity" are in Tajikistan. The term "clan" often is shunned on the Tajik side of the border, but nevertheless ethnicity and familial affiliation are invoked when the status of a family name or connection is useful. The next section focuses on defining clans, tribes, and sub-ethnic groups both in the scholarly materials and in the local vernacular.

Sub-ethnic groups: clans and tribes

There are many definitions of Central Asian clans and warlords. Moreover, these same words mean different things depending on which group, dialect, or alliance is involved. Even local residents living in the same neighborhood had different words and different definitions for what are often referred to as clan, tribe, and local leader. Therefore, the translated meaning into English may mean something completely different from one person in Tajikistan to the next person as understood through one dialect or another.

Clans and kinship

Informal ties are known to be vital to state stability and governance in both Tajikistan and Afghanistan. "Simply put, a clan is an informal organization comprising a network of individuals linked by kin-based bonds. Affective ties of kinship are its essence, constituting identity and bonds of its organization" (Collins, 2004: 231). Additionally, clan-based politics remained pervasive during the Soviet period. Collins argues that sub-ethnic political rivalries are primary for understanding how the political process works in Tajikistan. This

Table 5.1 Local terms for leaders and local informal sub-ethnic identity groups

| | Group | | Leader | | | | | | | |
Person Interviewed/ Location	Tribe	Clan	Neighborhood	Leader	Neighborhood Leader	Streetleader	Warlord	Drug Lord	Spiritual Leader	Clan Leader
Sher (Korog)	Qabila	Qawm	Mahalla		Mahallah Lideren	Rahbar	Commandon/ Jange Salar	Narcobaron/ Qachaqbar	Khalifa[1]	
Jamshed (Khorog)		Qawm, Zot, Qabila		Rahbar			Boevik (post-Soviet, Russian)	Narkobaron (post-Soviet, Russian)	Rahbari ruhoni	
Sohrab (Shughnan. Afghanistan)										Khaydar/ Rahbari Qawm/ Awloder Rohbar (Tajik/Dari)
Nilofar (Shugnan)							Thed Talabi (Shughni)	Qachaq bar/ Qachaq che (Shughni and Dari)		Malik (Dari) Aqsaqal (Tajik/ Uzbek) Qabilah Rahbar (Dari/Farsi)
Ahmed (Balkh, Afghanistan, all in Dari)		Qawm or Khanawada					Ustad Genural Jange Salar Mujahed	Hashafurush		Kolontar Khana, Aqsaqal

also is true for Badakhshan. But too often politicians and scholars apply the term clan in a negative sense. People assume that tribes and clans are pre-modern "primitive" groups opposed to state-formation or development schemes. "From a teleological perspective of presumptive developmental end points, to invoke the term 'tribe' is to make a normative claim" (Schatz, 2004: 25).

Kinship ties are either fictive or blood-based. Fictive ties are cultivated by the ruling elites and central power structures, while blood ties are based on a combination of actual family connections and perceived ethnic group identification. In the Soviet region, the networks of cooperation shifted from "blood" clan (pre-Soviet), to "fictive" clan (Soviet), to a combination of the two in the post-Soviet era (Collins, 2006). The clans' persistence confirms that they are a key informal institution and political organization that people regard as legitimate. Others (Dagiev, 2013) contend that Soviet institutions displaced clan-based politics during the Soviet period

I asked locals and officials in Khorog and Dushanbe about this issue. Many said that they still relied heavily on their family networks to get things done during the Soviet era—and even more so now. Soviet officials distributed administrative posts among different clans so that no one clan had too much power. This was even the practice at the local level, where a local apparatchik from one clan had a deputy from a different clan.

According to a local scholar:

> The political system of the Soviet Union in Tajikistan used a specific scheme here. When the first person in a district or at the country level was Tajik [from the north] the second person was always Russian and then, the head of police was from Kulyab, the head of the local KGB mostly from Pamir, the local trading system was under control of Gharmies. It was political division of regions in order to keep them silent.

I heard many locals assert that this division of labor according to Soviet-defined ethnic groups helped maintain order and limited inter-clan tensions during this period (see also Hughes and Sasse, 2002: 2–9).

But in many places, particularly Gorno-Badakhshan, clan has less to do with ethnicity and more to do with territory, family, and religion. In fact, when I used the terms clan or tribe with locals in Khorog, many became offended. They said that they were not primitive like that and that I was mixing them up with the Afghan side of the border. They wanted to make clear that the social divisions were based on territory and/or religion, not family blood-lines. They also asserted that clans were a pre-Soviet form of social organization, one beyond which they had evolved. But on the Afghan side of the border, locals agreed completely that many of the local divisions/ borders were clan-based, although territorial- and religion-based identities also exist.

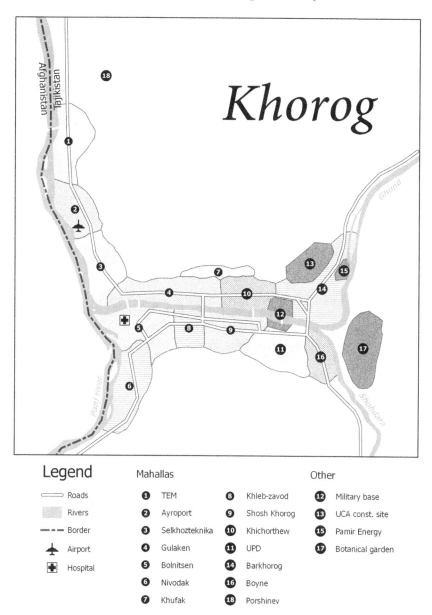

Figure 5.1 Map of the city of Khorog in Gorno-Badakhshan, Tajikistan
Source: Map created by Suzanne Levi-Sanchez (with technical assistance from Federico Rossi).

Tribes and territory

In the past khanates, emirates, and statelets defined a territory led by one leader. The territory also typically had a cohesive religious identity, linguistic identity, and common practices and customs and functioned similar to a clan or a tribe.

The boundaries of these territories were their greatest source of stability and instability. When local groups and leaders defied central authorities to assert their control over territory along their periphery of the khanate/emirate, instability increased both at the boundaries and also within the khanates/emirates themselves. The same is true today. The borders are areas of potential resistance and when outside pressure increases, it is likely that inside resistance will increase, which causes instability at the border. The identity groups, and in Badakhshan, the kinship networks, are a key component of these rivalries.[2]

The challenge is that these ties of self-asserted identity are fluid and based on many things at once. If we can pinpoint the components of group affiliation, it will help us to recognize "changes to the character of those affiliations and, therefore, what impact they have on politics" (Schatz, 2004: xxi). The logical starting point is to first define the words for clan, village, tribe, and various informal leaders in the local vernacular, but as shown in Table 5.1, the many interpretations of these words make even this a rather murky process. For example, tribe and clan are used interchangeably in the local languages, as are the terms for the leaders of these groups.

Defining leaders and groups in Badakhshan and Gorno-Badakhshan

I spoke with local scholars, villagers, community members, sellers in the bazaar, and local development workers from Khorog and Ishkashim (Tajikistan) and Shughnan, Ishkashem (Afghanistan), the Wakhan Corridor and Balkh (Afghanistan) about how they conceptualized the meanings of the many words for leaders and local networks. Even people from local groups who worked closely together, such as academics working in the same university, answered my questions with different words and offered different definitions of those words.

What is clear from my fieldwork is that in each village, village cluster, neighborhood, district, province, or region, the meaning of the term shifted based on context, person, and group. As an outsider to the area, I provide the meanings and explanations shared with me by the local population as well as scholars with this disclaimer: Table 5.1 is only a partial list of how local leaders are defined in the local dialects and context. The table has definitions of local leaders and local organizations provided by five different people.

The list in Table 5.1 only encompasses informal local leaders and organizations and territorial/familial/ethnic groups. It does not include the names for official leaders. The definitions capture not only the importance of local leaders and social groups, but also that they hold many different positions within their communities. Moreover, perceptions of whom and what they are and/or mean in the community shift regularly. For example, in Khorog all drug lords are warlords, but not all warlords are drug lords. The terms *Mahalla* and *Mahalla Lideren/Raise Mahalla* (neighborhood and neighborhood leader) are quite important on the Tajik side of the border since the partitioning of physical territory holds more significance there than clan-based networks.

In Afghan Badakhshan, territory is divided into village clusters and/or villages and districts. "Neighborhoods," as such, do not really exist. *Qeshlaq* or *Qaria* are the most common terms for village in the districts I worked. But, *Qawm*, which translates to clan, holds much more significance. For example, a friend of mine who lives on the edge of the Wakhan Corridor on the Afghan side, explained to me that if families did not show up for communal duties, such as building a house for a newly wedded couple in their *Qawm*, they were *Bevafa*, which could be translated as completely shunned.

There is not always a conceptual distinction between a drug lord and a clan head because the two types of leaders are so intertwined. In fact, there are almost no powerful leaders who do not traffic in drugs. On the Afghan side, some drug lords are called *Ustad*—a learned person or respected teacher. But other drug lords are simply *Qachaqbar*, which loosely translates to "full of corruption." A drug lord also could be referred to as *Hashafrush*, which literally means hashish seller—usually because they sell *Taryak* (Opium). On both sides of the border, the drug lord's title often delineates his influence or status as well as how much people perceive he has helped his community. It also defines the extent of his influence over a given territory.

The different meanings of leaders and social groups highlight that the definitions of informal local leaders are different in the local vernacular and usage than in the way scholars use the words to describe these same groups. In the vernacular, the terms have nuance and more aptly describe the actual position or standing of the informal leader within the community. More important, local leaders' status varies according to the perceived amount of public service they have done for their community as well as their ability to be physically strong and control territory as a means to project their power. A leader's intellect is also valued by the community.

The following series of vignettes provides a window into the complexity of the different identities and how outside pressure can mobilize local informal leaders and associated organizations. The following section is a case-study of the social organization in Khorog, Tajikistan. Chapter 7 focuses on the other side of the border in Shughnan, Ishkashem, Zebok, and the Wakhan Corridor, Afghanistan.

The social organization of Khorog, Tajikistan

During the majority of my fieldwork on the Tajik side of the border, I lived in Khorog, the capital of Shughnan district and Gorno-Badakhshan province.

Gorno-Badakhshan is made up of eight districts, which are split along sub-ethnic and ethno-linguistic groups.[3] Each district is divided in many ways, including by family (sub-ethnic groups), sector, neighborhood, and street.

Khorog also has numerous divisions. Ongoing tensions among these divisions sometimes rise to the level of physical conflict, but more often they simmer out of sight, invisible particularly to outsiders. The friction among local groups became apparent later in my fieldwork. In the beginning, I knew that Khorog divided into neighborhoods, but I did not know the extent to which these divisions also created borders for access to security, economic opportunities (and access to certain sectors and markets), and competition for resources in both licit and illicit trade. Partitions along lines of educational level and family standing also exist.

At the time of this research, Khorog was informally divided into 17–18 sub-districts or neighborhoods (*Mahallas*). Each sub-district elects a leader in a non-state sanctioned election. In addition to the informal leader of each sub-district, four higher-level leaders, locally referred to as warlords and/or drug lords, govern using their own security forces. Within each sub-district, each street has a leader and associated mini-security force made up of local young men. Leaders of civil society organizations, religious groups, business, academia, and development organizations also have influence locally. Some of the individuals have more than one position of authority.

At the time of my fieldwork, human trafficking was a growing concern in Khorog. The story of a young woman I'll call Gulya provides a point of entry into the intricate social organization of Khorog. Gulya's story highlights the growth of informal networks that have widened the disconnect between the formal state and the citizens.

Searching for "Gulya"

Gulya was a 16 year-old girl from an impoverished family living at the margins of their community in Bar-Khorog, a sub-section of Khorog. In late January 2010, she and another 16 year-old girl had been kidnapped from Khorog by two local drug-dealers and given to an Afghan drug lord to pay off a drug debt. Gulya was taken across the border, into Afghanistan, but the other girl escaped. I tracked Gulya for several months, and, in the process, I also gained a better understanding of the cross-border networks and the importance of local leaders to the local community as mediators and protectors.

I first heard about the Khorog kidnapping from an NGO working on human trafficking in Dushanbe, the capital of Tajikistan. As I asked around Dushanbe about this young woman, it became clear that human trafficking had increased along the border between Tajikistan and Afghanistan, but how much and the reasons for the spike were not clear. Most people, even those working directly on the issue, had very little reliable information.

Over time, the Pamiris living in Dushanbe started reaching out to me. They offered me assistance in the form of free translators, research partners, transportation, and lodging for my upcoming fieldwork in Afghan Badakhshan. They also wanted me to find Gulya. From the outpouring of offers, it was clear that many people wanted to know what had happened to this girl, why she had been kidnapped, and why human trafficking had moved eastward along the border. I had no idea that I was about to step into a tangled web of stories about this girl, a maze that would become increasingly impossible to sort out and even dangerous to study.

After speaking with a wide range of officials, NGO workers, and others in Dushanbe about human trafficking and its links to drug trafficking, I had confirmed that human trafficking was indeed on the rise.[4] I also knew that drug dealers in Badakhshan were in debt to the Afghan drug lords and were kidnapping young women who were then used to pay off their debts. If families could raise enough money to buy the hostage back, the dealers would pay off their debt to the drug lords, and their captive would (usually) be returned to their side of the border. This, I learned, was a long-standing way to deal with an unpaid debt to a drug lord. It seemed acceptable to some Pamiris in Khorog who viewed women's bodies as belonging to the community.[5] Eager to unravel the mystery, I packed my backpack and headed to Khorog, where the girl had last been seen.

Once I arrived in Khorog, it did not take long before I again heard about the kidnapped girl. Over lunch with a scholar at a local university, I heard the local version of the story. An official from the Tajik Drug Control Agency (DCA) office in Khorog named "Ali"[6] sat with us. He worked with my friend's brother. Ali claimed to have spoken with Gulya's family and with the girl who had escaped from the kidnappers. He offered to take me to visit both families, and I agreed. However, speaking with the families of the girls involved in the kidnapping would be extremely sensitive.

Ali told me that human trafficking was increasing in Gorno-Badakhshan. He also said that rising levels of drug addiction in the area had created rising debts to the Afghan drug dealers and lords. Apparently, lower-level Tajik drug dealers lacked business savvy and often ended up in debt to their Afghan counterparts. Using human hostages as collateral until the actual debt is paid in full has been a common practice in the area for centuries.[7]

Ali tried to clarify the tensions among local informal security groups, the community, and the state security forces through Gulya's story. He, and many in the community, wanted to stop human trafficking but did not know what to do. They could not turn to the state security forces, since they were believed to be involved in the drug trade. Furthermore, people were scared of the security forces after hearing stories about their torture of locals and mistreatment of local women.

Once people knew that I was investigating the kidnapping of Gulya, many came forward to speak to me about her, but also about drug trafficking, addiction, and human trafficking in general. People told me their fears about state security personnel. They said that the police and soldiers harassed or tortured people if they did not pay enough in bribes, argued with them, or for any number of other reasons. One local father said his son had been arrested after he fought with a drunk policeman from Dushanbe who was harassing a young woman in their neighborhood. The son, now in prison, was a respected local street leader known for his volunteerism and service to the young people and his neighborhood.[8] With him locked away, his neighborhood became more vulnerable. Many residents of the street that this local leader protected complained bitterly about the incident.

Ali brought me to the families in secret, not in the course of official business. He acted on his own and against the directives of his employer that he drop the case. He, like many others, told me that the girls had been kidnapped to pay off a debt incurred by drug dealers associated with high-level officials within the Tajik Customs Agency. I never proved or disproved this assertion. As an official of the DCA and an Ismaili Pamiri, Ali had conflicting roles between his professional and his religious duties. As an Ismaili, a citizen of Khorog, and a resident of the Mahalla, Bar-Khorog—the same neighborhood as Gulya's family, he had a duty to find her. As a DCA official, he had a duty to drop the case. In this instance, his identity as an Ismaili living in Khorog trumped his identity as an agent of Tajikistan's government.

Gulya's family

The next morning Ali and I went to visit Gulya's family in Bar-Khorog. "Bar" means upper, and indeed, the area is located in the northern section, on a hill above the main part of the city. The adobe house had one room. The family had moved there from another village outside of Shughnan district due to poverty. Because the family had few familial ties in Khorog, they had little informal protection. Instead of the police, local leaders provide security services for the people in their section of the city. The larger your family and the longer you have resided in the area, the more power and protection the members of your family have. Gulya and the other kidnapping victim were from families with little power; Gulya's family had even less due to being lower income newcomers.

I ended up visiting Gulya's family two times and spent a considerable amount of time with her uncle, in particular. Her father worked in Russia to support his family, and they lived with the uncle and his family. They told me that Gulya and her friend were snatched as they walked home from school in November 2010. They said that the girls were not addicted to drugs and not involved in that life. Rumors had circulated in Khorog about the girls' involvement in the drug trade—even prostitution—and many locals blamed the girls for what had happened to them.

The uncle wanted to go to Afghanistan to retrieve his niece. But the family conceded that even if she were rescued, because of these rumors, she could not return to Bar-Khorog because people would view her as tainted and "spoiled" since her virginity likely would no longer be intact. This was a very serious issue. They suspected that an Afghan drug lord had either kept her as a sex slave or had taken her as one of his wives, as was common practice. They showed me a picture of Gulya. She was striking, with large greenish-blue eyes, very dark brown hair, and large, beautiful features. The uncle said that if he could secretly buy her way back from Afghanistan, he could spirit her into Russia where she could recover and remain with her father. At that point, however, they had no leads as to where she was in Afghanistan nor even if she were alive.

"Umed": the community organizer

I need to explain Ali's network further before I continue with the story of Gulya and the kidnapping. First, Ali was close to "Umed" the leader of an important and very active Tajik civil society organization based in Bar-Khorog. Umed not only worked on a number of local projects such as youth sports, drug demand reduction and education, and local informal politics, he also was vocal about wanting an independent Gorno-Badakhshan.

I spoke with Umed a number of times at length about the NGO he directed. I also visited several buildings associated with his organization. According to many locals, during the prolonged search for Gulya, representatives of the Tajik government threatened to shut down one of the buildings that housed recreational programming for local youth. The government of Tajikistan owned the building and allegedly did not like the local community's persistence. Umed's NGO also was involved heavily in local underground politics. He said his organization was trying to consolidate some of the sub-sections (and associated street leaders) into larger groupings so that issues could be negotiated more easily between groups and there would be less competition at the micro-level for control and power. He even drew a map of how this would work. However, the most powerful warlord/drug lord in Khorog, who led a competing network, did not agree with this proposal, reportedly because some advocates were close to *his* rival on the opposite side of the city.[9]

While searching for Gulya, I learned of a longstanding rivalry among the districts in the area, in particular Shughnan, Roshan, Darwaz, Vanj, and Ishkashim. There were even rivalries within districts. When some of the men in Shughnan found out that the two alleged kidnapping drug dealers were not only from Roshan, but that Gulya had been taken over the border from a village in Roshan, there was a discussion (that I observed) about attacking Roshan. This did not occur, and the anger faded in a matter of weeks.

Locals acknowledged and accepted these informal leaders and security arrangements, although they were deliberately hidden from outsiders and from Dushanbe.[10] Even the majority of the citizens of Khorog who worked for the government of Tajikistan or supported a more consolidated Tajik nation-state took part in and followed the informal rule of law that mediated and structured so much of the legitimate authority and power in Khorog.

Ali allied with Umed because of Umed's close relationship to the war-lord who controlled Bar-Khorog. Moreover, as an Ismaili, Ali's search for Gulya was both a religious obligation and a duty to his community. He had networks on the Afghan side of the border he had gained through his job as a DCA official. Ali chose to secretly continue his search for Gulya, at his own peril and directly against the will of the state security apparatus, particularly the local KGB.[11] Like many others, Ali believed that the state security forces were not there to protect him, and, therefore, he had to take the law into his own hands. He met with a number of organizations in Khorog on behalf of Gulya's family including the Ismaili Tariqah and Religious Education Committee (ITREC now ITREB).[12]

ITREC had an office in Khorog. Ali and a group of local concerned citizens had a number of meetings locally and with officials (including the KGB) in Dushanbe about Gulya. Many locals felt that ITREC cooperated with or was infiltrated by the KGB and therefore did not trust them. Locals told me that the ITREC's meetings in Dushanbe had not gone well. In fact, they were told to stop looking for Gulya and that the circumstances surrounding her "kidnapping" had all been fabricated.

When locals did not believe the story about fabrication, ITREC came up with a new story. They allegedly said that Gulya was now happily married to the druglord in Afghanistan and therefore it would be pointless to rescue her. Yet another version that spread through the community was that the girl had jumped into the river and committed suicide. None of the locals I spoke with believed these stories, and their appearance made a number of them not only more suspicious of the state security apparatus but also of ITREC.

Pressure from ITREC and state security personnel only increased coopera-tion among local networks within Khorog and cross-border networks. Threats by state security forces about the private search for Gulya only increased dis-trust of the state. Finally, locals took the law into their own hands and searched for Gulya both on the Tajik side of the border and through networks along the Afghan side of the border. Locals regarded the presence of state security forces as a threat, not a guarantor of their protection and safety. Therefore, they had to find security through informal and local means, including providing their own weapons, increasing networks of cooperation across the border, and creating their own informal security organizations.

"Lutfiya"

In March 2010 Ali and I visited "Lutfiya,"[13] the girl who had escaped the kidnappers. Her family lived in a village far above Khorog and even above Bar-Khorog. The remote area looked like something out of a fairy-tale. The ground was covered in thick, green moss, while farm animals grazed in pastures framed by hand-made wooden fences carved from branches of trees. Female dogs, descendants of indigenous wolves, watched as their puppies scampered around under the spring sun. The crisp air had a fresh smell that comes with spring and the melting glacier snow. Villagers spoke about the water shortage due to the shrinking glaciers and how they worked together to share the limited but vital natural resource in the remote section of outer-Khorog.

Lutfiya also came from a socio-economically disadvantaged family. She looked terrified when we sat down. She kept glancing at Ali. I assured her that she had no obligation to speak with me, and I offered to leave or just stay for tea. She nodded her head. Her father told me they were worried for their safety because the local KGB had threatened her. I suggested that we just talk about their family and Lutifya's life instead of the trauma she had been through. Lutifya said she had been outcast since her escape and could not leave her house. Many in the community blamed her for what happened, and she did not feel safe. She said that a network of locals were involved in the kidnapping, but her story was confusing. She said that a young man involved in the kidnapping might want to speak with me. She said the men who kidnapped her were from Roshan and that Gulya was being held in a village on the Tajik side of Roshan and had not been taken to Afghanistan.[14] Lutfiya also said that the KGB had threatened her and told her not to talk about the issue. When she told me this, I said that it would be best if we did not speak about it any further.[15]

This part of Gulya's story highlights a few important issues. First, the DCA official, who is paid by the state to work on counter-narcotics trafficking, had to conceal his investigation into Gulya's kidnapping for a drug-related debt from state security personnel, and the KGB in particular. Second, most of the locals I spoke with insisted that the two drug dealers were associated with high-level Tajik officials and therefore would not be punished for their crimes. They also assumed that if they wanted proper justice they would have to seek it themselves. As a result, street leaders, civil society groups, drug lords, warlords, and religious leaders held a series of secret meetings to discuss justice for Gulya and how to make sure such kidnappings did not happen again. It was at this time that I decided to go over the Afghan side of the border to see if anyone had heard about a Tajik woman being taken across the border.

Female leaders of Roshan district in Afghanistan

Roshan district lies to the west of Khorog and Shughnan, Afghanistan. The Afghan side of Roshan is one of the most poverty-stricken and opiate-addicted in the area.[16] While I was in Shughnan, leaders from the Shurra (village) Councils and local informal leaders talked to me about the addiction problem in their district and in neighboring districts. They also reported that, in a number of villages in Roshan, entire communities were addicted to heroin and wasting away. Later I met with a group of female Shurra Council leaders from Afghan Shughnan and Roshan who confirmed that addiction is a growing problem. One of the female leaders from Roshan said she had been working on both starting drug treatment programs and getting young people to stop using drugs in her community. She said that the seedling programs had been more successful in Shughnan than they had been in Roshan.

I asked the female leaders if any of them had heard of a young woman from the Tajik side who had been taken over the border into Afghanistan. One of the women, the president of the Shurra Council in Roshan, had heard about a young Tajik woman who had crossed the river the preceding February. An Afghan drug lord reportedly held her as a hostage for a drug debt and took her to a village near Faizabad, in Afghanistan. This could be Gulya. The dates matched what I had heard, and the President of the Shurra could not have known the information I already had gathered since I had not talked about it there.

A few days later I crossed the border back into Khorog and told Ali about what I had heard. Ali had an informant who lived near Faizabad and called him. Later in the week, Ali's informant confirmed the rumors about the girl. People in Khorog began mobilizing to rescue her. Upon hearing this news, the local commander for Bar-Khorog, one for the four warlords controlling sections of Khorog, called Gulya's uncle and requested a meeting with me. We met the next day.

Divisions among local leaders in Khorog

The Commander of Bar-Khorog

Prior to meeting the Commander of Bar-Khorog, Ali and Sher told me about him and how I must act around him. Sher said it was a rather big deal that he had requested my presence. They said he had a large following even beyond Bar-Khorog and that many locals respected him and viewed him as a protector and one of the true leaders of the people in Khorog, and even Gorno-Badakhshan. They also warned me that he hated Tajiks and that I had better not speak Tajik or Persian around him because he might get offended and throw me out.

At the time, I did not fully comprehend what the Commander's role was in Khorog or Bar-Khorog, other than that he had been a formidable foe to his enemies (who were now in charge in Dushanbe) during the Tajik Civil War and that people respected him and his leadership, even if they did not like him. They called him a warlord, not a drug lord. Many people said that he had the support of the local population and that they would take up arms against outsiders at his order.[17] During the Civil War, the Commander had organized and designed the strategy to fight off and keep the Tajiks out of the area by forming an impenetrable perimeter along a mountain pass. Many felt he had helped save their area from being invaded by the Tajiks. This also meant that he had helped maintain local autonomy, protected local women from being raped, and kept the land safe.

We met in a local community building. The single-story cement structure had an open plot of land with a large area in front with trees and plants; a few men waited for us. They were part of his informal militia, and all carried weapons. I was told that about three-quarters of the residents of Bar-Khorog owned weapons. Since it is illegal to own such weapons, many residents hide them by burying them in their yard or other places.

The Commander talked to me for over an hour about the rising addiction in the area and the fact that the drug lords were enlisting young locals into their business and putting them in harm's way. He asked if I could help him set up a proper drug treatment center. He explained that they had one in Bar-Khorog, but it had little funding and treated people with HIV as well as heroin users. He said that the EU had promised to open one but it had been sitting unfinished for over a year.[18]

The Commander took me to visit the government-funded drug/HIV treatment center. The old single-story, rather decrepit cement building had a small yard. The center had one well-trained doctor who was the director. They had over two dozen patients in treatment, but very few women. The doctor said there were likely many more with HIV and/or addicted to heroin in Khorog but too scared to come forward. He also said he had run out of the pain medication (they were not allowed to use methadone yet in the area) used to ease the painful process of withdrawing from heroin.

Next, the Commander took me to visit a building that he owned and wanted to use for a drug education and treatment center, but he had been unable to find funding.[19] The Commander felt it was the only way to help his community and protect them from the adverse effects of the drug trade, lack of employment opportunities, and poverty. The majority of the people living in much of Bar-Khorog looked to the Commanders for assistance with their problems including mediation, monetary assistance, and security. The same was true for the other three informal leaders in Khorog. Rather than relying on the state, locals relied on local leaders to administer and enforce unwritten local agreements.

As I was leaving, the Commander opened his large army green overcoat and showed me a cache of weapons in holsters and pockets throughout the inside of his coat, including two hand grenades, a Kalashnikov, a handgun, and a large knife. The Commander clearly was ready, as were his men, for a fight. He explained to me that he hated the Tajik government. He even reviled the Tajik language and said he was ready for the *Chakhts* (an expletive commonly used to refer to non-Pamiri-Tajiks locally and translated as "crooked") to invade his territory. He was prepared to fight them. He also felt a personal responsibility for those living in both Bar Khorog and Khorog. He explained that Gulya and her family came from Bar Khorog and he was the leader of this mahalla. He told me that since she had lived in his neighborhood, he felt personally responsible for her family and for finding her. He thanked me for my humanitarian work in trying to understand where she was and what had happened to her. At the end of our meeting, he stuck out his hand and told me that I was now under his protection, and therefore I would remain safe and no one would bother me. He made good on his promise for the duration of my time in Khorog, even on the Afghan side of the border.

The Commander from UPD

I heard about the Commander of UPD long before I met him. This Commander was another one of the four neighborhood warlords. UPD is one of the mahallas in Khorog. It sits on a hill located directly across the Ghund river and south of Bar-Khorog. Next to UPD is a sub-section of Khorog called Khleb Zavod; translated from Russian this means "bread factory." At the time of part of my fieldwork (2010–2012) this "bread factory" was allegedly a local drug lab. Essentially, the area was controlled by yet another warlord. Competition and infighting between the warlords and those whom they commanded was common.

In my mind, the Commander of UPD had become a mythical presence, a legend often invoked during discussions, dinners, meetings, chats, and gossip. Locally, this commander epitomized the concept of hero in the region because of his bravery and leadership during the Tajik Civil War, which had left him paralyzed and in a wheelchair. He was also beloved for his service to his people: the citizens of Khorog and the Ismailis. One day he called Sohrab, a good friend of mine, and requested that I have tea with him.

Like Ali and Sher, "Sohrab" briefed me ahead of my meeting. Sohrab had worked for the Commander of UPD. He had accompanied the Commander when he traveled to Switzerland for surgery related to his wartime injuries. This commander's connections extended far beyond Gorno-Badakhshan. Throughout their trip from Uzbekistan to Switzerland, Sohrab recalled, they were met by government dignitaries and the Commander was treated as a celebrity wherever he went, including in Switzerland and various EU countries. Sohrab said this was due to his boss's vast international business network.

I met the Commander one afternoon. Over a pot of green tea he delivered a blunt warning: If I ever wanted to come back to Tajikistan, I must accept that Gulya had jumped into the river and committed suicide; end of story. Right before he delivered his warning, General Abdullo Nazarov, the head of the Gorno-Badakhshan branch of the State Committee on National Security (GKNB/KGB) came and sat with us. The two of them clearly knew each other pretty well and chatted about their sons' soccer games, their families, and gemstones. After General Nazarov left, I asked the Commander if they ever collaborated. He said that when things became tense or there were security issues, he informed the General and that they had a good working relationship. The Commander made it clear that not only was he a leader in his section of Khorog, but that he also believed in a strong and secure Tajikistan. Therefore, when he was assassinated a few months later during an incursion by the Tajik military, given his positive cooperation with the government of Tajikistan, I was quite surprised.

Khorog conflict of 2012

General Nazarov was killed on July 21, 2012. Many residents told me that the Commander of UPD and General Nazarov collaborated on illegal business and were the main contact point in Gorno-Badakhshan for high-level Tajik officials involved in the trafficking in the area. This appeared to be common knowledge. I have a map from 2011 that I had created with a local. The map shows where each "drug lord," "warlord," "drug dealer," "deputy commander," and "drug lab" were located. The Commander's house is shown on the map and labeled "drug lord."

Many locals told me that General Nazarov was assassinated because he had increased his percentage of the local trafficking profits in Ishkashim district, so locals from Ishkashim had killed him. But others alleged that General Nazarov had increased his levy and that officials associated with the Tajik government were angry at him and had him killed but made it look like locals did it. This also would give the Tajik Government an excuse to raid Gorno-Badakhshan. Indeed, early on the morning of July 24, soldiers poured into Khorog and immediately targeted the local warlords. They were repelled by local forces who had prepared for this moment by stocking up on weapons (albeit antiquated ones) and designating safe houses and groups who would fight together. Hard numbers are difficult to come by, but reportedly 200–300 soldiers and 20 locals died in the fighting.

There were many other stories circulating about the deaths of General Nazarov and the Commander of UPD. In either case, both men were working for and with the central authorities in Tajikistan—General Nazarov officially and the Commander unofficially. Once they were gone, the state's ability to engage the region via relatively well-institutionalized and locally legitimate channels was diminished. Moreover, since the Commander possessed the most respected form of local leadership and had the most power and legitimacy, assassinating him only increased the existing rift with the state. Many locals told me that they would not forgive or forget what the Tajik Government had done to their community and their local leaders.

A couple of months after the raid, almost all communication was still limited and encompassed only mundane topics and chats about family. Many believed that the government was actively listening in on conversations in order to identify people they believed to be resisting them after the raid. If the government decided a person had any inclination to resist, including talking about their frustration with the government of Tajikistan publicly, they were put on a blacklist, which allegedly included over 200 names. Friends told me about harassment, forced informing on friends, interrogation, torture, and imprisonment. Officials posted "wanted" photos of protestors and other undesirables in the local airport in Khorog. A number of my friends fled to

Russia to avoid being caught and tortured or killed. Some have returned, but others remain in Russia, struggling to find work and living on meager means. A few local youth have been arrested and some killed since that time. Locals assert that these young men were on this hidden blacklist. One of the leaders told me he would get a copy of the list and give it to me, but he never did. After October, there was a lengthy communication blackout. I heard nothing from my friends and contacts in Gorno-Badakhshan until mid-January.

When the Commander of UPD was assassinated in the summer of 2012,[20] over 3,000 people held vigil over his body, which they had brought to the main square in Khorog. They also protested his death.[21] He was the most respected and legitimate informal leader in Khorog. After the Commander's death, I heard that a group of local men from UPD had met a number of times in order to elect another local informal leader. In 2014, I met with the new leader. We talked about the tensions in the area and cross-border networks. Later, I heard that the new leader had not been selected unanimously, and some in UPD did not accept him as their new leader.

The late Commander of UPD, similar to the Commander of Bar-Khorog, mediated between the state and the locals. He was a leader of the territory, a Pamiri, and a respected Ismaili. Killing him has only alienated the locals further. By further alienating the locals from the state, the government increased instability at the border. This drew locals closer together due to their increased reliance on local security, increased resistance to oppression by the state, and a greater assertion of local, rather than national, identity.

While both commanders were part of the Soviet-era Tajik elite, rifts exist among other former apparatchiks in the region. One could say that one group is more allied with a western-style democratic approach with a free market economy while the other supports the old Soviet system which provided all necessities to its citizenry.

Communalism versus capitalism

Within the local AKF network in Khorog there are competing sub-networks. Some support a more capitalist, free-market-based region while others believe in a communal, more "socialist" system of resource allocation loosely based on the former Soviet system. For example, take the different approaches of the local president of one NGO and the president of a successful business (owned by the AKF). One believes in providing food, shelter, and energy to all people for free. The other believes that people should pay for what they consume.

The president of an NGO versus the president of "Energy Khorog"

The first time I spoke with the president of a large Khorog-based NGO in his rather plush office in Dushanbe, I told him that I had found an affordable room in Khorog. He looked at me and said, "Wouldn't it be better if it were free? Should we really have to pay for such things?" In our conversation he made it clear that he believed in sharing resources and opposed making a profit by charging people for basic necessities. He offered to provide transportation, accommodations, and data for me when I was in Khorog. The president of AKF, Tajikistan was a member of the former Tajik SSR elite, as were most members of the network tied to him at that time.

When I later arrived in Khorog, it was clear that the tension between this president and the local staff ran deep as many people approached me from various groups complaining about these issues. Not only were there rifts between the local staff inside the local organizations and networks, many of the local and national leadership positions within the Aga Khan Foundation (AKF) and Aga Khan Development Network (AKDN) institutions were staffed by men from Pakistan, which presented a completely different form of discord. These institutions include a wide range of local development, humanitarian, and service-oriented NGOs including the Mountain Societies Development Support Programme, the Pamir Eco-Tourism Association, Aga Khan Health Services, University of Central Asia, and the Aga Khan Lycée to name a few.

The locals told me that they resented the Pakistanis for telling them what to do in their own territory, as well as for making higher salaries and often treating them as inferiors. Similar tensions also existed between the local staff and higher-level administrators originally from Khorog but working in Dushanbe. These "émigrés" worked closely with outsiders or internationals and often had not lived in the area for decades. Some locals told me they viewed these "émigrés" working in management positions as being only concerned for themselves, not their birthplace. Ultimately, the amount or the type of help I received depended on who introduced me to the different networks of local development workers. The rival networks in the development sector also controlled different aspects of cross-border trade, parts of the formal and informal economy, and some of the local security groups.

In the beginning of my fieldwork I had not begun to unravel the sensibilities of all of these interlinking dynamics, I was like "an elephant in a China shop" as one person jokingly called me. For example, I called some of the local staff and said that the President of AKF had offered to help me with my research. This was a mistake on two levels. First, the Pakistani Director of the Afghan AKF program felt I had gone over his head. Second, the locals working in the area, who had dual roles of development workers and protectors of their community, were skeptical of my intentions, particularly because the President of AKF supported my work. The local staff resisted helping me, saying that most of their operations were private and they did not know what my intentions were and what they could do for me. After a few weeks, and with the help of a few locals who knew people working at AKDN and AKF, the local staff warmed up to me. From that point forward, they helped me immeasurably, and I could not have completed my research without their assistance.

The rifts inside of AKF/AKDN were not the only ones. The difference in leadership I alluded to above, communal versus capitalist, also ran deep in the community. One of the recurring issues revolved around the definition of a legitimate or true leader. One of the key measures was the amount that leader was "in it for himself/herself." Clearly, this creates a tension between local norms of resource sharing and allocation and the goals of capitalist enterprises.

This became clear to me when I began to spend time with the President of a local energy company I'll call "Energy Khorog" headquartered in Khorog. This President was also a member of the very powerful Ismaili Council, which was the most direct link the locals had to the "ear of His Highness, the Aga Khan."

After hearing about my work on Gulya, the President of Energy Khorog asked to meet with me. During our meeting, he expressed his concern about Gulya and offered his financial and logistical support on both the Afghan and Tajik sides of the border. Indeed, he provided numerous helicopter rides between Dushanbe and Khorog, accommodations and transportation in Afghanistan, and we talked on many occasions.

In time, a number of locals came to me with complaints about Energy Khorog and about the president specifically. They said that he was stealing from the locals and that they could not afford their energy bills. They accused him of forcing people to go without heat and electricity in the winters. Some people even accused him of falsifying energy bills. A group of locals asked me to investigate his alleged fraudulent and predatory behavior, so I asked the President about billing policies. He told me that Energy Khorog had an elaborate formula for calculating people's energy usage and costs. They also had a program for socio-economically disadvantaged families. The problem was, many of the families in more remote villages either did not know about the program or did not know how to fill out the application. This was the case with one elderly woman that I met. But this did not satisfy everyone; locals said that the rules were deliberately unclear and helped the company to prey on people who did not understand them.

In the end, it was difficult to know what was really going on. It did become clear that most locals resented the President for trying to make Energy Khorog not only sustainable but also profitable. As a result, they viewed him as corrupt and self-serving. Because of his dual role, as President of a capitalist business owned and controlled by the Aga Khan, and as a member of the elite Ismaili Council, the locals considered him a local leader, but one who was not there to serve the people. Instead, they saw a leader who presented a distorted view of their needs to the one and only true leader they needed to communicate with, the Aga Khan.

These divisions within the local organizations also transferred to the Afghan side of the border. In Afghan Badakhshan, the locals were linked to various networks on the Tajik side. The aid, projects, and cooperation were mediated through these networks. This cooperation also included access to the border crossings, people in the community, and other linkages such as local security and assistance.

When I arrived at the AKF office in Shughnan, Afghanistan, I made a similar mistake to the one I made when I had arrived for the first time in Khorog. Namely, I asked for the support of the AKF-Afghanistan office in Shughnan at the request of the President of Energy Khorog. The locals viewed the President as an outsider, not as someone who was there to support them. Although they did not express the same kind of vitriol as their counterparts in Gorno-Badakhshan, nevertheless, it hindered my initial fieldwork in Shughnan. I finally received vital assistance when a Tajik Pamiri who worked for AKF who helped me by leveraging his local network.

Rostam: the free-trader

According to a number of locals, Rostam had been a high-level Soviet apparatchik and he had maintained many of his connections within the Tajik government, in Russia, and internationally. While he had worked high up in the Tajik SSR elite, he had transformed his network and skills into that of a free market and open trade advocate for the region.

Many said that while he was quiet, he had a lot of power among different elite groups, particularly as it pertained to international trade. While he publicly identified with non-Ismailis and non-Pamiris for purposes of trade and economic gain, Rostam privately fought for a more developed and secure Gorno-Badakhshan. In his role as international arbiter of trade through the region, he had no official position except with his small NGO, but he had a high level of legitimate authority among the groups working to open up the trade routes in the area. Additionally, he had authority as a leader for helping to plan and implement the BBP and the open customs region in Ishkashem. As a local leader he was respected—both in the former Soviet circles and in the Ismaili circles, although in the Ismaili circles there are several other groups working on the BBP as well.

Many people told me that Rostam could diplomatically mediate between different networks and effectively implement projects and develop trade. They also said he was the best and most connected person working on international trade issues in the region. This is a key leadership position in an area with a long history of negotiating trade agreements, resource exchanges, and territorial issues dating to the time of the khanates, emirates and the Silk Road. Rostam's mediation among many trade partners while also advocating partial territorial autonomy simply advances and updates practices that have long been the norm in the region.

I met Rostam for the first time in 2010. The primary mission of his NGO was to increase legal trade in the region—between the countries that border Badakhshan (as a whole), including China, Pakistan, Kyrgyzstan, and Afghanistan. One of Rostam's projects involved creating a free-trade zone in Ishkashim that would span both sides of the border. Another project aimed to build a road from Tajikistan to China through the end of the Wakhan Corridor, thereby opening up another trade route between China, Pakistan, Tajikistan, and Afghanistan. Of course, these new trade routes would also open up alternative routes for illicit trade. Therefore, this project piqued the interest of a wide range of people and networks, locally, regionally, and internationally.

Rostam's office sat atop a hillside above Khorog in a mahalla formerly called TirChid but now Bolnitsen (meaning hospital in Russian) which bordered Khleb Zavod.[22] The office was housed within a larger international NGO.

Rostam spoke primarily Russian and Shughni. His Tajik was limited. During our meeting, he described his plans and shared that he was friends with the president and other official and unofficial leaders from all the relevant countries. He had organized one meeting and was in the process of organizing another one that included corporations, trade representatives, and officials from all participating countries as well as EU and U.S. representatives. He told me that officials from all of these countries were interested and he was optimistic about its eventual success. After explaining his "official" project, he decided to tell me about his "unofficial" one—the Badakhshan-Badakhshan Project. Rostam spoke about the importance of the BBP[23] for the local population and said that many people were working on it. The project is a poorly kept secret. I was already familiar with BBP, but Rostam did not know that. BBP is designed to increase partnerships between the two sides of Badakhshan in order to open trade, provide humanitarian exchanges, and insulate the Ismaili community from humanitarian and environmental risks, such as hunger, poverty, and the impact of climate change. People assert that if President Rahmon or other leaders knew of the plan, he would not allow it, and he might expel some if not all AKF/AKDN organizations operating in Gorno-Badakhshan. Moreover, he would view it as a potential separatist movement.

Rostam explained to me that there were approximately 21 unofficial crossings between the two countries. These informal border crossings are for humanitarian purposes. They were part of the Badakhshan-Badakhshan Project (BBP) at the time of the interview and the purpose of the BBP was to increase cross-border cooperation for humanitarian purposes. On the Afghan side, for many decades the district of Shughnan was completely isolated until the road to Faizabad was built in the past few years. The same is true for the district of Vanj on the Tajik side of the border. Opening up the border to these informal crossings allowed much needed aid to be passed to the districts made more isolated by the creation of the border. Without access to the other (Tajik) side, Roshan and Shughnan would have difficulty surviving at different times of the year, particularly in the winter due to food and energy shortages. In fact, up until 2005, Shughnan, Afghanistan had never had electricity.

Pamir Energy, owned and operated by the AKF, started to supply energy to Afghan Shughnan in 2005–2006 and since that time, many people in

Shughnan told me their lives had transformed immeasurably because many now had heat, hot water, some had stoves, and lights. Many women told me that before Pamir Energy opened, most of their day was spent cooking over the fire—if they had fuel to light one, and working to get things done before it became dark. Now they had time to learn to read, study, and do other things to improve their own lives and those of their children.[24] By enhancing different aspects of cooperation between the Afghan and Tajik sides of Badakhshan, these women's lives had improved through access to electricity.

So far I have discussed leadership by local Pamiri Ismailis, both living in Khorog and Dushanbe, and only marginally referred to the national government. While I was in Khorog, the president of Tajikistan visited Gorno-Badakhshan and Khorog. In preparation for his visit on June 27, 2010 President Rahmon's staff ordered the locals to put up posters, propaganda, and national symbols and to take down the symbols related to the Aga Khan. It was during this visit that I witnessed the relationship between the Pamiris in Khorog and their central government.

President Rahmon's official visit to Khorog

In 2010, the first time I attempted to cross the border into Afghanistan, the border ended up being closed for ten days due to *Ruz-e Vahdat* (Reconciliation day), a major Tajik holiday, commemorating the end of the Tajik Civil War in 1997. I am grateful for this closure that serendipitously left me in Khorog for the President of Tajikistan's visit.

The city of Khorog had been given a facelift for his visit, as was the custom of President Rahmon. Every Reconciliation Day he visited one city in Tajikistan. For the particular province he chose to visit, he overhauled the buildings and infrastructure as a gesture of kindness and a symbol of reconciliation (although only the portions of the province that he would visit). Locals often joked that it was like a Potemkin village—only there to help him pretend he was being a good leader.

Along with these cursory renovations and local upgrades, President Rahmon also inundated the city and surrounding areas with posters and slogans about reconciliation, his great leadership, the great country of Tajikistan, and whatever pet projects he was promoting at the time. In this case, it was the Roghun hydropower station being planned on the border between Tajikistan and Uzbekistan. For this project, which has been on the drawing table for several years, President Rahmon required all citizens to pay a ten percent income tax toward its completion. Many experts believe the project is impossible because it would be the largest and highest dam ever constructed in the world and because it is located on unstable land prone to erosion and earthquakes. But, as the many slogans reminded, President Rahmon "will ensure a strong and prosperous future for Tajikistan," and therefore the project is necessary and inevitable.

The forced decorations of the province with posters of the Tajik President and the removal of some of the symbols of the Aga Khan actually incited local groups to begin to organize an uprising. The Aga Khan had to step in, through the Ismaili Council, to stop the rebellion. He personally asked residents to support President Rahmon and to leave the president's signs in place. The locals, since they believe His Highness to be their true leader, obeyed.

President Rahmon's visit did two things simultaneously. It forced the locals to snub the Aga Khan, whom they regard as their true legitimate leader who provides guidance, love, and protection. And if they have to turn their backs on the Aga Khan, what does the Tajik government do to protect them? Second, while many locals expressed gratitude for what the President of Tajikistan had done for them, they also expressed frustration that KGB forces were flooding into Khorog and that the Tajiks were taking over the city. Moreover, many of the citizens I spoke with (at least the ones whom I was closer to) privately mocked the posters and the president, saying that he is an oppressive narcissist. This has echoes of Lisa Wedeen's (1999) scholarship on President Bashar al-Assad of Syria. In Khorog, locals whom I did not know (or who thought the security services were listening to them) would speak highly of the president in public, but privately they often made fun of both him and his propaganda posters. Indeed, the forced rhetoric certainly asserted that President Rahmon was in charge. But, at the same time, it also illuminated the shortcomings of his leadership in Khorog.

Ironically, the goal of Reconciliation Day is to bring the citizens of the country closer together and create a more unified Tajikistan, but at least in Khorog, it revealed that locals do not trust their government and have to rely on local networks to protect and provide for them. This reliance on local informal leaders and security over state authorities further marginalizes those living along the borderlands. The locals asserted a desire for more autonomy in reaction to increased state presence (such as increased infrastructural development and outside security forces). In reaction to the locals' push for more autonomy, the state viewed the local leaders and organizations as more of a threat, and in turn, increased militarization of the border. It is hard to say what is going on within local organizations and groups at the moment, but what is clear is that they feel even more strongly about the importance of local informal networks of cooperation as a means for their own safety and prosperity. Speaking of local security, I am fairly certain the reader is wondering what happened to Gulya. I am loathe to report, that the storybook ending we all would hope for did not happen.

Still missing

A few months after I left Khorog, I went to London. It was there that I spoke with a group of Ismaili scholars from Gorno-Badakhshan about Gulya. All of them had heard of the case of the missing girl from Bar Khorog. They had no idea of my involvement in her search. When they found out they told me that the Ismaili Council (the main advisory body of the Aga Khan) had spent a couple of months trying to rescue her and negotiate her release from the druglord. They raised money in secret. Ali told me that the druglord wanted two thousand dollars. These scholars from the Insitute for Ismaili Studies (IIS) reported to me that once the drug lord found out it was no longer just the two young men from Khorog who were going to pay him but a major international NGO, he raised the price for Gulya to 20 thousand dollars. The IIS refused to give him the outrageous sum. Gulya remains near Faizabad allegedly and a number of Afghans told me that she had a child but I had no way to verify any of these claims. Gulya's father still contacts Ali for help to rescue his daughter or so I am told.

As for the two drug dealers/kidnappers, eventually they were caught and put in the local jail in Khorog. Soon after their capture they were set free without a proper trial. After their release, locals staged two protests. When I spoke to a number of local leaders at this time, they threatened to do far worse than just protest. Some local leaders raised the possibility of a separatist movement, saying that they were tired of Tajik security forces and other government officials forcing them to pay bribes and harassing their women. The one positive outcome from this case is that the kidnappings which had been on the rise all but completely stopped. This was largely due to local community activism and organization done through the informal local institutions.

Conclusion

The analysis of the cases on local leaders highlights the different networks of cooperation both within Khorog and across the border in Shughnan. First, there are the networks dividing the local AKF workers and the outsiders, both the locals working at the management level in Dushanbe, and the Pakistanis. Second, there are divisions (and networks of cooperation), between the locals who believed in the communal economy versus the capitalist one. Third, networks exist which work together to provide local security and protection. These networks, when not united against other outside networks, also split along neighborhood lines and compete for resources based on these local territories. Lastly, all of these networks cooperate in different ways with the networks across the border.

Some of the networks were associated more with the religious identity (such as the Ismaili Council, and parts of the AKF system); other networks were more territory-based, while still others were based on ethnicity (including local, domestic, regional, and international ethnic differences). Lastly, outside pressure by the government, when perceived as a threat to any of these identity networks, mobilized their members, united the groups, and increased assertion of their self-identification. But, when the domestic or outside pressures decreased, these local networks competed more among themselves, and the national/country identity (Tajik versus Afghan).

In the following chapter I discuss the development of the border institutions themselves, including the training of personnel, the infrastructure, and the cross-border bazaars. These institutions and officials function directly on the border. They govern the periphery of each state, providing either access or obstacles to people, trade, and aid. I had the unique privilege of working with several organizations working on border development while doing my fieldwork and the following case studies cover my experiences and observations.

Notes

1 According to Sher, "khalifas can't take this responsibility [for true spiritual leadership] because they are controlled by ITREC which in turn is controlled by KGB." In the past, the Tajik KGB controlled the majority of Khalifas. There existed a parallel group of Khalifas who were operating outside the bounds of the government. Today, most of the Khalifas in Gorno-Badakhshan also are controlled or under the purview of the Tajik GKNB (the successor to the Tajik KGB). There are a few Khalifas who are not working within the bounds of the GKNB as was the case during Soviet times.

2 The main behind-the-scenes strategy right now in Afghanistan is to empower local leaders and their associated groups in order to increase stability.

3 Only seven are officially listed: Vanj, Roshan, Roshtqal'a, Darwaz, Shughnan, Ishkashim, Murgab. While the Wakhan Corridor is a district with important historical heritage it is not listed by the government of Tajikistan as a district. Each district has its own language, some having more than one.

4 Interviews in February to March, 2011 with officials from the Drug Control Agency of Tajikistan, Border Management Project for Central Asia, AKDN, AKF, Pamir Energy, Khirad, Madina, Girls Support Services, the Children's Legal Centre, and International Organization for Migration and others. Fieldwork from June to July, 2009; May to August, 2010; February to May 2011; and September to November, 2011 as well as constant dialogue over social media.

5 For some in Khorog, the women's body belongs to the community both for religious reasons and to keep the Pamiri ethnicity from being mixed with outsiders. More than once men told me of women who had either married or had sexual relations with people from outside the area and that they should be punished. Some even said they should be put to death, but that was an uncommon view and on the extreme end.

6 Pseudonym.

7 During my fieldwork in the Wakhan Corridor in June to July, 2010 and September to October, 2011, many of the families told me that one of the goals of AKF's DDRP is to reduce the need to pay off debt incurred from addiction to opiates by providing treatment, education, and jobs training. Prior to the program, selling of children, property, trees, and animals was endemic throughout the region. Many of the families are still in debt today to the local drug traders and struggle to keep up with the debts which they have to pay back in bits each time the traders pass their villages. Numerous families complained about their enormous debt burden and lack of food and other necessities due to the burden. Selling of children and property, due to the rules created by the DDRP, was significantly reduced after 2006 but still occurs. Due to the shame surrounding selling children or property, it is done in secret—or kept from the assessment personnel and employees of the AKF and AKDN.

8 The family told me they were keeping quiet because a presidential amnesty day for prisoners occurs once a year and they were hoping that their son might be released.

9 The Tajik military raided Khorog, in July 2012. Another local leader fled to Russia where he remains. Imum, one of the most respected local warlords, was assassinated.

10 The Tajik security services were well aware of it.

11 Tajikistan's State Committee on National Security (GKNB) is the successor to the Soviet-era KGB. All of the locals I have met in Tajikistan still refer to it as the KGB, hence I am using that in my analysis as well.

12 "Ismaili Tariqah and Religious Education Committee is one of the educational and cultural projects launched by the Institute of Ismaili Studies (London) years ago. The main objective of the project is to educate the Jamati members and learning constituencies about the heritage, history and cultures of Muslim peoples, in general, and, of the Shi'a Ismailis, in particular, as well as to facilitate the implementation of Ta'lim (an international educational program) within the Ismaili community." Quoted from an educational pamphlet distributed among Ismailis.

13 Pseudonym.

14 This was news she had not told anyone and, in the end, turned out to be true, in part. Gulya had indeed been there. I spoke with Lutfiya in March, and she did not know that Gulya had been taken across the border a few weeks earlier.

15 This means she was being protected by the local security group operating in Bar-Khorog and the surrounding area.

16 This is according to AKF staff members and Shurra Council Leaders from Roshan and the surrounding districts.

17 Many people said that about 70 percent of the population supported Boqir but there was no way to verify this information since any formal discussion about his leadership (meaning consistent, on-the-record acknowledgement) was unavailable due to local fears of retribution by government officials. Commander Boqir is the democratically elected informal leader of the Mahalla, Bar-Khorog, in city of Khorog. Many consider him a hero because he was a leader (warlord) in Badakhshan during the Tajik Civil War (1992–1997).

18 It has since been completed and now provides treatment.

19 One evening, I met with the head of the International Committee for the Red Cross (ICRC) for the region and asked him about funding and drug treatment in Khorog. He had just arrived in Khorog and insisted that the ICRC had needle-exchange programs funded in the area. I asked him if he had visited them. He assured me he had. He left early the next morning on a helicopter, never having checked out the programming that he insisted was available.

20 The Commander of UPD, as he was commonly known, was assassinated in July, 2012 during a raid by Tajik soldiers into Khorog over the assassination of the local KGB head for Badakhshan. For an overview of what happened see http://www. neweurasia.net/tajikistan/qa-with-man-nistam-what-really-happened-in-gorno-bada khshan/. The assassination of the Commander, the attack of Oyambekov, and the assassination of General Nazarov, Head of the GKNB for Badakhshan, all happened after I finished my fieldwork. The motive and killers of both of these men have remained unclear but were likely due to issues related to drug-trafficking and power struggles. Also, the leader of the Islamic Revival Party (IRP) for the Badakhshan region was assassinated, and another one of the drug lords was shot and severely wounded. Additionally, a number of informal deputy leaders were killed. The leader of the IRP was attacked in 2012 as well.

21 Protest: www.youtube.com/watch?v=PpclU16mP0k; Vigil: www.youtube.com/wa tch?v=660fsBhbDuU.

22 Some of the locals wanted to separate the area into two sections, Shashkala and Nasiri Khusraw, but this was being negotiated at the time of my fieldwork.

23 On many occasions, President Rahmon has competed openly for authority with His Highness the Aga Khan. A move to unite the autonomous provinces on both sides of the border would not be welcome.

24 One of the tenets of the Ismaili religion is that if a family has several children and only the means to educate one of them, the family must educate a female first. This is because, in their belief, the woman educates the children and it is therefore of primary importance to educate her first. Additionally, education in the area for both the Ismailis and the district of Shughnan in particular, is considered to be of the utmost importance. That is, for everyone to be able to get an education. When the Taliban banned education it went directly against local customs—both cultural and religious.

6 Border institutions

Ruling the unruly or unruling the rulers?

For centuries, rulers have built walls, constructed fences, set up patrols, erected guard towers, and made many other efforts to physically "control" a particular territory. But border enforcement is really the assertion of an idea, not a geographically fixed and temporally specific place. As "James," a British project manager of a major inter-governmental organization (IGO) in Dushanbe with decades of field experience told me, "Border 'control' is an oxymoron. There is no such thing as controlling a border. People say that, but it's bollocks."

In practice, border security is really about influence. Individuals, entities, institutions, and governments can influence the way a border is conceived, securitized, or institutionalized. "If a state has influence over the border," James added, "they can compel adherence to the rules."[1] The assumption driving many border projects is that through development and enhanced security, a border will become more stable. But the opposite is often the case.

Borders are inherently in a constant state of flux. On a daily basis they are traversed, transcended, breeched, and enforced. The best any country can do is create institutions that convince people on both sides of the border to accept that (1) the borders are there, (2) the borders belong to a particular place, and (3) the borders include a particular set of state-sanctioned rules. The border between Afghanistan and Tajikistan is no different; yet, there are over 30 ongoing projects trying to permanently fix this fluid boundary, including major infrastructural development projects, surveillance systems, nuclear material monitoring, and customs systems. These projects are intended to increase "security" and to facilitate trade and humanitarian efforts.

As a result, Badakhshan is in a state of constant, widespread, quiet protest against multiple incursions by outside elements, whether from another country, central authorities, or another clan. Many of these border development projects go against the well-established local practice of "unruling the rulers," meaning, the local informal leaders find ways around the rules the formal/official leaders are either working to enforce or devising.

Throughout the documented history of the area, the people in Badakhshan have successfully used barriers and force to remain outside of neighboring empires. The unusually challenging mountainous terrain has helped limit outsider's access.[2] Locally, the people have developed a complex set of cultural scripts that allow outsiders access to certain levels of insider knowledge, while hiding other aspects through language, religious practices, and other customs. These scripts control how and when an outsider might understand a given issue.

Given the importance of distancing outsiders, it would seem that the goal of increasing state stability through developing border institutions might be not only difficult, but detrimental; particularly if development is done by outsiders. Moreover, if these outsiders ignore the networks that are already in place, they do so at they own peril. These informal networks will strengthen, as an ever-increasing array of illicit activities continues to exist outside—or within—formal channels.[3]

This chapter offers a series of case studies that focus on the interplay among the newly developing border institutions, local people and the networks of cooperation, and their associated identities. These identities function within, among, and around the border institutions and associated development projects. The following sections reflect my time in the field working alone and with several IGOs and NGOs including: (1) the cross-border bazaars and the recently built bridges, (2) the training of border personnel, (3) and border infrastructural development.

Building bridges and cross-border bazaars

Between 2002 and 2011 the Aga Khan Foundation (AKF) and the Aga Khan Development Network (AKDN) sponsored the construction of four bridges along the border in Badakhshan, while the European Union and United States underwrote the establishment of three cross-border bazaars. A cross-border bazaar is a marketplace that extends into the territory of two countries. Citizens residing on both sides of the border can buy and sell at the bazaar during a designated, agreed upon time. Citizens of both countries are allowed to attend the bazaar without needing a visa. Prior to 2002, much of the cross-border trade required traversing the fast-moving currents of the Panj River. The first bridge opened in 2002, at Tem, which is an area located within Khorog, the capital city of the Tajik province of Gorno-Badakhshan. Tem is the border crossing that connects Khorog and Shughnan.

The opening of the bridge at Tem provided increased access to medical care, food supplies, household appliances, and measurably changed the lives of the majority of people living in Shughnan, Afghanistan. People in Shughnan told me that in 2005 when Pamir Energy started supplying them with electricity, it was the first time they had light in the evening. The energy initiative was another aspect of increased cross-border cooperation. When Pamir Energy began supplying energy, electric ovens started being sold in the bazaars. Many women told me that the new access to electricity had shaved hours off of their work day. They also said that having heat in the winter had saved a lot of lives.

In 2002, the first of four bridges opened in these borderlands of Badakhshan. The fourth bridge opened in 2011. More are under negotiation as of the writing of this book. As the bridges developed, so did the cross-border bazaars. In 2006, Afghans were allowed to cross and shop in the bazaar in the Tajik village of Ruzwai near Darwaz. Five years later, two more cross-border bazaars began operation in Ishkashim and Tem (Shughnan). While the bazaars provide few opportunities for local producers—most of the goods come from China or Pakistan—they do provide locals access to items such as watermelons for Afghan shoppers and Afghan rice for Tajik buyers. Afghan yellow rice is prized in Khorog for those who have had the privilege of eating it. The fragrant yellow rice has a sweet taste and is the perfect combination of firm and tender for the Tajik national rice dish, osh.

The price of some goods has risen due to increased demand for certain products, which can be problematic if some traders seem to benefit more than others. Data from the AKF indicated that the cross-border markets have a small, but positive impact on the Tajik side of the border and make a growing economic contribution to the Afghan side. However, some residents on the Tajik side, as well as representatives from AKF, complained that the bazaar had caused a spike in the price of honey and a few other commodities, which was hurting the rest of the local economy. Many Shughnis commented that they could now buy cheap watermelons from the bazaar and resell them throughout Shughnan. The Tajik side has benefited more because most of the traders are local, while on the Afghan side many of the traders are from Pakistan or Kabul.

Prior to the construction of the bridges and cross-border bazaars, a considerable amount of trade and other types of exchanges were managed through informal networks and agreements. The bridge formalized these exchanges. But the formalization also made some existing humanitarian exchanges more difficult for locals on both sides of the border, particularly the Afghans. For example, crossing the border for medical help now required a passport and an expensive visa. Similarly, cross-border trips for foodstuffs now required a visa and passport. During each of my trips I observed border guards and border commanders enforcing these laws to their fullest extent; they even went so far as to show me the rules they had to enforce if I wanted to cross the border. Additionally, I received a copy of the customs manual and the handbook the border guards were to follow from a Tajik customs officer who was kind enough to share it with me. The manual was convoluted, and the customs guards told me that they were unable to decipher all of them, but they certainly attempted to enforce what they could, at least when I was there. Many people reported that enforcement was quite flexible and rules could and would be broken with a payment by the person crossing the border.

The bridges and the cross-border bazaars also created opportunities for increased cooperation among illicit networks. In the past, most of the drugs came across the river on tires, on other flotation devices, and in the stomachs of animals. Now they flow freely in trucks and other vehicles. Only petty traders trying to smuggle small amounts still cross the river since the bridge opened. Any river crossing is done at considerable risk, both from the strong currents and from border guards needing to prove they are doing their jobs.

I conducted a small survey in Khorog that alleged that there is relatively little drug trafficking or illicit activity at the Tem border crossing, particularly during the Saturday cross-border bazaar. In private, locals told a different story. They said that the bazaar was used to coordinate the illicit trade, not for actual transactions, and that many parts of the criminal networks met at the bazaar weekly.

The fact that the locals presented a different interpretation (in part) even to a trusted local, a fellow Ismaili from Khorog who conducted the survey for me, highlights the common practice of feigning ignorance about informal and/or illicit activities. The survey was about the cross-border bazaars and included questions about illicit trade and drug trafficking. While the people surveyed clearly had knowledge about such activities, based on private discussions, if they viewed the survey as official, they would not disclose what they knew even if it was supposed to be anonymous.

Privately, during parties, dinners, walks, and other social events, the more I partook in these events the more the layers of knowledge came out. What became clear was that everyone knew everything about each other—period. There were no secrets among community members, whether a village or group of villages or a city spanning both sides of the border. During my many visits to the bazaar, I witnessed many unlikely pairs, including border commanders and drug traffickers, chatting with no shame—openly, for all to see.

For the border guards, since they are not allowed to catch the "larger fish" as the locals refer to the higher-level drug traffickers, they target the smaller, inconsequential traders. This satisfies the international funding agencies such as United Nations Office of Drug and Crime (UNODC) and legitimizes the efforts of the Tajik Drug Control Agency (DCA) and the entire border security system. The larger shipments, controlled by the "larger fish," are just part of a complex web of informal cooperative networks running from China and Russia to Pakistan by way of Afghanistan and Tajikistan. Moreover, these are just a fraction of the links in a very long chain of networks of cooperation that have financial remuneration as the primary goal for inter-group agreements and collaboration. The government of Tajikistan is not going to dissuade these traders from doing their business as long as they are profiting personally. Some referred to this profit as a "cash cow" for the government and one they were not likely to part with even with intense international pressure to do so.[4]

The cross-border bazaars are newly formed institutions with official rules and regulations including procedures for entering and exiting, stall rental fees, and times of operation. Each bazaar has a different set of procedures and a different framework within which it operates. In the cross-border bazaars, I was able to observe how informal institutionalization and informal networks interact within and around the formal institutions. They occur as daily practices and often as quiet protests against the formal structures that are viewed as illogical, impractical, or as tools of oppression by the state. The official procedures often impeded transactions and informal networks are simply an easier means to an end.

Informal institutional practices in the cross-border bazaar are both overt and covert, embedded in the legal and illegal transactions. By practices, I mean the taken-for-granted, common-sense behavior that is a part of every inter-action at the border. The exchanges can be between people of equal standing, unequal standing, a person with official position, unofficial position, or just a passerby. Generally, these transactions are hidden from international donors and/or outsiders by those working or conducting business in the bazaar. I witnessed these overt and covert informal practices by both participating in and observing the cross-border bazaar. The following vignettes provide some of the flavor of the bazaars.

Bazaar at Tem (in Khorog/Shughnan)

The cross-border bazaar at Tem is not the sprawling sort of bazaar I had experienced in many other parts of the world. It was a small patch of land with a dusty dirt floor and a rickety, tent-like structure covering some of the merchants. The rest of the merchants had plastic ground cloths or bits of plastic on which they spread their various and sundry wares: cheap plastic shoes, bracelets, tchotchkes, and clothes from China and Pakistan. They even had slippers—a Chinese version of the popular Bulgarian house shoes. Local Tajik women traditionally wear these slippers, only the cheap Chinese knockoffs wear out quickly and left women with exposed feet.

Many of the local *bazaaris* (traders working in the bazaar) thought they were selling stuff manufactured in Faizabad, India, or Kabul, but, in reality, that is just where they picked up the goods. Most of them were actually from much farther away, such as China. A few merchants were selling local crafts, clothing, and semi-precious stones. Foodstuffs on offer included milk, rice, flour, and a few spices. Soap, cell phones, and dishware were also available, all from China and Pakistan. Some of the women sold Surmah (kohl),[5] a local rock that has religious significance in Islam and is believed to have healing properties throughout South Asia and the Middle East. Women and Afghan men in the borderlands use it for eyeliner.

Women in the bazaar: roles and rules

The roles of Afghan women and the rules governing them in the bazaar were hotly debated among the men and women (gathered in separate groups) as well as the internationals working in the area. Many of the men believed there were strict laws governing women in the bazaar, but each group seemed to have their own "clear" version of these laws. I had one particularly heated discussion with an Afghan man named "Farid" in Shughnan on this subject.

I asked Farid why women were not allowed in the cross-border bazaar. He said that I had an ill-conceived U.S.-centric view of the Afghans. I told him that I had been spending time with different groups of women in Ishkashem and Shughnan and they all had told me that they were not allowed to go to the bazaar. Two women even confided to me that they had snuck out and gone to the bazaar in defiance of their husbands. They said they were just so curious to see what it was like. Farid said that I must have misunderstood them, because this just was not true.

I asked many other women, and all of them categorically said they were not allowed to go to the bazaar. Finally, I asked them who it was that forbade them. The Afghan women all said the same thing: the male head of their household would not allow them. The men were scared that the women would be kidnapped by Tajik men or that something else bad would happen to them and they would be "ruined."

During my trip in 2011–2012, Kabul appointed a leader for Shughnan who was Sunni. Reportedly, this leader had issued a new law banning women from going to the bazaar. There was so much hearsay about what was allowed for women and what was not. Regardless of the laws, the men in the family, namely the father or husband, made the family rules, and for the most part, that meant females were not allowed to go to the bazaar. A similar discrepancy between law and practice also applied to the leaders, in that some leaders believed that women should be allowed and others were against it. This became clear after speaking to many people about this issue, and it likely contributed to the confusion.

In Afghan Shughnan, Ishkashem, and the Wakhan Corridor, family customs, local practices, and norms within village cluster trumped any official laws of the state. In fact, each village cluster had different rules pertaining to leaders, based on local practices as well as the local leaders' acceptance and ability to govern in the area. Moreover, different networks had different systems in which they accepted leadership. For example, in the villages in which I conducted my fieldwork in the district of Shughnan, Afghanistan, much of the legitimate authority split between the local religious leaders and the Shurra Council leaders. Shurras for each village had separate councils for men and women. In many of the villages, the female shurras did not have places to meet or funding for their councils. In many villages, however, the female shurra leaders did have legitimate authority to settle disputes among women or help women who were having problems at home.

By contrast, in the Panjsher province of Afghanistan, the networks mediated through the local militias and associated leaders and had a less communal form of local governance, and there female shurras or shurra council leaders did not exist.[6] It was difficult to ascertain whether the central government had any real influence or control over the districts I studied, particularly as it pertained to female access to leadership positions within the local governments. The unwritten agreements were diffuse and non-uniform across territories and at the same time deeply embedded and enmeshed within small groups of people such as clans and village clusters.

While Shurra Council positions are elected locally, other positions are often not. Many locals complained bitterly, when they felt safe to, about the appointment by the administration in Kabul of outsiders to official positions in their districts. They felt the government was stealing local authority, disregarding local customs, and forcing informal taxation from outside, all of which was the opposite of what they wanted their government to do for them. It was almost unheard of for women to be appointed to these positions. The lack of female leadership at the district or provincial level limited the ability for women to gain access to services, legal structures, and goods. This lack of access includes the bazaars, whether cross-border or in-country. At the cross-border bazaar, a few Afghan women were allowed to sell. The following section describes these women.

Surmah and the Afghan female bazaaris

At the entrance to the bazaar was a group of older Afghan women, since it is more acceptable for them to be at the bazaar as opposed to younger women who are either unmarried or taking care of their children. These women, four in all, kneeled on the ground, displayed an array of local handicrafts, Surmah nuggets, and some semi-precious stones carved into beads. In Dari, they asked if I would like to buy some of their wares. I had seen the dark lines drawn under the eyes of many of the local women on both sides of the border and even some of the men. They explained to me that the make-up from the surmah was good for the eyes. "Nilofar," a friend of mine, had said the same thing a week earlier. She wanted to buy a stone and applicator for me, so we went to the bazaar together. I ended up buying five of the rocks and applicator pens from these women, thinking I would give them to my friends and my daughters. Nilofar, pleased that she had persuaded me to try this custom, smiled and helped negotiate the purchase of these items.[7]

After Nilofar and I left the bazaar, we went to the house of our friend, "Malika." It was then, much to my surprise, that the truth about the Surmah came out. The Surmah I had bought from the bazaar was not Surmah at all. It was simply rocks collected from wherever and dipped in battery acid, which makes the stones look silvery. My friends said that they believed that the Afghans did it on purpose, to blind the Tajik women. Furthermore, the Afghan traders could not be trusted since they did not care about the well-being of the Pamiris on the Tajik side of the border. Malika and Nilofar told me that the Surmah was considered to have almost magical healing properties and they felt the Afghan women were tainting it and blinding their Tajik sisters with the very stone that was supposed to heal the eyes. Then the conversation shifted to rumors about Tajik women being kidnapped, which is why Malika's husband had forbidden her from going to the bazaar. Afghan men, according to my friends, liked the beautiful women from the Tajik side and had taken them as brides.[8]

Later I heard that the Surmah supplies were dwindling and that remaining sources were in difficult-to-reach locations. The local Afghan women had discovered the battery acid trick, since some of them did not have access to the actual mineral-laden rocks. They did not seem to understand just how toxic the battery acid was. Due to the shortage of the stone, it was an economic choice, at least according to the women and men in Afghanistan I spoke to about this practice. However, the characterization of the Afghans by the Tajiks as uncivilized or backwards, certainly became more deeply entrenched on the Tajik side of the border through the practice of lacing eye make-up with battery acid and kidnapping of the women.

Both the rule disallowing Afghan women from the cross-border bazaars and the rumors about battery-acid laced stones show a distrust of their counterparts across the border. While I often heard locals from both sides of the border talk about how the area belonged as one and they were all Ismailis and mountain people, the assertion that the other side was not safe or to be trusted also existed. There were clear contradictions. In one context, the border very much existed and delineated and protected one side from the unknown of the other side. At other times, the locals on either side of the border felt a kinship and a desire to be unified.

This may seem contradictory, but in the borderlands it makes perfect sense. In one context, the networks cooperate with each other to do business, provide humanitarian aid, and have the same ethnic, linguistic, territorial, and religious identities. Conversely, they do not believe that they are always safe with those on the other side, as is evidenced by human trafficking. They were both united and divided by identities, nationality, and most importantly, networks of cooperation (which were both negative and positive). The positive unification between local groups increased when outside pressure or penetration occurred, such as state monopolization of power at the border. Divergence occurred more when the local informal networks of cooperation were perceived as violent or harming the locals.

The gemstone trade

It was a bright, sunny and beautifully crisp early morning in Khorog when my phone rang. It was an official in charge of the border for one of the leading international organizations. He was bringing a delegation of international officials. They were coming at the behest of AKDN in order to view the ongoing development projects and make decisions about future donor participation. He asked me if I could meet them at the cross-border bazaar and give the delegation a tour and talk about Khorog and the bazaar, essentially to be an informal guide. He then asked for a rather interesting favor, given his position, the status of the delegation, its relationship to AKDN, and my own position as an independent researcher. He wondered if I could introduce a couple of members of the delegation to some gemstone traders because they wanted to buy some of the region's famed precious stones. I asked if he wanted to buy them within the networks I was researching (which he knew about). He replied yes, that would be great. I agreed to set something up, if my contacts were willing. He said he would arrive by helicopter within two hours and would call when he reached the airport at the border. We hung up.

I went to the bazaar where I knew a number of border guards and commanders from both sides of the border were involved in various types of illicit trade. A friend of mine at the bazaar who worked for the DCA of Tajikistan was there. I spoke with him, but he said that he could not help me. Then I saw an official with the cross-border bazaar and asked him. He nodded toward a border guard on the opposite side of the bazaar but said nothing. I strolled over to him and explained that a delegation would like to buy some precious stones, that its members had money to spend, and would he kindly introduce me to a trader who would be willing to sell some of his wares.

At first the border guard demurred, saying he knew nothing about it. Then, he went to another border guard and a friend of his from across the border, the three of them all looked at me while I tried to pretend I did not see them, and then the border guard gestured for me to talk to him. He said he knew someone who could be there in about an hour. I thanked him and said that I would tell the delegation when they arrived. A few minutes after that, the delegation arrived, but they only stayed at the bazaar for about 30 minutes. They had to go to another venue and then to lunch and requested that I bring the traders to the place of their luncheon after about two hours. I said I would be there as soon as I could. After about a half an hour, one of the gemstone dealers showed up. He showed me some beautiful stones, gave me prices, and other details. I called my contact with the delegation, who confirmed that the officials were interested and said we should bring the goods to the luncheon. The trader said he was going to go home to get some more of his goods and would meet us at the hotel in two hours. I thanked him and promised he would be safe in the meeting because I knew the man we were working with quite well and he had assured me anonymity.

My worry was that the delegation members would be sold stones and then arrested at the border or airport, as the gemstone traders might have been working with the government of Tajikistan. But, as it turned out, the trader was worried about getting caught as well (and was actually a gemstone trafficker). He told us that he hated and feared the government of Tajikistan. In fact, he was one of the many I subsequently met who said that they would prefer to be a separate country from Tajikistan, a sort of united Pamiri territory. This was not the first time I had heard this. Another group of friends had jokingly asked if I would be the national security advisor for the United Pamiri Nation. The question was said with enough bitter irony that it was clear this was not an idle pipedream.

This gem trader was associated with one of the local warlords who wanted an independent Badakhshan, entirely separate from Tajikistan. Since the civil war ended, he had created his own militia and stockpiled hundreds of weapons to make sure that if the government of Tajikistan "invaded" again, they would be trained and ready. Many said this warlord had the support of the majority of the residents of Gorno-Badakhshan. True or not, he was supported by many living within his sphere of influence.

A few weeks before meeting the gemstone trader, I had met with the warlord he was allied with. I later learned that this was the main reason the trader had trusted me. Most of the people in and around Khorog had an informal leader they were allied with or attached to as a means for security, dispute resolution, and other forms of protection. Ultimately, the warlords made money through a mix of illicit and licit trade and local businesses. This informal leadership provides local stability and dispute settlement locally when the government of Tajikistan cannot.

The gemstone traders believed that the money earned from their trade is from locally acquired gems and therefore the profits belong to the local population. They also felt that if they shared the local resources with the government of Tajikistan they would not get their fair share and neither would the Pamiris in general.

The trader, whom I got to know later on in my fieldwork, gave me a detailed history of what he called the "genocide" during the civil war from 1992 to 1997. He explained how, in his view (and, it turned out, that of many others I spoke with) warlords in the area had protected the community and that without them, particularly the warlord he was allied with, many more civilians would have died. He said that the warlord in his area was one of the only leaders looking out for his section of Khorog and that people viewed him as the true leader for their area (aside from the Aga Khan, who was the leader of all their leaders). The trader said that the warlord settled disputes and helped the people in a number of ways, including the poor and marginalized (which, while true for many, was not unanimously the view of those living in his area).

In fact, one local resident lost a five-year court battle over a property dispute in Tajikistan. In the end, he turned to informal channels to resolve the dispute. The gentleman who had lost in court said it was because he was less connected and powerful than his opponent. He said he would keep fighting but did not hold out much hope for the courts to administer real justice. This is all just to say that the formal justice system had little ability to enforce the law, while the informal leaders and their mediation processes were where people turned. The gemstone traders were under the umbrella of these informal local leaders and followed the rules enforced informally by the leaders under whom they operated. The distrust of the formal government and trust of their local leaders empowers the informal trust networks that cooperate over and above any of the formal institutions in the area.

The border guard and the drug lord

On a crisp day in late spring, I was at the bazaar with a woman who worked for the Tajik government. She pointed out a big white SUV. When I asked whom it belonged to, she laughed, not wanting to tell me. When I pressed for an answer, she gave me a long look and spilled the secret. Sitting in the SUV with unmarked plates were the main drug lord from Khorog and the Afghan Border Police Commander. Now I began to understand how things really worked—through back channels. Both of these men were clan leaders with considerable informal authority in Badakhshan. Both men were also drug lords. Both men worked with their governments, one officially paid by the government and the other a willing partner in both security cooperation as well as illicit trade.

The border guard and the milk trader

One day the Third-Secretary from the Afghan Consulate in Khorog asked me to accompany him, his wife, and their children to the Tem bazaar in Khorog and to have lunch afterwards. They had asked me to come and live with them so that I could teach the family English. I was in the process of deciding whether to move my stuff to their apartment or not. The gentleman from the Afghan consulate introduced me to the official "Manager" of the bazaar and to a number of border guards from both sides of the border.

During one of these introductions, I noticed that the Tajik border guard had a case of prized Iranian cream under his arm. The Tajik bazaari was angry. The cream had real value—milk products were scarce, especially in the winter, and Iranian cream was considered the richest and tastiest. The other cream sold at the bazaar, made by Nestlé, was cut with hydrogenated vegetable oil, giving it a synthetic taste. It was clear the bazaari was upset by having to give up a whole case of his product—and judging from his language, he had not been paid for his product.

I later asked a local friend if this was a form of bribery. She confirmed that it was and added that while the official fees for the rental of a stall in the bazaar were rather small, often the border guards and other government workers appropriated various products and items as an informal surcharge. The informal system of payment was overt, done in the light of day, for all to see. It was a routine transaction.

Ishkashim bazaar and Mr. White Suit

I witnessed a similar case of rent-seeking at the bazaar at Ishkashem. When I first began visiting, this leader kept his rent-seeking covert, but as he got to know me he no longer bothered to hide his informal dealings. I had met the gentleman before, when he helped me cross the border when it was closed.

As I got to know the local border guards and commanders on the Tajik and Afghan sides, I increasingly was allowed to cross at will, thanks to the various informal leaders. This informal leader had been governor of the area and a key apparatchik during Soviet times. He no longer had a formal position, but he was still a leader. Most of the time he wore a white suit, bowler hat, and patent-leather shoes, clearly a demonstration of his position within the group. He often was accompanied by an entourage of younger men from the Tajik border command in Ishkashim. Many of them wore sunglasses and clearly had the power to decide who or what went across the border.

At first, I observed Mr. White Suit leaving the bazaar laden with bags of goods that usually were not sold in bulk, such as soap, milk, and fruit. He would have 20 or 30 bars of nice soap, lotion, and similar luxury items. Nearly every day he left with two or three bags of this stuff. I wondered if the traders purchased his cooperation or assistance with commodities.

My suspicions were later confirmed when I crossed the border with the UN. A driver with a truck full of cigarette cartons was trying to cross the border. The border guards stopped the truck and began questioning the Afghan driver. Next, they dumped a valuable pile of around a hundred cigarette cartons on the ground behind the truck. Then, the group began haggling about whether it was enough or not (they thought I could not understand because they were speaking in a thick dialect). Finally, Mr. White Suit decided the terms were acceptable. He turned to the commander and his deputy, said "*bechara*" and nodded toward the driver. He told the other men that they had taken enough because it was clear the Afghan trader was impoverished and struggling. Satisfied with the pile of cigarette cartons stacked on the road, Mr. White Suit let the driver go because he recognized his desperation.

As the border guards and informal leaders accepted me more and more, they made no effort to conceal their activities and carried on in the "usual" way. Whether crossing the border, selling in a bazaar stall, or trafficking illegal goods, all activities required some type of an informal "rent" or payment. Any official leader could levy rents for access. But on the Tajik side, the informal leaders often had as much, if not more, authority to charge rents as the formal authorities. On the Afghan side, the clan leaders, drug lords, and official arbiters of the border were often one and the same person. In Ishkashim, one informal leader controlled the border crossing, while at Shughnan, Tajikistan, three local leaders and the border command shared power, depending on the commodity or service desired or requested.

In the end, the bazaar appeared to work like every other institution at the border, meaning the modus operandi was to leverage legitimate authority, whether formally or informally sanctioned, against a form of informal taxation for access to markets or to cross the border. These informal rents and agreements usually trumped the formal mechanisms in place for doing business and crossing the border.

Personnel training and infrastructural development at the border

Infrastructure development along the border of Badakhshan includes buildings, training for border and customs guards, trade agreements, rules, regulations, and methods of enforcement, surveillance equipment, and delineation of crossing points and inaccessible areas. The goal is not just control, but also influence since, as James pointed out, this is usually the closest a country can come to control. And in Badakhshan, it was local leaders who benefited from greater infrastructure.

In Badakhshan, every written law has a corresponding informal arrangement. When the two rules clash, the informal practice usually prevails. This includes legal and illegal trade, human flows, and visa/customs-related issues. Moreover the customs and border guards on both sides of the Afghan/Tajik border belong to both formal and informal networks of power. For example, an Afghan border commander working for the government likely is also a powerful clan leader and drug lord. The official appointment by the state enhances his unofficial position.

Currently most infrastructure development schemes focus on the formalization of border institutions, but the majority of the interactions and transactions continue to occur in the underlying informal agreements. To learn more about this process, I lived near some of the project sites. I assessed the infrastructure—including buildings, bridges, personnel training, and security equipment—and participated in workshops training Afghan and Tajik customs agents and border guards. Participating in development projects with five international organizations helped highlight the roles that stakeholders, local, national, and international, play along the border and how local and informal agreements trump formal institutions and rules.

Customs agent and border guard training

Customs (ghumrok) versus customs (sonat)

In the Tajik language there are two different words for customs whereas in the English language there is only one. It is precisely this intersection of the two types of customs (security and norms) that I examine in this chapter. Customs (*ghumrok* in Tajik) means the agency that monitors border trade. Customs (*sonat* in Tajik) means the typical practices of a group of people. At the border, the customs officers function somewhere in between their own customs and the laws they are there to enforce.

I had the unique opportunity of participating in border development projects and programs with five organizations. For the UN, I assessed their Border Management Project for Badakhshan, Afghanistan (EUBOMBAF). With the OSCE, I provided situational awareness and video documentation of their training of Tajik Customs agents and commanders. For AKF, I assessed their Drug Demand Reduction Program (DDRP) in three districts in Afghan Badakhshan. For the Deutsche Gesellschaft für Internationale Zusammenarbeit (GIZ), I provided training and a workshop for experts working on cross-border trade development in Badakhshan, and I worked with their staff on documenting successes and failures of the three cross-border bazaars in Badakhshan. Lastly, I observed the training of Afghan and Tajik border guards by the International Organization for Migration (IOM) at the military compound in Khorog.[9]

Many of the border workshops and counter-trafficking simulations inadvertently provided opportunities for developing more entrenched networks of cooperation among traffickers and other illicit trade networks. The trainings taught border guards and others employed by the state not only how to protect the border but also divulged methods on how to avoid getting caught. Locals claim that most customs and border guards and officials are involved in the drug trade,[10] so the more they learn about how to catch traffickers, the more they learn how to avoid being caught themselves. This awareness helps them to "play the part" of the good customs guards for international donors, while abetting criminal networks in practice.

What was independently corroborated by numerous sources was the fact that almost all of the customs agents and officials act as mediators between traffickers and officials involved in trafficking. Customs jobs reportedly are the most lucrative, due to the sums of money made through bribes. Not all of the customs agents and border guards are corrupt, but certainly the majority seems to be, either out of necessity or peer pressure.[11]

The workshops and trainings also provided a window into the various identities the border and customs personnel had to present on an ongoing basis including: an instrument of the state; a member of their community; a member of a criminal network; and a religious person. The border personnel's group affiliations intertwined with their individual, family, and, particularly in Gorno-Badakhshan, community's security. The borders of the state were just the beginning of the many borders people had to traverse. The symbolic borders of delineation encompassed far more than just the border between nation-states including: territory, religious, economic, and ethnic. Therefore, as state and international institutions asserted influence (and national identity) through training, workshops, infrastructure, and newly implemented rules, local identity groups, networks of cooperation, and organizations, reacted in turn, sometimes more and sometimes less. The first of these observations describes the role of the international community and trainers in this process.

The project manager and the expatriate party

Before going to the border, I spent a few weeks in Dushanbe talking to international development workers about the ongoing border projects. I soon realized that most were living a life of luxury far removed from the local population and that few had even been to the border to see their projects in action.

I was invited to a dinner party that would be held at the home of the director of a large IGO who lived in a mansion in an elite area of Dushanbe. He had invited a small group of EU development officials and workers over for fondue and a photo presentation by an ice climber who had recently returned from the remote and previously unexplored ice cliffs in Badakhshan. Shortly after I arrived at the party, I sat down at a table in a courtyard across from my host, the president of a major development bank from a European country. He had a half wheel of Gruyere and melted it slowly on an open flame, preparing a traditional Swiss fondue.

The decadence of the expat community stood in stark contrast to the villagers and the lives of the majority of the citizens of one of the poorest countries in the world. While the host prepared his evening fondue, most Pamiri villagers were having a cup of *Sheerchoi*. This is a salty tea made with powdered milk, chunks of flat bread, and perhaps butter or some other kind of fat. Many locals eat this meal three times a day, particularly in the winter, due to the food scarcity and extreme poverty. The scene at the party was something I had only read about—and heard about from locals. Foreigners living like royalty, often making ten and even 20 times the pay of a local working alongside them in the same or similar position. The locals often told me that they were treated with disrespect or just plain ignorance by many of the internationals. Indeed, I witnessed such behavior. The division between insider (local) and outsider (international) could not have been more obvious.

The partygoers were a mix of people from EU member countries—I was the only American—along with Tajiks from elite families and young beautiful Tajik women. All of the internationals had good salaries, luxurious living quarters, and drivers. Some had visited the villages and hiked in the mountains in and around Dushanbe. Very few had been to Gorno-Badakhshan, which occupied 50 percent of the land of Tajikistan, and where many of the cross-border development projects—*their* cross-border projects—were located.

Even fewer had bothered to learn the local language. There would be some locals at these parties, and when they found out that I was a graduate student who spoke Tajik, they would make comments to me in Tajik when they thought no one else could understand. One Tajik woman said to me, "When you come to our country and don't learn our language, get rich, and never talk to us, how can you expect us to respect you?" She said this in front of a group of well-paid expats from her office. She smiled the whole time, acting as if she were saying something else to me.

At the IGO Director's party, I met two Tajik women who worked for the OSCE. When they asked what I was doing there, I told them I was doing fieldwork for my dissertation on cross-border security and cooperation. They giggled and said, "Have you spoken with Pierre yet?" "Who is that?" "Oh, you must speak with him! Come, we will introduce you." Then, quite by accident, I met the Director of Border Management for a large IGO, "Pierre."[12] Pierre had deep experience in Tajikistan, Central Asia and many other parts of the world. He spoke 13 languages and had a disarming, dry sense of humor.

In the corner of the large patio was a small, non-descript Frenchman with a rather unruly mass of gray hair. He had a gorgeous young woman next to him (as I later found out was his habit), and he looked at me dubiously. Pierre said he had heard about a Ph.D. student "sniffing around about borders." We then began a rather animated conversation about drug-trafficking and the borders in the region. He told me that he suspected precursor chemicals were being shipped via North Korea across China and into Tajikistan and from there, splitting between Tajikistan and Afghanistan. I had heard the same thing from two other people. I asked him if labs for drug-processing were moving over the border into Tajikistan. Pierre said that some existed there and some were in Afghanistan, but most of the officials in Tajikistan were involved in the drug trade. I asked him about all of the new buildings that had sprouted up in and around Dushanbe. He laughed and said, "What do you think? They certainly aren't getting the money for this from other businesses."

Pierre's program trained customs agents, border guards, and commanders on both sides of the border in interdiction and counter-trafficking/counter-narcotics methods. Of course, the very people he trained were the ones who trafficked. Pierre believed that if one or two of those trained moved up the ranks into a position of power at some point in the future, then perhaps policy could be implemented to begin to positively change things through these people. After talking to Pierre for over an hour, he invited me to participate in a customs training workshop.

Policy was developed and implemented by these international and local elites with scant input from the actual locals that the policy ultimately would impact. This disconnect was not only evident in the nightlife of the expatriate community in Dushanbe, but also in Kabul, and, most importantly, along the border in Gorno-Badakhshan and Badakhshan. Many in the local community did not understand why outsiders were imposing laws on their autonomous territory.

The following sections are from the part of my fieldwork in which I worked with, around, and/or observed the implementation, planning, and training of border personnel by IGOs. The seminars and workshops took place along the border in Khorog (Tajikistan) and Shughnan (Afghanistan) in Badakhshan and on the border of Tajikistan and China in Gorno-Badakhshan. The border and customs personnel training and workshops that Pierre allowed me to attend reflected not only the dissonance between project planning and implementation, but also the discord among local, domestic, and international staff. The stories give insight into how the development of border infra-structure both on the personnel level and the physical, structural level, impact stability at the border and the state. They also underscore the role of local leaders, organizations, and the community in both project implementation and overall development of the border institutions in Badakhshan.

OSCE training: Murghab and Khorog

In July 2010, the OSCE provided training to customs officers and agents in Khorog, the district of Murghab, and at the Kulma Pass, at the Chinese border with Tajikistan. Two retired senior customs officers, one from the UK and one from the US, taught the seminars. The OSCE Program Manager was French. They taught physical search techniques, psychological profiling and methods, and document inspection. Some of the customs officers appeared to be truly interested in the training while others clearly viewed it as a formality they had to go through for both the internationals and the Tajik government.

There was a large poster of President Rahmon in the classroom. Because of the president's impending visit for the *Ruz-e Vahdat* holiday (discussed in Chapter 5), there were additional posters and pictures of the president papering the city. During the workshop we heard workers outside hammering as they hung a large banner outside of the customs headquarters. A number of locals taking part in the training mocked the images and even took down the framed poster of President Rahmon and flipped it over to face the wall.

The customs agents were divided into five teams of four and told to act like smugglers. Some pretended they were illegally crossing the border; others were tasked with smuggling goods in a truck or plane. One group had to pretend to use false documents to get into the country illegally. The Tajik customs personnel were creative in their problem-solving and clearly knew exactly how drugs, weapons, and other items were smuggled across the borders.

When the agents and officers were asked if smuggling and trafficking was a common occurrence at the border, they said that it was not so much of an issue. But when they were asked how they themselves might smuggle goods (and drugs in particular), they had many useful ideas. When the trainers asked them how they knew all of these methods; they said they had a lot of experience with them. There was a tacit acknowledgment among the trainers and trainees regarding the smuggling. The agents could not admit that the illicit activity was endemic because then the low seizure rates might expose their complicity in the trafficking. Everybody knew it was going on so if they could show what they knew, without actually acknowledging it, that appeared to be okay.

This workshop uncovered how well the customs agents already knew their jobs both formally and informally, and how disconnected the two were. I mentioned this to the trainers, and the general consensus was, "We don't care if the customary norms contradict the laws they are being asked to enforce. They simply have to enforce the law." But it seemed that the locals enforced the law only when it would not harm them, their family, or their immediate community. Otherwise, the informal institutional norms/unwritten agreements were their guiding principle.

When outsiders such as non-Pamiri Tajiks, state officials, and/or internationals worked to monopolize power at the border through formalization of the border crossings and customs, the locals not only hid the fact that illicit trade was endemic, but they also mocked the visual presence of their president in the room. The illicit trade, not unique to the border in Badakhshan, was something in which both the locals and the non-Pamiri Tajiks participated.

The internationals, domestics, and locals each had their own networks of cooperation but the network of the internationals (at least those involved with the customs training for OSCE) interacted more with the locals and their associated organizations. While the locals kept their distance from the non-Pamiri Tajiks, they generally befriended the internationals; certainly more so than the non-local Tajiks. The internationals seemed aware that both the official institutions of the state as well as the locals and their associated groups held sway at the border. The locals also understood that influencing and gaining the trust of the internationals would benefit them when/if they had problems with the Tajik central authorities. The tension between the local (Pamiri) and non-local Tajiks revealed itself in many ways. The following two vignettes highlight religious-based tensions, in particular.

The Islamic psychologist, the customs agents, and the commanders

I observed the underlying dislike between the customs agents and their local trainers bubbling to the surface during an OSCE workshop on interdiction and counter-narcotics methods. The workshops were in Murghab, a district in Gorno-Badakhshan that borders Kyrgyzstan and China, in the most north-eastern corner of Tajikistan. The harsh climate makes living there difficult since it is above the tree line and the elevation ranges from 11,000 feet to close to 15,000 feet. Water, arable land, and food are scarce and it is bitterly cold and windy. Because of the high altitude, workshop participants had altitude sickness, limited food and water, and consumed large amounts of vodka. As a result, two members of the OSCE staff, an interpreter from Ishkashim, and a doctor from Dushanbe who was also the deputy program manager from Dushanbe, became ill. The doctor had to leave the workshop and return to Dushanbe and the interpreter was hospitalized for over a week. The difficult living conditions also exacerbated certain tensions.

The OSCE had hired two Tajik "psychological profiling" experts to lead the seminars. One was the Deputy Head of Customs and the other was an "Islamic religious psychologist" studying at the Islamic University in Dushanbe. The majority of the attendees were Ismaili Shi'a from the district of Shughnan in Gorno-Badakhshan, although a few were Kyrgyz-Tajiks from the district of Murghab. The Deputy Head of Customs wanted to introduce the importance of the role of Sunni Islam for the study of interdiction and profiling at the border.

One Ismaili Shi'a participant found the training offensive since it was entirely based around Hanafi Sunnism—one of the least conservative Sunni sects. The majority of the residents of Tajik and Afghan Badakhshan are

Ismaili Shi'a, while the majority of the people in power in both countries are Sunni. The Ismailis in the workshops complained that the trainer (the "Islamic psychologist") had a very low-level of education and spoke a "street Tajik" and could not speak Russian or English. All of the Ismailis attending the seminar were fluent in Russian, Tajik, and Shughni, and many of them also could speak English.

The customs personnel from Gorno-Badakhshan took pride in being Tajik (as opposed to being from Afghanistan, China, or Kyrgyzstan). But the training, forced them to listen to doctrine that directly contradicted their core religious and philosophical beliefs and discounted their religious identity. As the workshops progressed, they increasingly asserted the differences between them and the Sunni Tajiks. This included beliefs regarding differences in ethnicity, education level, women's rights, familial practices, and other local customs.

Additionally, the Sunni Tajiks forced the Pamiri/Ismaili customs guards to recite Sunni prayers at each communal meal and to train in traditional Sunni religious practices that differ quite a bit from Ismaili Shi'a practices and beliefs. This forced the Ismaili customs officers to subordinate their core beliefs and their status as citizens of a secular state. By framing a workshop for Ismaili Shi'a participants around Hanafi Sunnism, the OSCE and the Tajik Deputy Head of Customs, who advised OSCE on this training, de facto excluded the Ismailis from a key developing state institution at the border. Moreover, the fact that they would advocate a "proper religious way of life" while representing a secular state and provide psychological profiling individuals to the customs guards through Hanafi Sunnism appeared to contradict President Rahmon's new mandates for both increasing religious inclusion and dampening religion within institutions.

A week after the training ended, one of the customs agents told me that three of the customs commanders who had been involved in the training had been fired, all of them Pamiri-Ismaili. One was the deputy head of counter-narcotics, another was a well-regarded local general, and the third was well-respected within his community. Apparently there had been a dispute between the local Ismaili commanders and the customs officials from Dushanbe (all Tajik-Hanafi) during the training, but the customs agent did not know any details.

According to the locals, the positions of the customs agents and commanders were the most lucrative government jobs due to the ability to get the most in informal rents (bribes). Most extended family networks share salaries and income among the group. Therefore, by taking three lucrative jobs away from the local economy, many more people were negatively impacted than just the immediate families of these three men. Many locals told me that they felt the officials in Dushanbe were corrupt and increasingly pilfered scarce resources from their local economy without providing anything in return. The loss of the positions by local elites was just one more example of this for them.

Ultimately, while the customs guards participated in the seminars and were taught some practical skills such as proper search procedures and passport inspections, the underlying difficulties caused by rampant bribing, trafficking, and oppressive, hierarchical governmental power structures made it difficult for these customs officers to implement or properly utilize what they were taught. Moreover, forcing outside cultural and religious practices on local border and customs personnel by non-Pamiri Tajiks only amplified the rift between the local and central authorities.

Debates on religious identity

I witnessed numerous debates about religion in Tajikistan, ranging from the policies regarding religious freedom to the philosophical, even mystical, underpinnings of Islam. Some of these discussions included the importance of religious freedom as a means of avoiding radicalism or, conversely, developing governmental policies to quash religious freedom in order to stave off extremism.[13]

In 2011, I spent time with an informal leader in Dushanbe who was close to the president of Tajikistan. My friend was in the process of drafting a legislative proposal on religious freedom and religious regulation. President Rahmon had just banned children under seven from attending mosque and practicing Islam. The Tajik government was monitoring the mosques and mosque leaders and had compiled a list that contained cell phones, addresses, and close associates of all religious leaders in the country.[14] This included "shadow" or underground mosques. The government crackdown on Shi'a mosques had forced many to congregate in secret.

Around this time, residents became concerned that religious institutions had been compromised, since the KGB was paying—or forcing—leaders to inform on mosque members. This practice has increased over the past three years becoming more and more formalized. When I was in Qurghonteppa in 2014, locals did not want to meet me in the mosque even to talk about benign issues such as local farming practices because it would lead to a visit from the local security services. In Khorog the government offered salaries in 2014 to all of the local Khalifas (Ismaili religious leaders). All but two of them accepted. Standing up to the government increased the respect and authority of the two who refused; many groups now regard them as the only legitimate Khalifas left in Khorog.

At the other end of the Islamic religious spectrum—meaning those actively working against the government and promoting more extreme ideologies in Tajikistan—were the Salafists from Saudi Arabia. They distributed DVDs to locals (mainly youths) and held religious discussion groups. Both the Tajik central government and the international community were growing concerned about these developments. These DVDs had been confiscated from a few mosques in Dushanbe. With the education system in disarray due to corruption and low pay, and few productive free time activities available, youth might attend the religious meetings funded by Saudi Arabia. The goal, based on the content of the DVDs, was to convert the young traditionally Hanafi Tajiks to the more conservative Salafi sect. The Iranians also were attempting to influence religious identity inside Tajikistan through the underground Shi'a mosques. They donated a large sum of money in support of the Tajik school system.[15]

During the Soviet era, religious practices were left up to the people as long as they kept them private. But in Gorno-Badakhshan, religious observance was completely secret, and people did not even reveal to their children that they belonged to the Ismaili faith. After the fall of the Soviet Union, people still primarily practiced religion in private, although tensions among different sects of Islam became more visible during the Tajik Civil War (1992–1997).[16]

Many times, I heard disparaging remarks from both sides of the religious spectrum. The following case studies contain two specific interactions that characterize what I frequently heard. The first one, a rather unexpected inter-action on an 18 hour drive from Dushanbe to Khorog, occurred between "Akbar," a Tajik Sunni Hanafi interpreter from the UN, who had recently been on Hajj to Saudi Arabia and "Nur," a Pamiri Ismaili who was a teacher and scholar (and had studied Islam, all sects, quite intensely for a number of years).

Akbar and Nur

In Darwaz, a primarily Sunni section of Gorno-Badakhshan, we stopped at the border crossing of Afghanistan. As part of the assessment of the United Nation's border management program, Akbar and I spoke to some border guards and a border commander for about an hour. When we came back to the car, Nur was holding a religious pamphlet in Tajik that a local had given to him. It spoke of why people should practice Hanafi Sunnism and not other sects within Islam. It provided a short history of Hanafism and its founder. The story left out the fact that Hanafi was a disciple of a respected and well-known Shi'a religious leader, Imam Ja'far al-Sadiq. This omission particularly irritated Nur.[17]

During the rest of the ride to Khorog (about six hours), Nur urged me to read sections from the pamphlet out loud as fodder for debate with Akbar. Nur had wanted to find a way to engage Akbar in a religious discussion since the beginning of the journey for two reasons. First, Akbar prayed five times a day, as many observant Sunnis do. Each time Akbar prayed we remained quiet out of respect. Nur found this to be an imposition and quietly expressed his annoyance. Second, when we stopped to relieve ourselves along the side of the road (since there are no public toilets), Akbar pointed out to Nur that he should urinate in the direction of Qiblah (or Qaaba/Mecca). When Nur urinated in the opposite direction, Akbar pointed out that what he was doing was *haram* (a sin). Since Nur is an Ismaili, this is not part of his religious practice, and he found it offensive that Akbar was imposing his beliefs on him and accusing him of sinning. From this moment forward, Nur wanted to explore religion with Akbar as a means to expose Akbar's religious knowledge or, rather, lack of knowledge. The pamphlet on Hanafism provided the entry-point for Nur.

After I had read a few sections of the pamphlet aloud, Nur asked if Akbar knew the history of Hanafism. Akbar said that he did not, but that he knew the principles of Islam and that is what was important to him, not its history. Nur asked Akbar if he knew that the origins of Sunni Hanafism were in Shi'ism. Akbar denied this and became angry. In fact, he remained upset on and off for the remainder of the trip.

The debate between Akbar and Nur led to a debate about who the founder of the Persian language was, another subject in which Nur was well-versed from his graduate studies. This topic cuts to the heart of the Tajik nationalism, which was created by the former Soviet Union. As I discussed in Chapter 4, at the inception of the Tajik Soviet Socialist Republic, the Soviets rewrote the history of the origin of the Tajik language to separate the people from their Persian (and Iranian) heritage.

When Nur asked Akbar about this, Akbar predictably said that Rudaki (Abu Abdollah Jafar ibn Mohammad Rudaki) was the founder of the Persian language because he was the first author to write explicitly in Persian. In one sense this is true. Rudaki is a key figure, a symbol at the heart of the Tajik nation (and he was promoted during the Soviet period) in that he was from the area and many historians assert that he was the first poet to write in the newly transliterated Persian alphabet. The newly created alphabet used Arabic script, added three specifically Persian characters, and was transliterated from the Pahlavi (middle Persian) alphabet. So on one hand, Rudaki did help crystallize the Persian alphabet. Hakim Abu al-Qasim Ferdowsi Tusi, however, helped preserve and codify the Persian language.

Ferdowsi, who came after Rudaki, decided that the Arabization of the Persian language was happening so quickly that he had to find a way to preserve it. The Arabs invaded the region in the middle of the seventh century, and at that time Islam began to replace the prevalent Zoroastrian religion in the area.[18] For 30 years Ferdowsi drafted the *Shanameh*, which is written in what he hoped was "pure" Persian. It also preserved many of the foundational myths of Zoroastrianism thus making Ferdowsi more relevant to Nur given he is from Gorno-Badakhshan, a territory with deep Zoroastrian roots and with many archeological sites from Zoroastrian times. Gorno-Badakhshan also has linkages to the Persian culture in that the original families all came from an area now part of Iran (Kerman).

The debate between Nur and Akbar ultimately was comparing apples and oranges. One referred to the Persian alphabet, the other its language. Both are important and relevant in their own right. Nur knew he was chiding Akbar in a way that would make him angry. The debate between Nur and Akbar about Rudaki and Ferdowsi, while seemingly academic, was similar to the debate on the origin of Hanafi Sunnism as it was steeped in the roots of conflict between some in Badakhshan and some in other parts of Tajikistan. It embodied differences asserted repeatedly. The above are just two examples of an endless stream of narratives about who has the "purest" roots in the region or who is practicing the proper form of religion or has a superior culture.

Four days after our drive, Akbar brought up the issue of the Ismailis and the Pamiris with me. We were with another non-Pamiri Tajik from Dushanbe. They asked me what I thought of the architectural style of the traditional Pamiri houses. I said I thought they were beautiful and connected to ancient roots in the area, including Zoroastrianism.[19] Akbar shook his head and said that the way they lived was *haram* and disgusting. They are primitive. "They all sleep together like a pack of animals. They even have sex right in front of their children. This is like molesting them. It is disgusting. And they are not proper Muslims." "Soheil," the other non-Pamiri Tajik, nodded his head in agreement. I asked them if perhaps they just had different customs than other Tajiks and that the Pamiri house is a key part of their culture and religion. They just shook their heads and said that it was disgusting. I had heard this many times before, but in more guarded ways. Akbar's outburst revealed a prejudice and dislike on a very deep level. It also showed how much he felt (and Soheil as well) that the Pamiris were not the same as them and not safe to be around due to their "dangerous" practices.

The tension between Nur and Akbar is only one example of something I witnessed countless times. It is important because it shows the tension between insiders and outsiders in relation to Gorno-Badakhshan. It also highlights how locals react to the state, and officials from the state when they enforce laws, increase institutionalization of borders, and use outsiders to train locals in their border development workshops. The tension between people belonging to different religious sects, while somewhat under the radar, permeated many interactions in subtle and not-so-subtle ways.

The UNDP EUBOMBAF Assessment

I crossed the border three times for the United Nations Development Programme European Union Border Management for Badakhshan Afghanistan Program (EUBOMBAF). My job was to assess the infrastructure that BOMBAF had designed and built over the past five years. I interviewed the border commanders, documented problems and successes, and analyzed what needed to be fixed and/or revised. For this assessment I crossed the border into Afghanistan at Rusvai/Darwaz, Tem/Shughnan, and Ishkashim/Ishkashem.[20]

As our vehicle descended into the valley between the high peaks surrounding Darwaz on the Tajik side of the border, the haunting beauty of the mountains sank in once again. At the same time I was reminded of the many challenges people faced in Tajikistan and in Gorno-Badakhshan due to this striking terrain. And yet, as we drove down the main street children played soccer, groups of men chatted animatedly, and cell phone stores, a new gym, and a number of businesses lined the streets. While waiting for one of the UN staff members, I had several groups of people invite me for tea, and a group of young boys took me over to the newly built gym where they took wrestling classes three days a week. I took a tour of the gymnasium led by the group of boys and then went to a craft store run by a group of local women. They shared the local cultural roots of the various items in their store—embroidered coverings (called *Suzani*—*Suzan* means needle), dolls, purses, and textiles from the area.

Once the border command was ready for us in Afghanistan, our small team then crossed the border into Afghanistan for our first visit to the border outpost, border command and military base in Nusai. We stopped at the Afghan bazaar in Nusai because I wanted to buy a new Burqa for my upcoming trips into Afghanistan. As I was trying on the Burqa, a tall Afghan security officer came up and started yelling at me. At first I had no idea why. Then I remembered my camera. He accused me of taking pictures of women, which is against Islam. I told him that the Commander had given me permission to take pictures. He became even angrier. The group of border military I was with started yelling back at him. Before I knew it, there were about 15 men yelling at each other about me. I went up to the security officer and offered him my camera, telling him that if I had breached any rules or done something wrong I would be happy to delete my photos. He refused and looked a bit embarrassed. I took the camera and showed him the pictures as I deleted them. He thanked me and was calm again. But the Border Commander, who had been shamed by the security official for yelling at his guest, started yelling at the man again and the altercation resumed. I quickly jumped into one of the cars and left for the base, leaving the group of men to sort out their differences.

The Border Commander arrived at the base shortly after me. He explained to me that the security official was a Pashtun and likely had to answer to the Taliban and needed to prove that he did not want an outsider/American in his territory. I asked if there had been problems for the border command due to this type of issue. All of the border guards and the commander agreed that the Pashtuns in their command informed on them to their "enemies" and put their lives in danger. They did not trust them and said that even on secret operations information had been leaked to the insurgent groups. This was in 2011. It was shortly after this that the insider attacks within the Afghan National Army began. After this incident, I spent a few hours having lunch and tea discussing issues related to trafficking, poverty, and the border with this group of officials.

Crossing the border for the infrastructure assessment meant that I encountered all of the procedures, formalities, and rules of the institutions the development projects and training of personnel aimed to formalize. Therefore, the border guards wanted to show the UN assessment team that they were following procedures to the letter. They carried out many of the procedures they had learned during the border and customs training by the UN and OSCE in which I had participated. Our re-entry into Tajik Ishkashim from Afghan Ishkashem was markedly less formal—and less conflictual.[21]

Border infrastructure development

EUBOMBAF had constructed new buildings, trained personnel, and installed new equipment on the Afghan side of the border in Shughnan, Iskhaskhem, and Rusvai. My job was to assess the new buildings, including the plumbing, electricity, and technical equipment (computers, generators, etc.)

The border commanders (both police and military)[22] showed me their vehicles, sleeping quarters, and surrounding areas, and introduced me to their personnel. They briefed me quite openly about the challenges they were facing and their attempts to address these challenges. They all said that they worked in a difficult part of the world, inherently encumbered by mixed signals (official rules versus unofficial, but relentlessly powerful unwritten agreements).

The newly built infrastructure was riddled with engineering and technical problems. The border guards found the faulty construction simultaneously offensive and puzzling. The windows for the passport inspection booths in two of the border stations were coming apart at the frame and held together with Scotch tape. The border guards pointed out these problems and said that the buildings were so cheaply made that after one year they had started to disintegrate and a lot of the equipment was inoperable, including almost all of the Polaris off-road vehicles.

Equipment was provided, but training in how to use it was not. For example, every border station I visited had new computers and scanners that would have been useful had any of the staff understood how they worked. Moreover, the intermittent access to electricity caused by malfunctioning electrical lines installed by EUBOMBAF made proper use of this equipment difficult at best and most often impossible. Most of the computers in the buildings had fabric covers and other decorations. None of them was being used. The scanners for goods and luggage sat unplugged and covered in dust.

The border commanders said that the architects and construction contractors had neglected to take the terrain and context of the area into account during the planning phase. For example, local engineers had bought substandard materials from China and pocketed the remaining unused funding. Pipes had cracked because they were made of cheap iron not rated for the extreme weather conditions in the area and the cement had been cut with sand (some reported to me that it was supposed to be 70% purity and was only 40%) so that it was crumbling a year after being poured.

In all three locations, there were significant electrical and plumbing problems caused by the low-grade materials and poor engineering. Buildings were riddled with faulty electrical lines and most of the generators, if not broken already, lacked the proper fuel. Some of the commanders said that people had poached the fuel once it arrived. Others said it never even made it to the border stations. Whatever the reason, the generators and electricity, for the most part, were not being used.

The plumbing also presented major challenges. First, most of the border guards did not use the new indoor showers and toilets, as they often did not work. Also, many of the border guards preferred using toilets located outside the buildings they lived in, as toilets are considered unclean and should not be part of the main living space. They used these rooms as storage facilities or just abandoned the space altogether. In one of the buildings, the roof had leaked, letting water seep into the second floor dormitories, and the resulting mold made sleeping in these rooms unbearable. In two of the locations they had to shut off the plumbing lines due to the cracked pipes.

Shughnan had more problems with faulty construction materials than did Rusvai. The main issues in Shughnan included ongoing water leakage in the main building (and flooding during parts of the year), cheap construction materials that caused broken door handles, buckling ceilings, peeling floors, and the like. Additionally, there had been no water line installed in the border police barracks, so the functionaries had to wash themselves outside in the unforgiving winter. The buildings were designed to be heated with solar panels, but installation was incomplete, non-existent, or the panels had cracked since they were not rated for the cold winters. This made the buildings almost unlivable since the indoor heating did not work and the winters (which I have personally experienced) are bitterly cold.

The EUBOMBAF border-crossing project in Ishkashem was plagued with problems. The Border Commander there had no kind words to say whatsoever and berated me for over an hour about the shoddy construction and lack of follow-through. His anger was palpable. He also asked why the UN command building in Qunduz had a guard tower and he did not. Why should international border or command posts be more secure than the ones for Afghans? A week later, locals attacked the guard tower in the UN command post in Qunduz and burned it down.[23]

The commander in Ishkashem had a long list of complaints, including random electrical surges that caused all of the light bulbs to explode. He said that the UN had ignored the local environment when they designed the buildings. The walls of the barracks were too thin and did not protect his soldiers from noise and the cold. He added that numerous door handles were broken, two out of the three generators were broken at the military post—they had fixed the third one but did not have diesel fuel for it. Without diesel, the boiler did not work, which meant the barracks had no heat in the winter. The commander pointed out that coal would have been a better choice. He also said that the staff were never instructed on how to operate the boilers and therefore they remained unused.

The cement sidewalks were crumbling, the toilets did not work, and there was no water, drinking or otherwise, in the headquarters. The border personnel had to bring water from a river which is about 0.5 km away. The border commander asserted that money was not spent on the project but was stolen instead.[24] His office was too small, he continued, and therefore was a sign of disrespect, and why didn't the original plans include a VIP guesthouse?

All of the commanders implored me to pass on to the UN their urgent need for a VIP guesthouse. They all said that this was necessary for the proper functioning of the border posts. Each had picked out the piece of land at the border crossing on which the guesthouse could be built. Why was a guesthouse so important for the commanders? In the area, the ability to properly host guests is a sign of power and status and has been for centuries. It also can be used in exchange for favors. Ultimately, it is a sign of legitimate authority and without it, the command posts—given the local cultural framing—lack appropriate status.

While it is clear that the infrastructure projects had institutionalized the Afghan Border Command in Badakhshan to some degree, it was also obvious that the poor engineering, implementation, and cheap construction materials greatly diminished the overall sustainability and long-term success of this goal. If the stations are already falling apart, how are the border guards supposed to uphold official rules, regulations, and security? They lack basic equipment, skills to operate provided technology, proper pay for their jobs, and decent living quarters. Also, since the local commanders used the stations as a means to garner informal power locally (hence the desire for the VIP guest houses) the development of the border stations institutionalize informal networks of power. As the infrastructure becomes less and less useable, it is easy to extrapolate that the local border and customs personnel will revert to traditional practices.

This denigration of a key institution of the state at its periphery had a negative impact on both border and state stability. This, in turn, has allowed for easier trafficking flows as was highlighted by the illicit activity I witnessed being coordinated at the crossings. Moreover as the infrastructure deteriorates, the local commanders seek the ability to influence in other ways such as through the illicit networks operating along the trafficking routes that cross the border in Badakhshan.

In reaction to the illicit trade, militarization of the border by the Tajik side has increased (largely at the behest of the international community), and in turn, caused the illicit networks to cooperate more since they have to work harder to coordinate the illicit trade. This cycle, once started, has the capability to rapidly increase and therefore the potential to cause instability not only at the border, but also at the state, and even the region. Currently, we are seeing the beginnings of this trend.

Conclusion

James said repeatedly that development is slow and, "if one border guard or two decides that the rule of law is something he wants to support," and then, over time, that same border guard moves up into a position of power, perhaps, in some small measure, things change. Paul and Rod, two trainers working for OSCE, both said the same, only each at different times. They all said we need to think not in five year or even 20 year terms, but in a 100 or 150 year terms. "Just as England took 150 years to settle down, why should we expect differently of others?" But, as he said, we never do see the long-term. We expect things to rapidly change and not only set ourselves up for failure, but those we are trying to help sometimes end up worse than when we started. James's insights into the actual development process versus the goals and/or implementation of the development projects highlighted what I also had observed at the border. Projects were conceived with a particular context in mind but that context was not the one that existed at the border. The disconnect between the temporal goals within each project and the actual temporality in which both formal and, more importantly informal institutions and local organizations change or transform, were eons apart.

The process of rapid formal institutionalization did two things. First, it increased cooperation between informal networks and illicit trade groups both locally and regionally. Networks span the territorial and clan divisions and even borders of states throughout the region. Second, it decreased the ability of the locals to gain access to basic necessities such as medical care, food, and other commodities. This created the perverse effect of institutionalizing the informal networks, decreasing formal institutionalization of the border, and then, paradoxically, decreasing border stability. Rapid formalization increased the cooperation between aforementioned informal networks. The informal institutionalization occurring in and around the formal institutions tends to entrench and legitimize informal networks by having something to counter or oppose. Through this opposition, the identity and "norms" of the networks become more defined and institutionalized.

At the border this is exactly what is going on, although it is not becoming a "formal" institution, the process is causing deeper entrenchment of informal institutions. It could be argued that this is indeed turning the informal into formal through: "authorization," which came through officials at the border (not from the state); unwritten agreements became more clearly defined; the networks of cooperation were not only legitimate at the border, the main trafficking networks were also legitimate at the state level; and finally, as the formal institutionalization process increased, the locals at the border mobilized within their networks.[25] The former increased the latter; but the informal remained just that, informal. Namely, all of the funding from the IGOs and international community would dry up if the informal institutions became official/formal because of the endemic illicit trade and narco-trafficking. Therefore, as institutionalized as the informal becomes, it will never be an official part of the state apparatus.

The formal institutions installed by various "outsiders," domestically or internationally, implants a veneer of legitimacy and formal state intervention and control at the border crossings and cross-border bazaars. At the same time the formal institutional infrastructure provides a system through which the informal channels hide, divert, and coordinate. Because it requires more effort, they also become stronger in their opposition, paradoxically system-atizing these informal networks. This layer of interaction is potent and aids in the institutionalization of the informal since the informal is often covert or unseen by outsiders of all types, but overt to insiders.[26]

Here is the logic of the informal institutionalization and increased coop-eration between informal networks aided and increased by the development of formal institutions:

1   Informal institution and network is in place. While it is "informal" to outsiders, it is the way things have been negotiated and have operated for decades (and sometimes centuries).
2   Outsiders enter and decide that this informal institution is not a proper and official arm of the state and therefore must be "developed." And, by developing this institution it will not only aid the local population, it will also increase the stability of the state.
3   The locals accept the formal institution and are grateful for the funding for various things like uniforms, buildings, equipment, and titles/jobs. But, they find it hard to incorporate these new institutions into a network of their own institutions they have developed over centuries and, more-over, they are being implemented and enforced by outsiders. While taking the money from the outsiders is fine, submitting to their institutions is not.
4   As the operation of the formal institution flows along on the surface, beneath the waters are complex networks of informal institutional modes of operation. Since the informal networks have to both work harder to navigate the mine-field the outsiders have set along the river's edges, they also have to hide from the funders/outsiders in order to continue the ways in which they have been cooperating, engaging, and operating for centuries. This not only internally enmeshes these groups within these informal institutions (institutionalizing them), it also unifies them against the formal perceived incoherence of the outsiders' formal institutions (which to them are really the informal in that they make little sense within the context of their work and region).
5   Conversely, the formal institutions allow for the informal networks to control various aspects of what crosses the border with a veil of legiti-macy in the form of a set of official by-laws. Again, this façade of legiti-macy allows those operating within the formal institutional matrix to enforce higher rents (or bribes) for access. Should people refuse the "rents," they now have a set of by-laws from the Customs manual to "consult" and find a reason to deny access. Moreover, the cost of getting caught (as an official) has gotten higher because the "outsiders" or "foreigners" might pull their funding or take other punitive action if the officials are caught not following the rules, or the formal institu-tions. The Customs manual and formal procedures allow officials to hide behind the bureaucracy should someone complain about being forced

to bribe (called a fine or tax or whatever) when crossing the border or denied access.

All of these examples of unwritten agreements across informal networks of cooperation take different forms at different times, but what was clear during my fieldwork, was that if one does not know the "secret handshake" or what is commonly held as acceptable behavior within a group, one is not going to be included in that group's activities or knowledge-generation. This includes all types of cooperative networks from illicit trade to access to the border crossings.

One way to think about the unwritten agreements is through the idea of "cultural scripts". Linguistic norms put constraints on daily language and, in turn, on people's communication. Similarly, unwritten agreements mediate the silences as a set of unspoken rules through which one is expected to navigate.

In the above case studies, I provided highlights of descriptive episodes from my fieldwork which are emblematic of not only the assertion of different identities within the formal institutions, but also how the formalization process itself is increasing the assertion of local identity as a means of protest. The IGO party showed the interaction of the international community with some of the citizens of Tajikistan. The Customs training detailed some of the rifts between some of the Pamiris and the non-Pamiri Tajiks, as did the drive with the small UN team, particularly the religious tensions. The EUBOM-BAF infrastructure assessment case study provided a window into the actual structural development and its impact on the border. Together, these case studies explain how the build-up of the border, both physically and institutionally, has created certain tensions between locals and outsiders. Moreover, they show the resulting increased assertion of local identity as a means of silent protest in order to maintain autonomy and limit encroachment from the state or outsiders.

Notes

1 James added that, in his view, while developing the infrastructure is important, getting buy-in from citizens and border personnel is even more important. For James, the symbolic border trumped the physical border when it came to "control" and/or "influence." Moreover, according to him, for any border to develop, it should be considered a long-term project. The reverse is also true. When development is forced or sped up beyond its capacity, negative consequences occur such as resistance by locals to encroachment by outsiders particularly if these changes are viewed as violating local unwritten agreements, customs, or norms. I worked for and with James for four months in 2011. His name is changed to keep his identity anonymous. He was one of six border management directors I worked/participated with during my time in the field.

2 For about six months a year, the inclement weather of the mountainous terrain surrounding the borderlands of Badakhshan blocks access to outsiders although slightly less now that the roads are more developed. Until 2005, much of the area had no electricity and in many areas, Pamir Energy is still building infrastructure

for electricity. There are even some villages in which they do not have plans to build as of yet. These areas are isolated and the villagers rarely see anyone from outside of their village. For centuries the region was left largely unexplored by outsiders (Cobbold, 1900; Habberton, 1937; Tanner, 2002; Rashid, 2000). Most of the historical maps do not include the region and when they do, it is shown as a remote area and ill-defined. See James Scott (2009: 256) on radical constructionism of "tribe."

3 Over a two-year period, I visited the Saturday bazaars at Tem and in Ishkashem numerous times.

4 See Greenfield *et al.* (2007) and "Drugs in Tajikistan".

5 "Kohl (Surmah) may be defined as an eye preparation in ultra fine form of specially processed 'Kohl Stone' (galena) incorporated with some other therapeutically active ingredients from marine, mineral and herbal origin for the protection and treatment of various eye ailments. The other ingredients blended to develop special Kohl formulation may include Kohl adjuvant, (e.g., zinc oxide, silver leaves, gold leaves), gemstone (e.g., ruby and emerald etc.), marine coelenterates (e.g., coral, coral reef and pearls etc.) and herbs (e.g., neem, saffron, mumeera and fennel extract etc.)" (Mahmood *et al.*, 2009: 109).

6 This interpretation of the different styles of governance came from an international civil servant who has spent decades in the region.

7 We chatted a bit with the woman. One of them had five sons, which in Shughnan means that she was likely extremely poor due to the traditional property laws on the other side of the border in Badakhshan. Property is divided up among sons at the time of their marriage. This means that over time, families who have had a lot of sons have gotten more and more land poor unless they have other forms of income, such as money from drug and other forms of trafficking. I also bought three bead bracelets and two necklaces for my daughters. The bead work had geometric patterns common to local craftwork and was a deep red, indigo, gold, and yellow, green, and red together. The beads were tiny and the string was white cotton holding them together in a delicate web, in parts almost like lace.

8 This practice might be considered a very old custom—not that common in this region—called bride-knapping. Ironically Malika had been bride-knapped by her husband. But, according to Malika, he was saving her from a horrible man she was slated to marry through an arranged marriage by her family.

9 For the UNDP I wrote a 42-page report on the border infrastructure built in 2010 in Badakhshan, Afghanistan. For the Aga Khan Foundation, I wrote a 70-page report assessing and offering recommendations for a redesign of the DDRP in Ishkashim, the Wakhan Corridor, and Zebok, Afghanistan. Currently, this project has received more funding and is expanding (or is in the planning stages). UNDP said they were going to fix the many problems I found, but the last time I was in Ishkashim and Shughnan, Afghanistan in late 2011 (and according to staff at UNDP in 2012), the recommendations in my report had not been addressed, much to the dismay of the local Afghan border personnel. GIZ, after talking to me, revised their policy designs for the border since they had been basing their projects and planning on a report that had fabricated all of its data related to cross-border trade. IOM blocked my access to training after I observed the workshops. From what I understand, The U.S. Embassy was not happy with some of the fieldwork I conducted at the border. Even with all of this access, the majority of my observations came from living with local families and spending time living in the area.

10 Based on interviews with customs agents, border guard officials, and traders from Tajikistan and Afghanistan, as well as officials from UNDP, UNODC, and OSCE between May, 2009 and January, 2012. Additionally, observations by the researcher along the border and at the cross-border bazaar supported these assertions.

11 The border guards all participated in the formal institutions at certain times—when that role was required of them. When the role of the enforcer of the informal institutions including community norms, customary law, or the informal economy was the role required of them, they played that (for the most part).

12 Pierre introduced me to many key people in the beginning of my fieldwork. He also provided logistical assistance on and off during my entire time in the field.

13 The underlying tension between the majority Hanafi Sunnis and the other minority religious groups, in particular the Ismaili-Shi'a, who inhabit much of the province of Gorno-Badakhshan often came up in conversation.

14 This list was shared with me by one of my research participants.

15 In return, the Tajik government added the study of Islam to its core educational curriculum. Many in Dushanbe talked about how some of their friends began praying five times a day, wearing a hijab, and adhering much more closely to Sunni Islam. In my immediate circle, one of my friend's mothers began praying five times a day and attending the mosque frequently. She was in her forties and always had been secular. The increase in religious activity fueled the fear of the Tajik administration, which cracked down further. These were unexpected developments.

16 These two groups allied for a short time, but according to locals, their differences, in part religious, separated them rather quickly. The Gharmis are somewhat conservative Sunnis while the people of Badakhshan are largely adherent Ismaili-Shi'a. During the civil war, due to the isolation from the outside community there was mass hunger and near starvation among the people of Gorno-Badakhshan.

17 See Daftary (2005).

18 Gross (2013).

19 The Pamiri House usually is made from a tree which is planted when a male child is born. By the time they grow up, the tree is cut down and a house is created. The floor plan is open with a sunken square center in the middle of the large room. There also is a fire pit. The whole family sleeps together in the room on the elevated parts. Every Friday the Ismailis meet in different people's homes and practice their religion which involves smoking the house from the fire pit. Above the fire pit in every Pamiri house is a sky light which opens and closes to let in air and let out smoke. Another feature of Pamiri houses is that they are built with five posts. Each post signifies a different member of the prophet's family. Other beams in the ceiling signify the four elements of nature, earth, water, air, and fire (the same elements which were important in the Zoroastrian religion).

20 im = Tajik side/ em = Afghan side.

21 Before I discuss what I encountered during the BOMBAF assessment, I want to provide one example of the procedures I went through at the border crossings while working on the BOMBAF assessment. This outline helps to clarify what the "official" procedures were (at least in our entrance into Afghanistan during this crossing. During our return, the procedures were somewhat less formal). The example below is from the border of Ishkashim/Ishkashem: Tajik side. We drove our SUV up to the gate. They asked for proper identification. They made us wait while they verified with their bosses. The gate was opened. We drove to the Tajik crossing station and they asked for our passports. They searched our vehicle. Our passports were analyzed by Customs and once they passed inspection with Customs they were given to the border station office for registration and stamping. In the border station office I was asked a number of questions about the many stamps in my passport and my position with the UN. They searched my backpack and the suitcases of my driver and translator. They then stamped our passports and opened the gate for the bridge to Afghanistan. We drove across the bridge and went through similar procedures on the Afghan side. They asked for our passports, then they searched our vehicle and belongings as they had on the

Tajik side. They asked us what we were doing and why. Then they registered our names and stamped our passports.

22 See Guistozzi (2013) on police versus military in Afghanistan.

23 There was some speculation regarding the timing of the attack on the UN guard tower and the border commander's comments by friends at the UN and others but I could not corroborate or even look into whether there was a connection at the time.

24 James negated this and said that the border commanders were complicit in the stealing. It was hard to know what was really going on except that the money was not spent entirely as the development project had budgeted it to be.

25 Kubik defines institutionalization through four criteria: "authorization," "procedures," "legitimacy," and "disruptiveness/mobilization" (1994: 135).

26 See Appadurai, 1990. The idea of "other," related to such dichotomies as insider/outsider or emic/etic, has a rich literature in both political science and anthropology. Some scholars also have written about the "third space" or the "ethnoscape" of the border. This is particularly relevant here. "Ethnoscape" refers to groups of people who transcend boundaries as a group creating a landscape of connected groups.

7 The social organization of opium in Northeastern Badakhshan

The districts of Shughnan, Ishkashem, Zebok, and the Wakhan Corridor abutt the Tajik/Afghan border and are traversed by key roads linking the capital cities of Kabul and Dushanbe. These are key strategic locations for opium traders smuggling their goods north through Central Asia. The opium trade is nothing new in Badakhshan, but the influx of heroin in recent years, particularly in the borderland districts, has broad implications. Opium, heroin's more benign cousin, has a variety of uses, and it constitutes one of the primary medicinal forms of pain relief. Heroin use, on the other hand, has been spreading like a slow-moving virus along both sides of the border. Given that the opioid content of Afghan-grown opium poppies is almost twice that of poppies grown elsewhere, addiction to Afghan heroin is doubly difficult to overcome.[1]

Outsiders capitalize on the opium addiction epidemic, exploiting it as a weapon and a means of resource coercion in order to acquire land, food and

Figure 7.1 Photo of Wakhi woman in the Wakhan Corridor, Afghanistan

people. Since the 1950s—and likely much earlier—families throughout Badakhshan have resorted to selling land, crops, and even children to repay opium debts. The harsh climate, endemic hunger, and long winters make the Wakhan and neighboring districts particularly vulnerable to opium addiction.

A study of opiate use in 2004 by Marc Theuss showed that 92 percent of people living in the Wakhan used opium. By the late 1990s, the Wakhis had sold over 40 percent of their land to outsiders to repay drug debts, ending up as virtual indentured servants to drug dealers from nearby districts. Many worked as migrant laborers in Sunni strongholds such as the towns of Baharak and Jurm. In these parts of Badakhshan, locals despised the Wakhis for their high level of addiction. The selling of family members for slave labor and into forced marriages was commonplace and a source of deep shame (Gardizi and Theuss, 2006: 9).

In 2006, a few years after the study by Gardizi and Theuss, the Aga Khan Foundation (AKF) launched a Drug Demand Reduction Program (DDRP). Originally, the DDRP pilot project included 30 days of treatment and several follow-up visits. The treatment included minor pain medication, monitoring, counseling, and job-related training. In subsequent programs, treatment times were shortened to 21 days with fewer follow-up visits. Later, as heroin addiction increased, those addicted to heroin also attended treatment but medication for heroin withdrawal was limited or not available, with success in treatment of heroin dependency nonexistent. The DDRP was designed to alleviate the need to sell land, animals, food, wood, and most importantly, people, to repay opium debts or to support opium dependencies.[2] The program registered successes in some communities, but not all. It is still ongoing.

Opium's enduring impact on the lives of the villagers in this border region has reached into every household. Moreover, the opium trade parallels the asymmetric and shifting power relationships in the region and provides a window into the daily lives, the leadership, and the social organization of the villages.

Opium has a long and rich history in the area. One oft-repeated myth is that Alexander the Great brought it with him many centuries ago. Others say it spread northward from India—a story far more likely, but much less popular. In either case, once opium arrived in the region, it quickly became popular for medicinal purposes as well as for celebrations and mourning rituals.

Opium grows quickly and needs little attention. The striking orange flowers bloom in diverse climates and yield an abundance of medicinal poppy, which remains in high demand both in the illicit markets and pharmaceutical industries. Afghanistan has no presence in the licit market; instead, it supplies the majority of the world's black-market opium. Although the Taliban banned opium production in the late 1990s, causing a huge spike in global prices, opium generally has been grown, sold, and regularly used in the area. Opium has been a regular feature of daily life for generations.

The resurgence of opium cultivation in Baharak, Jurm, and Balkh[3] coincided with a resurgence of addiction and predatory selling in other parts of Badakhshan that do not grow opium. Today, the Ishkashem, Zebok,

Shughnan, and Wakhan districts remain relatively free of poppy farming since the Aga Khan issued a decree ordering the Ismailis living in the area to stop *cultivating* it. The problem, of course, is that they did not stop *using* it. In a region with endemic hunger and severe winter temperatures, opium has been used commonly to numb the pain from both. It is almost impossible to disentangle legitimate medicinal use from problematic dependencies. Without homegrown supplies to draw upon, opium users became more indebted to outside traders. The increasing debt burden has caused uncertainty and insecurity in the lives of those who live in the Wakhan Corridor, Ishkashem, Zebok, and Shughnan.[4]

In Badakhshan, each family, each village, each village cluster, each region, and, most importantly, each clan (*qum*), have their own sets of practices that both interact and counteract each other, and each village has a distinct relationship with opium and heroin. For example, in the upper Wakhan Corridor, relapse is viewed as a failure in the eyes of the Imam (the Aga Khan). Conversely, in a village located in the lower Wakhan, relapse is viewed as a criminal offense and is often punished with physical beatings, fines, or other punitive measures. In another village in Zebok, opium and heroin use are viewed as individual choices.

Some families choose to banish relatives who use opium, while others support them, even though this use is generally detrimental to the overall well-being of the family. Some families hide their use from fellow community members while others see it as a sign of wealth and prestige. Family members may hide their use from their own households, even husbands from wives, while others use together socially and in groups.

Villages regulate opium use through formal and informal institutions. Each village has a *Shurra* (village council) that creates and upholds laws.[5] Some *Shurra* presidents use oppressive techniques to exert influence over the community and enforce laws in more punitive ways, while other *Shurra* presidents have little-to-no authority. In these instances, customary laws, local traditions, and less formal enforcement practices guide behavior.

In addition to the *Shurra*, each village has an Anti-Narcotics Committee (ANC) which is a central government body that has committees that function on a local level. The ANC advises and monitors drug use and addiction. Sometimes the ANCs had data that they gathered in the villages under their jurisdiction about relapse rates, drug use, and drug trafficking in the villages, but it was often unreliable and they rarely collaborated with other community leaders. Most villagers and local leaders said that the ANC is a weak body with very little authority, and that locals do not trust the central government in general. This creates rifts between the central authorities in Afghanistan and the local leaders.

The central government in Afghanistan shares control with the locally elected *Shurra* Councils, *Qawms* (family networks), and other local informal networks. Informal institutions and organizations largely control local politics and economics but are linked together by officially sanctioned political institutions such as the *Shurra* Council. Leaders range from outsiders appointed by the central authorities in Kabul to informal religious leaders to drug lords. Minor conflicts erupt and the various leaders act as mediators but base their decision making not on the villagers' needs or the law but on whomever or whatever will benefit them personally the most. This makes the daily lives of the villagers unpredictable and tenuous. Opium feeds into these shifting dynamics of murky allegiances and local governance structures both economically and politically, through the economic incentives as well as the dependencies.

To describe the impact opium has on the daily lives of the people, I provide brief case studies of three sections of the Wakhan Corridor: (1) Wakhan-e Bala, (2) Khandud, and (3) Wakhan-e Payan.

The upper, middle, and lower Wakhan Corridor

The Wakhan Corridor is a narrow strip of land wedged between Tajikistan and Pakistan and bordering China on its eastern-most edge. The local population is largely Ismaili-Shi'a and has a number of languages not heard elsewhere in Afghanistan. The Wakhi language is an entirely separate linguistic structure from Dari or Pashto. The customs, clan structures, local norms, and terrain also differ from other regions in Afghanistan.

Wakhan-e Bala (upper Wakhan): Sarhad-e Breughel Cluster

Sarhad-e Breughel Village Cluster (SBC), comprised of three villages, lies at the end of the road in the Wakhan before the Kyrgyz-Pamir mountain range rises along the border with Pakistan. The landscape is harsh in that there is little water, food, electricity, arable land, and developed infrastructure. Cold winters and hot, dry summers make existence there difficult. When the harvest is small, as was the case consistently during the years of my fieldwork, the people suffer from hunger. Given all of these challenges, the people still support each other; they work together to solve problems within the context of a tight-knit and highly networked community.

Over the years of my fieldwork in the Wakhan, I spoke with numerous people about their lives and about their opium use. In the following sections I highlight a few of these stories. All of the names I use are pseudonyms and even the villages mentioned are not the villages I actually visited. In all of the places I spent time studying, people (whether leaders or villagers) consistently told me on the first day of my visit that their villages had remained completely free of addiction since the implementation of the DDRP. On subsequent visits this story of being free any opium or heroin use almost always changed and people shared their struggles and need for assistance with their dependency.

Alim, the first young man I interviewed, told a story I frequently heard from people living in the Wakhan. He said that he felt oppressed by his addiction but did not know where to get help or how to stop. The young man said he had relapsed when he became ill while working in the Kyrgyz-Pamir Mountains. He did not have access to a doctor there. Alim took opium to alleviate the pain in order to continue working. Kyrgyzstan's Pamir Mountain range lies to the east of SBC, and many of the villagers living in this area work as shepherds for the Kyrgyz who have large herds of yak and other livestock.

When I met Alim for the second time, he brought me to a communal opium smoking room. He took out a *chilim* (an opium pipe) and showed me how it worked. He brought a number of other people who had relapsed after treatment to the room to be interviewed. They were uncomfortable and worried they might be punished if they were caught using drugs. I soon realized that what was being said here differed from what was actually going on in the villages.

Alim's family was angry with him for his "inability to stop using and his lack of faith and self-discipline." They wanted to know if/when treatment might be offered again. Many people working in the DDRP, as well as members of the local community, believe that individuals who relapse after quitting opium are being selfish, shunning God, and using scarce resources that should be available for others. As a result, anyone who relapsed after treatment likely would not be offered services again.

The village elders and leaders, including the *Shurra* Council Presidents from three of the villages and the *Shurra* Council President for SBC cluster, the President of the Ismaili *Jama'yat*, the President of the ANC, and the Deputy of the *Shurra* Council, convened to discuss opium use. For nearly four hours the group debated treatment options, addiction rates, and problems in their communities. One leader asserted that nobody was using at all and that the entire area had been completely clean since the implementation of the DDRP. Other leaders disagreed, saying that a number of people had resumed their opium habit after detoxification. Eventually, the leaders reached a consensus that eight people had started using again. The debate evolved into a discussion about the lack of work, the cold winters, the scarcity of food, and how hard life is in SBC.

I observed the same pattern over and over. At the beginning of most visits, officials would deny that anyone in their village used opium. But later, they would reluctantly concede that relapses had occurred, even though relapse or opium addiction meant that the villagers had failed in the eyes of their religious leader, the Aga Khan. In the end, all of the leaders agreed that additional help for people addicted to opium would be welcome and was needed, but they did not have a system or a common metric for helping people who had relapsed. When asked how the community had responded to people who started using again, all of the leaders said that no help was available for treatment and the families of the people using narcotics dealt with it in different ways. No consistent solution was in place. For example, they said that sometimes if the addiction was extreme, people were shunned by their families and communities and exiled to the Pamirs.

The high level of addiction in the Pamirs makes it difficult for residents to remain opium free. The group of leaders said the proximity of the Pamirs presented three challenges for their community. First, many employers in the Pamirs pay at least some wages in opium. Second, the men from the villages who went to the Pamirs for work often turn to opium to alleviate the unrelenting cold and hunger. Third, locals felt obligated to offer opium to visiting Pamiris because that is how Pamiris show hospitality toward visiting SBC guests.

The village leaders said that land had not been sold to pay for opium since the implementation of the DDRP. In fact, the village economy had improved quite a bit: people had more food, animals, clothes, and were healthier overall. However, debts incurred prior to detoxification and generalized poverty still plagued the region.[6]

During dinner one day, a young man named Mohammed came for a visit. He told me that a villager had relapsed and sold his land to buy opium and that the village elders did not want outsiders to know. After speaking with a number of people about the alleged land sale, I could not verify the story. I did learn that the man lived with his *Qawm* but not his parents.

Conflicting stories about relapse rates, new opium users, selling of land, animals, trees, wood, and family members made it difficult to grasp opium's full impact on the community. In the past, opium was regularly offered to guests, but now it is used but hidden from view in many places, although not all. In some villages the ability to buy opium and use it as desired is still considered a symbol of status. In other places opium dependency is a source of shame.

After meeting with Alim another young villager named Khurshed offered to be interviewed.[7] He set up meetings, outlined users' habits, and brought me to the place where most of the villagers go to smoke opium in secret. This young man had been struggling with his addiction for more than a decade. Prior to detoxification, he had smoked three *Gulees* (grams) three times a day. He worked in the Pamirs to make money to support his addiction. He said that when the outside traders came to SBC to collect money on his debt he "ran to the hills for four or five days to avoid them." He said that the traders were physically violent if the villagers did not pay their debts on time.[8] Along the Wakhan Corridor the debt burden among the villagers is endemic and opium use, either now or in the past, contributes to the problem. Other villages had similar problems as SBC although differences in leadership, location, and daily practices require village-specific approaches to the common challenges.

A very small village with a charismatic and forceful *Shurra* Council President neighbors SBC. Only a small number of families live there. The leader gathered all of the people who had gone through detoxification and asked them to share their experiences with me. The former users reported considerable community pressure to remain clean. Many said that the tradition of opium use had been transformed with the DDRP, and that opium was no longer used for weddings and funerals. After some discussion, it appeared that two people in the village who had begun using opium had been exiled.

Both villages in SBC struggled with prior debt, lack of medical care, hunger, and cold during winter. Opium appeared to be a constant temptation since it relieved the pain from the hunger and cold and was used medicinally. The villages in this cluster closer to the Kyrgyz Pamirs seemed to struggle more with dependency and many reported that the high addiction rates to opium in the neighboring mountains had spillover effects in SBC.

The middle of the Wakhan: Khandud Cluster

Khandud is the largest city in the Wakhan Corridor. It has a small, but busy, bazaar, as well as an active group of village leaders, including youth and elders. A Community Health Center (CHC) near the bazaar has doctors, nurses, medicine, and other medical facilities and treats patients from the entire Wakhan. The facility was accessible, free, and well stocked. However, locals confided that they did not trust the head doctor of the CHC. He was from Shughnan, a neighboring border district. Many ridiculed him and mocked the way he spoke (Shughni sounds very different from Wakhi). They also made fun of the way he walked, his customs, and his mannerisms. Many villagers told me that they thought he was mentally ill and therefore they did not go to the CHC. The availability—or lack—of proper medical care became a running theme in Khandud as did the marginalizing of outsiders.

The leaders in Khandud

The president of the Khandud cluster told me that while more drug treatment programs were needed, most residents of Khandud had stopped using opium and remained clean. Later, however, some villagers told me that this particular leader and most of his family still used opium. They also claimed that many of the other leaders in the area were using opium. How did anyone expect the community members to give up opium if their leaders did not? The same leaders who were using had no compunction about levying fines against the locals when they were caught using narcotics. The leaders would sometimes seize animals or other assets in place of the monetary fines and would not return them even if the person stopped using opium. In reality, the law regarding fines was supposed to have changed in 2010 ending these types of punitive sanctions against people who use narcotics. According to a number of leaders, the law requiring fines for using narcotics had been implemented in 2006 in the Wakhan (and 2008 in Ishkashem) in conjunction with the DDRP. The law had been promulgated by the *Shurra* Councils at the provincial level in conjunction with the DDRP Director but was to be enforced at the village level. Enforcement varied widely, with many villages opting not to levy monetary fines.

In Khandud, new users faced a much greater stigma than people who had relapsed, but the fear of disgrace did not deter them from trying opium or even heroin. Many young people said that use of narcotics was spreading among their friends. One young man offered to set up a meeting with a group of three young men who allegedly had started using both heroin and opium, but no one showed up at the appointed time. Later, the young man offered to set up the meeting again, saying he did not show up before because he had to work unexpectedly. When the second meeting occurred, he came alone and said that he had been wrong and that these young men were not using after all. It was clear that his friends were scared to meet with us.

One village, one man, and one woman

As was the case during many of my visits to villages in the Wakhan, by the second and third visits leaders began to express their concerns about opium dependencies and a desire for additional treatment. They also often talked about the lack of food, medical care, and salaried work.

One leader brought me to the house of a man named Ismail who had relapsed and asked me to speak with him. As I approached, Ismail started running in the opposite direction. I waved to him and said that he was not in trouble. He then stopped running and came over to me. I asked him if he would be willing to speak with me about his challenges with opium. He agreed to an interview and invited me to his house for lunch. It turned out that Ismail was relatively prosperous, with ample land, animals, and food. His son taught at the local school. After being clean for a year and a half, he had started again when his wife and daughter both died suddenly of an unknown illness. He cried and said he could not bear to live without them. He said he started eating opium, one Gulee two times a day (about two grams a day) to relieve his agony. He said that before he went through detox-ification he had smoked larger quantities daily for many years, but now he was using relatively small amounts to tame his ongoing depression. He said he did not want to stop because he was too sad. Without the opium, he simply would not want to live anymore.

During my third visit to this village, I heard of Dilbar, a woman who was struggling with addiction to opium. Women were often not allowed to share they were using or dependent on opium without the permission of their husbands and most often their husbands did not permit them to talk about it or seek treatment. The President of the *Shurra* Council accompanied me to Dilbar's house, and she agreed to be interviewed, although her husband and family members insisted on staying in the room. Dilbar had relapsed after treatment. Her husband went through detoxification as well but has remained clean. She said she had turned to opium after her husband had been away for work and she was lonely. She had concealed her habit from her husband for the previous year and a half scared that he would be ashamed at her weakness. Her husband then spoke to me, saying he was angry when he found out about her opium usage. He then turned to his wife and accused her of being weak-willed and lacking faith. The wife said she was lonely and sad and the opium helped her but that she only chewed one Gulee three times a day.

One constant from our interviews is that female users face a much greater social stigma than male users. In more extreme cases, women were not even allowed to tell DDRP workers that they used narcotics because their husbands would not allow it.

Wakhan-e Payan (lower Wakhan): Qozideh Cluster[9]

The lower Wakhan is near to the Ishkashem bazaar, where widespread drug dealing has complicated an already difficult situation. I conducted fieldwork in an area known as the Qozideh Cluster.[10] Two themes emerged from Qozideh Cluster: (1) the leadership-style of the *Shurra* is an important factor in the successful implementation of the DDRP, and (2) sanctions, fines, and other punitive measures have negatively impacted the goals of drug treatment programs.

After a number of visits to one of the villages in Qozideh Cluster, I realized that this village's powerful and influential *Shurra* President was struggling with his own addiction to opium. His family, deputy, and a few members of his deputy's family also were opium dependent. When I met with him for the first time, he insisted that his village had remained *kamalan pak* (completely clean) and that the DDRP had been enormously successful there.

Later, the *Shurra* Council President introduced me to two men who had completed the treatment program and had remained clean. These two men explained to me that the program had completely changed their lives and the lives of the villagers. The stories of these men became difficult to believe because it appeared that at least one of them was using. Both exhibited typical signs of opium dependency, such as yellow skin, weight loss, and generalized malaise.

After leaving this meeting, I met with a woman named Nilufar who had gone through treatment. Although she looked emaciated, glassy-eyed, and yellow-skinned, she said that she had remained clean and that the treatment had transformed her life. Nilufar's neighbors, however, told me that she was struggling with addiction and they were worried about her. A female informal leader asked to speak in private. She took me to a quiet location and said that three families in the surrounding houses in her area were using opium, including children and a pregnant woman. She said that many of the people living in her area had gone through detoxification but needed more help. She was particularly worried about the pregnant woman. When asked why they were hiding, she said that the *Shurra* Council President levied fines and sometimes physically beat and imprisoned people if they relapsed. This assertion later was confirmed during a meeting with two different leaders and a woman who had gone through detoxification. This woman reported that she had been locked up in a community room and food was only periodically thrown to her through a hole in the roof. A local teacher said that it was common knowledge that most of the village had relapsed.

The following day I had a meeting scheduled with a group of young people in the village who were supposed to be accompanied by the *Shurra* Council President. However, the President had left the village and the meeting had not been set up. After waiting for a while, I went to the house of a family with which I had scheduled another interview, but the young man I was supposed to interview was not there.

During another meeting that day, two people told a story about a group of four women and one man who had relapsed after treatment. They said that these women had been locked up for ten days and beaten with a stick. The man was let out after a day. Many people I spoke with supported punitive measures to deter people from using opium because, in their view, a more relaxed approach had led to addiction and economic collapse in the village.

The second village I visited in Qozideh was governed by the same *Shurra* Council as the first village since it was a small village in very close proximity to the other village. A group of six people convened in a private location under a few trees next to a stream. It turned out that every person who had gone through detoxification in this village had relapsed. They said that some of them had been fined, beaten with a stick by the *Shurra* President, and had their animals taken away. Despite the fines and beatings, many of the people in this village continued using opium. They said they needed more treatment; that they were extremely poor, hungry, and cold; and that a recent drought and landslide had made things even worse. They pointed out that the landslides had been increasing, water supplies decreasing, and that crops were getting smaller and smaller. They said the world was changing, the weather was changing, and it scared them. As an aside, many people I spoke with during the fieldwork mentioned the change in weather and the decreasing water supplies and the changing climate.

As I left this village, a group of women asked to speak alone with me. After a bit of discussion, these women disclosed that there were about eight women in the village who were addicted to opium but that their husbands had not given them permission to get treatment when it was offered. They were obviously scared to speak about these issues, and one often glanced across the field at a group of men who were with the village leader.

Across the region, it was clear that a double-standard existed for women using opium. Many women said that in order for them to admit they were addicted to narcotics, they had to get permission from their husbands. Additionally, a number of men confirmed that without their permission, their wives would not have been allowed to participate in a treatment program. This particular village had a high degree of opium dependency as well as debt burdens. The landslide and the low harvests had made life even more difficult.

While the villagers said they needed more treatment, it was clear they also needed more food, medical care, and water.

Ishkashem: Ishkashem Center, Khoshpak-e Bala, and Gulgan-e Payan

Ishkashem district is a main thoroughfare for trade between Tajikistan and Afghanistan. It is also where the centers of power for the northeastern-most section of Afghanistan sit in terms of border commanders, local authorities, and legal and illegal traders. It has a thriving bazaar and the main medical clinic is located near the center of Ishkashem. Due to its location and leadership structure, the community in and around Ishkashem has easier access to both opium and heroin, creating additional challenges for those in the Wakhan. For example, heroin addiction is increasing, in part because heroin is sold in the bazaar and is offered at initially low prices to people who are already addicted to opium in order to manipulate them into using heroin. The leaders from the Afghan government officially support treatment for opium dependency and drug demand reduction programming and oppose the selling and trafficking of opium and heroin in the area. In practice, however, they have not pressed to implement this policy in the area and many are benefiting from the trade.

The case studies for the district of Ishkashem reveal: (1) the effects of different leadership styles as perceived by the villagers (power equals control); (2) the impact of geography on the DDRP and opium and heroin addiction in the area; and (3) heroin addiction presents a different challenge than opium addiction and appears to have a much higher relapse rate and growing user base in the area.

Khoshpak is located just above Ishkashem Center and along the same trade routes as the Afghan/Tajik border crossing in Ishkashem. This same route also runs southwest toward Zebok and Warduj, which are transit points to Baharak and Faizabad and, ultimately, Kabul. The leading traders of legal and illegal goods regularly travel through these villages, allowing heroin use to spread in the area, enriching the dealers, and impoverishing the users.

Khoshpak-e Bala

Upon our arrival in Khoshpak-e Bala, the leader of the village cluster said that there were people who had relapsed after treatment and ongoing assistance was needed. He suggested that a permanent treatment center would help. He organized a meeting with a female member of the ANC (the first female official I had met during the fieldwork). He also brought two women who allegedly had gone through treatment. They said that the treatment had transformed their lives and that no one in the village of Khoshpak-e Bala had relapsed. One of the men I was working with knew some of the former users and asked her if she indeed had ever been addicted to opium. She confessed to him that she had never been addicted to opium and that she had never attended the DDRP for treatment. She had been brought to the meeting to pretend she had been in treatment. When I asked the President of the *Shurra* Council if it would be possible to meet with more people who had actually attended the clinic, he said that none of them were living in the village at the time. After speaking with other leaders and villagers in the community I found out that those who had gone through treatment had relapsed and some were still living in the village.

During one discussion with a group of farmers, a local drug dealer was meeting with another man in a white sedan. The local drug dealer invited me to dinner. I politely declined. This was the third time during the field-work that I observed drug dealers driving into the villages to do business. These dealers appeared to have considerable power and people were scared of them, since, according to the villagers, they were often indebted to them.

The same group of farmers took me to a cluster of houses, some belonging to their family members. A group of young women from the cluster agreed to be interviewed. They were shy and giggled a lot. They said that they did not know anyone who used narcotics in the village. Another woman, who lived next door, invited me into her house. She refused to be recorded and was scared but felt compelled to share her observations. She said that the use of heroin had spread and just about every house surrounding hers struggled with dependency. The entire family living next door to her smoked heroin and, in the house I had just visited, the mother of one of the girls who had said they did not know anyone using was addicted to heroin herself. She pointed out that lumber had been taken from the structure of one of the houses in the cluster and sold for drugs. This was a common practice in the past—paying off a debt by removing part of a wall, floor, or roof of the house. The struc-tural beams were missing from this adobe house. I had not seen the actual missing wood from a house up until this point in my fieldwork.

A number of people in Khoshpak-e Bala expressed concern over the growing heroin problem and they requested help for their communities. The spread of heroin in this village resembled that of a virus. When one house in a close-knit area started using, often neighboring houses became "infected" as well. The proximity to the opium and heroin trafficking that occurs on the road between Warduj and Ishkashem contributed to this spreading problem.

The ANC President for this village said that heroin was a growing problem, but the DDRP treatment was only for people addicted to opium. After the DDRP follow-up visits ended, people started using again because they had no help and nowhere to turn. Moreover, since the drug dealers were always around, it was difficult to resist temptation without outside support from the Aga Khan Foundation, Afghanistan (AKF-A) and the DDRP. The President of the ANC told me that the drug dealers had sold heroin in the Ishkashem bazaar for less than opium in order to get people addicted. Then they would drive up the prices for heroin after the people became dependent on it. He said that the treatment program had helped change the cultural perceptions about opium in the area, but that people needed more help with the issues that had propelled them to addiction. He recommended a permanent treatment center. Clearly, everyone in the village knew who was using, who was dealing, and who was clean in this area.

Village two in Khoshpak

The atmosphere in the community and its attitudes related to addiction and drug use were markedly different from the first village I visited in this cluster. The President of the *Shurra* Council wrote down a list of every opium and heroin user in the village and offered to take me to their houses. He pointed out a number of houses and set up interviews with these heroin users. The father of one family in which almost every member was addicted to heroin spoke openly with me about his personal struggles with heroin addiction as well as his family's struggles. This man said he went to the DDRP and detoxed but was only able to remain clean for two weeks because it was just too difficult. He also said that the withdrawal process was extremely painful and he was scared to go through it again. He realized that he needed more help and that heroin was ruining his family and their lives, but they did not know what to do. This man is a poet and a well-respected member of his community. He agreed that a maintenance or harm-reduction program would be a welcome form of help since detoxification and remaining off of heroin felt impossible.

Another woman addicted to heroin claimed to only be using opium, but she exhibited the physical signs of heroin use. The *Shurra* Council President and her neighbors confirmed that she was using. The stigma of heroin versus opium use is even greater for women, as is the case with opium dependency in general. In fact, during my fieldwork, not one woman admitted to using heroin, while many men readily shared their addiction to heroin. Furthermore, men admitted that their families used heroin but the wives, themselves, did not admit this. Many residents said that no one in the village who had attended the DDRP for heroin addiction had been able to remain clean. A number of people accused the President of the *Shurra* Council in this village of being weak and addicted himself, and they blamed him for the endemic addiction. They called for strong enforcement and punitive measures like those in neighboring Khoshpak-e Bala.

The two villages in Khoshpak-e Bala village cluster differed in the degree of people's openness about addiction. In the second village, where addiction was clearly higher, residents were quite open about their own addiction and the challenges related to addiction in their communities. But in the first village it was hard to get even one person to disclose what was really going on. The differences in attitudes about heroin use and addiction in general between the two villages shed light on how leadership style and village community life and culture vary greatly, even between neighboring villages.

Village number three

This village is located near the beginning of the district of Shughnan, slightly northwest of Ishkashem. It sits between the border of Tajikistan and the Pyanj River, and there is a steep mountainous wall with a Taliban stronghold on the other side of the mountain. DDRP workers were still making follow-up visits during my visit. Relapse rates were very low in this village but in the neighboring village, which is located a three hour walk up the mountain, many people had relapsed and become newly addicted. Many residents told me that they were scared that addiction would spread in the upcoming winter when people are cold and hungry. Others said that they would start using again when the follow-up visits stopped and they no longer faced random drug testing.

Two women who had relapsed in this village said they did so for reasons of untreated health conditions. They said that the small, emergency clinic did not have medicine for severe pain. One had a swelling on her neck which looked like a large cyst of some sort and the other had a severe tooth infection. They also said that drug dealers often crossed the border (illegally) nearby, making their lives difficult. The Taliban lived over the mountain and they were constantly scared for their security because the Taliban had killed people. A number of people were in debt to the traders, which exacerbated their sense of fear.

Zebok District Center

Zebok is along the main road going west toward Faizabad. It is a main hub of business activity of legal and illegal traders who operate in a small bazaar and along the road. Opium and heroin are sold in the bazaar, and traders from Warduj, a well-known Taliban-related group stronghold, frequent the area. It was challenging to find people who would speak with me in Zebok Center. Upon arrival, I found that the district governor, the President of the *Jama'yat*, and the President of the *Shurra* Council all were gone. I had to walk a couple of miles into a mountain pass to find the ANC President, who was also the *Asiabi* (grinder of flour for the village). The President of the ANC said that many people were relapsing soon after detoxification in Zebok. He felt that the program for detoxification was not long enough and there was not enough support for the people who detoxed after they went back to their homes, particularly for those addicted to heroin. He added that heroin use was on the rise and many of the leaders in Zebok Center used heroin (as was later corroborated during interviews with these leaders). The President of the ANC said that many of the leaders in Zebok Center were using opiates and were not particularly supportive of the DDRP. This made it difficult for the much-needed treatment program to take hold and succeed in Zebok. He expressed concern about the growing addiction to heroin among the villagers in Zebok Center.

After speaking with the President of the ANC, I went to the house of the President of the *Jama'yat*. His brother, his wife, and their daughter agreed to be interviewed. They had a son as well, whom I did not interview. All four appeared to be addicted to heroin. The President of the *Jama'yat* had gone through partial detox but then had gone back to using heroin. The brother said he used heroin while his wife said she used only opium (but she had the physical signs of heroin addiction). The daughter and son were glassy-eyed, unsure on their feet, and the daughter nodded off a few times. During the second visit, this was even more apparent. The 15 year old daughter attempted to kiss me on the lips and staggered out of the house in three-inch heels. I later found her lying on the floor of the house with a local man sitting next to her. She wore a red sequined dress and green spike heels, which was highly unusual for this area in Afghanistan.

The wife of the President of the *Jama'yat* said that opium had been part of the fabric of Badakhshan for hundreds of years and would continue to be. She said it was part of the air the people breathed and the land they stood upon and a drug treatment program was not going to make it go away. She said that she had no interest in quitting opium. When asked if she used heroin, she said no and that heroin was bad; it was the devil. For some in Zebok and some surrounding villages, opium and even heroin use—or having the money to do so—is a status symbol. And, the leaders of Zebok held this perception.

In Zebok Center I met with 12 men in the process of detoxification. They were all extremely grateful for the DDRP. When asked if their wives or any women were going through the program, they said that the women were going to attend the DDRP Center later and that for now, only men were going through detoxification.

The people who had been treated in Zebok were relapsing at a faster rate than in Ishkashem and the Wakhan. A number of people I spoke with contradicted the official list provided by local healthcare workers. It was unclear if the locals I spoke to, who appeared to know what was going on in their village areas, were inflating numbers of relapses, or if the list compiled by the medical staff in Zebok was incorrect. In either case, the program had (1) little support from the local leadership, (2) appeared to have a higher relapse rate than officially reported, and (3) heroin use was on the rise.

Conclusion

Villagers are all too aware that the drugs trafficked through their area make their lives more difficult. They would like help with combating trafficking since they think it contributes to opium addiction and increases the temptation to relapse after treatment. They often talked about wanting help from their government to stop the spread of addiction to opium that many view as causing hardships among their communities, but that their government was not working in their interest.

In every household and every village, people understood that opium was addictive and that this addiction could lead—and had led—to various socio-economic difficulties and health problems. On a cultural and social level, the norm of using opium for hospitality, celebrations or mourning, and pain relief has largely changed; now many people regard opium use as a choice that has negative consequences.

While education about the hazards of opium use has been successful in most areas, there has been relatively little community development that addresses, at least sustainably, issues of addiction, treatment, and prevention. In each community, after detoxification was offered and follow-up conducted for the initial groups, programming largely ended. The lack of follow-up, program cancellation, lack of second-round treatments in the event of a relapse, and fears of punishment make it virtually impossible to achieve a five percent relapse rate, which is the goal of the DDRP. Even with treatments that include two years of full psychological services, a 50 percent relapse rate is common (AKF-A Report, 2010: 11–12).[11] Additionally, given the challenges in the area for addiction—easy access to drugs, untreated health issues, severe winters, and poverty/hunger—this number seems unrealistic, putting undue pressure on people who are struggling with addiction and fear seeking additional, often much-needed assistance. Also, maintenance programs such as methadone were not allowed at the time of this fieldwork making treatment for heroin dependency next to impossible. This would take a change in policy among officials in Badakhshan.

One of the goals included integrated policy coordination among local political groups. This includes encouraging the *Shurra* councils for the village clusters, the ANC, *Jama'yat*, and village *Shurra* Councils to work together on issues related to drug use, drug trafficking and supply, and opiate addiction. Very few villages were actually able to attain this goal. The villages that had successfully implemented this "governance cohesion" aspect of the DDRP did appear to have lower relapse rates and, on the face of it, a less widespread addiction problem. The mechanisms of this relationship remain unknown. It could be because the community already had a healthier, more cohesive civil society with well-developed networks of cooperation, or it could work in the opposite direction—a lesser addiction problem might make it easier for governance structures to work together. This meant that the civil society groups were able to partner more effectively because there were fewer people struggling with addiction to opiates.

Many people asked for access to ongoing treatment and for treatment programs to be permanent and accessible. A number of people who had relapsed felt ashamed and stated that they did not deserve more help with their addiction. Many leaders also pointed out that without permanent treatment facilities, there was a danger that youth would start using and addiction would spread. Many leaders requested ongoing prevention and education programs as well as treatment centers in their communities.

While this goal is important and realistic, it is not being pursued at this time. The model from the Wakhan Corridor that was replicated in Zebok has not had much success due to cultural, political, and geographic reasons. People appear to be less open to outside influence or interference into their personal lives in Zebok. The villagers are more supportive of a rights-based approach and individual choice model, which is not what was implemented in the Wakhan. Geographically, Zebok is closer to trafficking routes, Warduj, and other negative influences, including some predatory dealing of heroin to locals. The Wakhan program did not address the problem of increasing heroin, so that was not included when it was transplanted to Zebok. Furthermore, politically, many officials in Zebok Center do not support the DDRP and, in some cases, appear to be openly hostile toward it. Once again, this was not the case in the Wakhan Corridor.

While leaders and residents have a sense of the level of opium use in Badakhshan, hard numbers are difficult to come by, because of people hiding their drug use to avoid fines and other punishments. What the fieldwork did show, on a consistent basis, was that after a second or third visit to a community, reported addiction rates changed radically from those given at the first visit. During almost every initial visit, leaders and often locals would claim that there was almost no addiction in their village. They would insist that while there were, indeed, people dependent on opiates in neighboring villages or village clusters, their villages were completely clean. After a second or third visit, the façade of lies would crumble, and people would begin to talk about their addiction or struggles with addiction issues in their families, and ask for help.

As heroin use spreads, treatment programs and support decrease, and the stakes for control of the trafficking networks rise due to power struggles inside of Afghanistan, these districts are vulnerable. While Ishkashem has remained free of large-scale Taliban activity over the long haul, this may not be the case in the near future. The networks that run the opiates in and through Badakhshan have much to gain by coopting power and governance in Zebok and Ishkashem, and those with dependencies on heroin are vulnerable to this cooptation. Since the fieldwork for this chapter was completed, hotspots controlled by the Taliban-related groups have sprung up in many locations in Badakhshan. In the past I could travel freely along all of the roads in the province, now I can barely cross the border in what used to be the safest districts. This is due to the struggle for control over the trafficking routes, the opiate trade, and the increase in addiction. The social organization of this part of northeastern Badakhshan is part and parcel of the trade and use of opiates.

Notes

1 During my fieldwork I did not meet a single heroin user who had stayed clean after treatment as opposed to the much higher success rate of close to 25 percent of the opium users in the same villages.
2 According to David Mansfield, poppy-growing spiked in Badakhshan in 2000 after the Taliban banned it in Taliban controlled areas. After 2003, when aggressive efforts to stop poppy growing in Badakhshan took place, the money from growing

poppy also left the area. It is unclear when the debts that are owed today were incurred by locals (Mansfield, 2004).

3 Pain (2011). See also David Mansfield: www.davidmansfield.org/all.php.

4 I assessed the AKF DDRP in late 2011 but had worked on issues related to opium and heroin use along the border already from 2009–2011 for a grant funded by UCLA.

5 For further information and analyses on the political heterogeneity see: Lorimer (1958); Barfield (2010); Daftary (1995, 1998, 2005, 2011); Payne (1989); Grierson (1920).

6 This assertion is corroborated by an extensive database on various aspects of the Wakhan compiled by the Aga Khan Development Network.

7 A number of times during the fieldwork a person struggling with their own addiction became a "guide" and transit point to contact with other people who had relapsed or had become newly addicted.

8 This assertion was backed up the research of Gardizi and Theuss (2006) a few years earlier.

9 From 2011 fieldwork.

10 Anecdotally, there appears to be a small number of people using heroin, but due to the stigma, it was hard to get information about this. One man did admit to me that he had been addicted to heroin, but he had not gone through treatment. For this reason, even though it appeared there might have been the beginnings of heroin use among the villagers, opium remained the primary focus of the fieldwork within two villages by the names of Ftur and Wurzhdragh. The heroin use appeared to be more within the village of Qozideh. However, since my guide lives in the village of Qozideh, there was a conflict of interest, and for this reason a detailed case study of Qozideh village is not included in this report even though the team did visit the village a few times. I did hear that in Qozideh the relapse rate was quite high and many people were struggling with addiction.

11 Additionally, "Several important findings emerged from the Integrated Drug Prevention, Treatment, and Rehabilitation Project in Afghanistan Integrated Drug Prevention in Afghanistan (IDPA) evaluation. Over all treatment sites, a 40 percent relapse rate was found. Badakhshan subjects had the second-highest rate of relapse. The report highlights the remoteness as a particular challenge for Badakhshan patients accessing aftercare services. Another important finding of the IDPA study is that the majority of relapse took place between 8 weeks and 6 months after detoxification, which is when the aftercare support in the IDPA treatment schedule was reduced. However, even those who relapsed reported lower levels of drug use than before treatment, which should be appreciated" (Aga Khan Foundation unpublished report from 2010 given to the author by the Aga Khan Foundation in Afghanistan: 11–12). While this evaluation was not of the AKF-A program it does highlight how this area, its poverty, remote location, and high level of drug trafficking, make it one of the more difficult terrains for treatment programs related to opiate addiction.

8 Conclusion

Overview

My fieldwork, research, and analysis were driven by several main questions. As explained in my introduction, I set out to answer these questions by first providing an historical background and discussion of the foundational myths of the borderlands of Badakhshan through local narratives. Then I supported my findings with three ethnographic chapters based on my own fieldwork. In my descriptions and explanations I used an interpretive approach, usually in the form of extended case analyses. In the following sections I briefly describe the importance of each chapter for answering my questions and supporting my findings. I then present my findings, make a few recommendations, and in conclusion, suggest some areas for further research.

Chapter 1 gives a broad overview of the relevance of borders to the study of comparative politics and international relations. While the periphery of nation-states are places of transition often rife with illicit activity, they also may be areas of constant institutional and infrastructural innovation. The paradox is that often the increased institutionalization at the periphery actually has perverse effects by decreasing rather than increasing border and state stability. This is the basic assertion my book explores.

To study this paradox, I went to Badakhshan, a border in the process of intense development and accessible for fieldwork. Little to no research had been conducted in this area on the impact of developing border institutions on local and state stability. Therefore, in order to answer my main question, I had to go and observe (and participate) in border development projects and the local community. I discovered that the border development projects contributed to increased coordination of informal networks of cooperation, which, in turn, aided powerful illicit traders. In contrast, legal traders and local humanitarian efforts encountered more and more obstacles. At the heart of my research was an effort to understand how these networks cooperated, what role local leaders and organizations played in these networks, and how local identities (as opposed to the national identity) reacted to pressure from outsiders.

Chapter 2 provides the main questions, concepts, and methodology that are the foundation of my research. I have one main question, three sub-questions, three concepts, and two main findings. Below is a short recap.

The main puzzle my book aims to solve is:
    What is the importance of local leaders and local identity groups to the stability of a state's border and ultimately, the stability of the state?

To answer my main question, I used an analytical framework comprised of three main concepts: (1) borders, (2) institutions/organizations (formal/informal), and (3) identity (national, ethnic, religious, and territorial). These concepts are used to formulate my main findings.

Finding 1:
    An increase in formal institutionalization at the border increases illicit cross-border cooperation (abbreviated).[1]
Finding 2:
    Marginalization of local leaders and organizations at the border decreases border and state stability and increases illicit cross-border cooperation (abbreviated).[2]
    The rest of my book supports these main findings.

The next section describes the methodology, methods, and theoretical foundation for my "fieldwork, deskwork, and text work." Theoretically, I am a constructivist and believe the world is fundamentally built upon social interactions (action/reaction/action and so on) via which we transact meanings (but also resources and power), and thus I assume that we need to study the ways in which these interactions shape our understanding of the world. Structure and agency, two sides of this interactive process, are in a constant conversation, one constraining and/or changing the other—a never-ending and evolutionary process of forever becoming and never arriving.

Because of this underlying ontological assumption, my fieldwork employed ethnographic participant-observation methods as well as unstructured interviews and focus group discussions as a means to study people's interactions. This helped me to not only observe, but also participate in the daily lives and practices of the borderlands of Badakhshan.

My deskwork and text work used an interpretive methodology based on extended case-analyses. With the large amount of data I gathered from my fieldwork, the fact that I lived with people for a significant amount of time, coupled with my assumption that structure and agency are bound intricately together, using an interpretive methodology (which I define in detail in Chapter 3) to analyze my data helped me to stay true (to the best of my ability) to my research participants and empirical material.

Answering the questions, supporting the findings

The analyses in each of my subsequent chapters support the main assertion of my findings—an increase in border development will decrease border and state security if local leaders and organizations are not included. The following discusses how the data analyzed in each chapter was used to develop my findings and answer my main questions.

Chapter 3 outlines the historical narratives of border development in Badakhshan. I concentrate on the past few centuries but also give a brief outline of the area in the pre-Islamic/Zoroastrian period. I highlight the different historical accounts pertaining not only to border development but also the pivotal role of local leaders and the relative autonomy of the region. I trace the changing definitions of the borders by the Russian Empire (1721–1917), the British Empire (c. 1500 to mid-1900s), and the Soviet Union (1922–1991).

The primary point of the chapter is that the local leaders successfully negotiated terms of territorial delineation in the form of khans, mirs, and pirs for centuries prior to the formalization of the border. As the border formalized (through terms imposed by outsiders) the locals did two things. First, they maintained their autonomy through negotiated agreements with the outside governments while allowing the areas to be subsumed into formal empires or, later, independent nation-states. Second, they resisted attempts by outsiders to formalize their local organizations and thereby resisted control by outsiders.

For the most part, the area has retained informal networks of power, built around religious, territorial, and familial leaders. They have trumped state authorities in a number of ways. For example, local informal leaders mediate most territorial, familial, and resource disputes. The religious authorities mediate larger conflicts and disputes related to religious traditions and customs (although these days they are allegedly in cooperation with the security wing of the Tajik government).

The state security forces (those not from Badakhshan) are viewed as corrupt and causing insecurity instead of security. Local street-level leaders and paramilitary groups provide security and protection to neighborhoods, while leaders of larger sub-sections of the district provide security for their areas. Also they work together with the other main leaders (four of them at the time of the fieldwork) to provide protection and mediate larger problems within the community; they find help for people who are hungry, need medical attention, and are addicted to drugs. While it is unclear how evenly distributed or accessible the help of the local leaders and organizations actually is, this is where residents go when they need help.

I also highlight how narratives of internally and externally imposed development underpin the locals' resistance to being co-opted by outside forces. Moreover, they increase informal networks of cooperation (including local organizations, illicit trade, reliance on local leaders) as outsider pressures increase. This directly supports my findings in that it shows how the presence of outsiders increases the assertion of local identity networks (territorial, ethnic, and religious) and thereby decreases the assertion of national identity in the area. This, in turn, has led to increased conflict along the border in the past and present, which has decreased border and state stability.

Chapter 3 shows that: (1) informal networks of cooperation have persisted over time and continue to be an important factor in local authority and governance; (2) formalization of the border has increased cooperation among informal networks, forced locals to seek their "true" historical origins (in order to prove outsider versions wrong and take ownership of their own past), and thus has increased the assertion of local identity by various groups and their leaders. (3) This, in turn, has decreased acceptance of the state and contributed to overall border and state instability. As George Orwell said in his novel, *1984*: "Those who control the present control the past, and those who control the past control the future."

Chapter 4 examines disputes about the foundational myths of settlement, culture, language, ethnicity, and naming. Moreover, I show how narratives of origin among locals, domestics, and internationals compete for legitimacy and, in doing so, frame the area in very different ways. Specifically, I examine how insiders and outsiders use the ethnic identity and myths to assert legitimacy locally, domestically, and internationally.

I conclude that the competing foundational myths and naming underlie contemporary tensions between locals and outsiders. Outsiders try to control the history, names, and foundational myths of the area, and the locals continue to point out how they are wrong. Moreover, the encroachment by outsiders, as the locals point out, is present even in the remaking and efforts to control their foundational myths and history.

Chapter 4 points out that even before the border was formalized, locals strongly resisted any outside presence through asserting their own names for the region and holding on to what they believe are the actual foundational myths. The debates about the myths and names going on today invoke earlier disputes of who belongs and who does not, and who is a true insider and who is not. The more outsiders try to create a history and identity for a group of people, the harder the target group works to find out the "actual" history of their territory and people. This, in turn, makes them assert their separate identities (territorial, ethnic, and religious) at the expense of the more recently formed national identity.

Chapter 5 provides a detailed study of the social organization of Khorog, Tajikistan. It is an extended case study of the kidnapping of a girl named Gulya. The social organization of Khorog (and associated areas) encompasses territorial, religious, ethnic, and familial (kinship) borders. The chapter focuses on how these different boundaries shift under pressure from—or due to the presence of—outsiders. It also describes the networks of cooperation, the rivalries between areas, and the importance of local leaders and organizations for local economic, physical, and social security.

During my fieldwork I observed patterns of local resistance to outside presence and interference. Whether that presence was in the form of the state security services or the institutional formalization of the border, the local leaders and organizations were the primary sources of security and assistance the locals sought out during crises.

The case study of Gulya's kidnapping is at the center of my analysis, but it also led me to other cases, including the release of the kidnappers without a proper trial, the arrest and torture of a local street leader, and the informal trafficking and trade networks of cooperation across the border. These cases also highlight how the assertion of local identities increased as outside/state presence increased, whether in the form of the intensified military presence, border police interventions, or within the locally based religious institutions.

While the chapter does not directly relate to the institutions that are being developed at the border, it helps to frame my analysis of how outside presence in the area mobilizes and further legitimizes local forms of political and social organization, and—as a result—increases the legitimate authority of the local leaders. My findings suggest that increasing institutional formalization decreases local and state stability and that marginalizing local organizations and leaders further undermines stability. Therefore, understanding the social organization of a key city directly on the border with Afghanistan is vital to my argument. This detailed description of the complexities and intricacies of local leadership and organizations provides a rich context for the next two chapters, which are directly about the development of the border institutions.

As locals seek help for their problems, such as freeing a local girl from her kidnappers, through local leaders and organizations instead of the state security forces, they are not only resisting state institutions but also concentrating power in local non-state-sanctioned organizations and associated leaders. The state security apparatus reacts to this increase in local governance by applying more pressure and increasing its presence in the area. The locals begin to assert the "local" identity of their groups more and, as a consequence, weaken the hold national identity has among the region's populace. This action/reaction between local leaders and organizations and the state security forces creates instability and raises tensions along the border as well as in the state. Being that Khorog is right on the border of Afghanistan, this decreased stability not only impacts the Tajik side, it also impacts the border area and ultimately spills over to the Afghan side of the border.

Chapter 6 delves into the actual institutions operating along the border, including the border checkpoints, border and customs personnel, and the physical infrastructure. I describe how the faulty infrastructure has aided in delegitimizing the border stations and personnel. I also highlight how tensions between locals and outsiders developed during training of customs agents.

These tensions influence religious, territorial, ethnic, and cultural identities. In reaction to the training of local border and customs agents by outsiders, the locals increase assertion of their local ethnic, religious, and territorial identity. Specifically, when outside trainers came to Khorog to train local customs agents on how to catch traffickers at the border, the training included a lesson in Sunni religious ethics. The problem was that the locals were all Ismaili Shi'a and they found this offensive.

Following this, I describe the actual process of crossing the border which, while quite formalized, actually operates with a complex set of unwritten agreements aided by informal networks of power. These informal networks transcend the border as well as the region and ultimately undermine state authority. Conversely, if they are threatened or attacked, they increase their cooperation, which further erodes the legitimacy of the state institutions at the border. But, if the state brings the local leaders into the institutionalization process, the local leaders and organizations cooperate and the area remains relatively stable.

The second half of Chapter 6 describes another newly forming institution at the border—the cross-border bazaars. Like Chapter 7, it shows how the bazaars are a place for local informal networks of cooperation to coordinate their activity. It also highlights how unwritten agreements trump official rules and regulations. Finally, it reveals how locals react to outsiders and how complicated the definition of an "outsider" really is in the context of Badakhshan.

The section on cross-border bazaars supports my findings in three ways. First, it shows how the development of the border infrastructure, meant to help institutionalize the border, actually decreased overall institutionalization and helped to energize informal networks of cooperation. There were many problems, including the use of cheap materials and faulty engineering. Second, the training caused increased tensions between state officials/trainers and local border personnel that in turn led to the firing of three local border command officials, intensified assertion of local identity, and decreased assertion of nationalism. Third, the border stations, which remain places for local leaders and informal networks of cooperation to wield power, highlight how the training (which taught the border guards counter-trafficking techniques) and the infrastructural development served to increase their local informal authority.

Chapter 7, the last ethnographic chapter, is a study of the social organization of opiate use and opium in three districts in Afghan Badakhshan. I explore the impact of opioid use and selling on the villages throughout the Wakhan Corridor, Ishkashem, and Zebok, Afghanistan. Opium and heroin use are endemic in these districts. In 2006, a drug demand reduction program focusing on people with opium dependency started in the area. At the same time, the Aga Khan decreed that the Ismailis in the region should stop cultivating opium. This forced those using the narcotic to buy from non-Ismailis, leaving them more dependent on traders from other parts of Badakhshan. Additionally, many of the leaders appointed by the government of Afghanistan are non-locals and from different ethnic and religious groups than the Ismailis in these districts.

While the drug treatment program has helped many people in the area, the lack of food, access to medical care, predatory opium trafficking practices, and extreme cold contributes to the continued high addiction rates. Trafficking through the districts, and in particular the district of Ishkashem, continues and is increasing. Heroin use has also increased and makes it easier for outsiders to recruit locals for nefarious purposes.

Findings

First, the increase in border controls has made locals not only frustrated, since they resent the increased presence of the state in their "autonomous region," but also has made them increasingly willing to work with entities or individuals within criminal networks who are willing to pay them money to feed their family. This is also true of the border personnel who are underpaid. Although the border guards have to operate within the official institutions at the border, their participation in and need for the informal institutions is not diminished by this "formality." In fact, it is likely increased. Both the guards and community members need to take informal rents to feed their families, which does not bode well for decreasing illicit trade along that border.

Second, since trafficking functions through local kinship groups and networks of cooperation, increasing security raises economic costs for doing business, which deepens already established illicit networks due to the increased challenges of doing business. Therefore, the reality at the border is that the traffickers (at the higher level) do not have a problem getting across the border either by bribing the border guards or through complex coordination of surveillance and logistics to which both the guards and others turn a blind eye. As the obstacles increased, so did the cooperation to circumvent them.

Third, locals view the increased presence of outsiders; especially state security forces (meaning Tajiks who are not from Badakhshan) as a threat to their security. This could be attributed in part to the limited development of roads (which isolated the region for many centuries) coupled with long-standing trade routes that traverse the region along these roads (which enhanced their autonomy). When locals are threatened either socially or economically, their allegiance to local identity groups and networks deepens. As a result, the effectiveness of the newly implemented development (and security) projects decreases, destabilizing the region.

Fourth, increasing border security increases the price differentials across the border, which increases the gains from successful smuggling. Last, I found that assertion of national identity and acceptance of the central governments decreased on both sides of the border, including weakened loyalty to the central authority, which decreased overall territorial integrity.

Finally, my research illuminated the multi-layered and complex ways in which identity and statehood are implemented and asserted through the actions of local leaders and organizations that are often involved in border development projects along the borderlands of Badakhshan. I found that the informal institutions—territorial networks, religious identity, kinship networks, criminal networks, and other forms of informal connections, very much trumped the formal institutions there. On the other hand, what was also true was that the formal institutions, laws, and procedures, were very much enforced in a kind of theatrical way to show the need for increased control, funding, and necessity of the "state" institution. They both existed together but with the tacit understanding by those working at the border that the unwritten agreements are the law of the land.

Conclusion, recommendations, and future research

As I assert in the beginning of my book, borders are the beginning and the end of every state. The state would not exist without them and neither would the symbolic delineation of each nation. Even in the increasingly connected world, the borders of the state, whether in our minds or as experienced by our bodies, remain primary to ordering our world. Illicit and licit trade cross these borders both physically and virtually. The informal networks of cooperation that connect different types of groups throughout the world, whether physically located, operating in virtual spaces, or constituted as "thought-groups" or "idea-spaces," span the "external" political boundaries but also maintain their local identity and thus reside within the "internal" cultural boundaries.

In the context of the borders of nation-states, pressure at the periphery from those at the center increases cooperation between the informal cross-border networks of cooperation operating at the periphery. The strengthening of these cross-border networks is, for example, reflected in the increased cooperation within transnational illicit organizations which, in turn, strengthens the local networks. Eventually, those living on the margins, after increasingly asserting local identity as separate from national identity (in reaction to outside pressure) move to separate and create their own identity that may be increasingly framed as a new "national" identity, at least by some actors. I am not saying this will happen in Badakhshan, but it has happened in many places around the world. Currently, the Baloch are waging a battle, as are the Kurds. Other conflict-plagued places on the periphery easily come to mind as well.

Outside pressure (or pressure from the state) on the periphery, since it increases the assertion of local identity, has the ability to fracture larger communities and states. These states, perhaps not fully formed (according to some international standards), have entered into "social contracts" with each other to accept the boundaries that demarcate the states and help to symbolize nations. If the borders of nation-states become ever more fractured by separatist movements at the periphery and transnational illicit economies operating out of the bounds of the state, the borders that order our world will become increasingly convoluted and diffuse.

In the extreme, this ultimately could erode the written rule of law and the institutions that mediate them, and allow for unwritten, informal agreements to concentrate power in potentially perverse and dangerous ways. If it is possible that increased pressure by outsiders, and marginalization of local leaders and organizations, coupled with formal institutionalization of the border, causes decreased border and state stability and can lead to increased fracturing of the nation-state system, my findings should be taken seriously.

Recommendations

My recommendations are three-fold. First, to include local leaders and organizations, if possible, in the development of border institutions. While designing the infrastructure and personnel training, talk to the locals, the commanders, and the local leaders and take the context and terrain in which they live into consideration. This means understanding what the local identity and political–social networks are, what tensions exist with the ruling elites, and how that is to be managed at the border, particularly if the region in question has at least some degree of autonomy.

Second, international organizations that fund border development projects should require a preliminary scouting mission as a pre-condition of the funding. The findings of such preliminary field research would be part of the proposed work plan, including how the IGO or NGO plans to navigate the local context and terrain. The "universal" logic often applied in development projects needs to be contextualized and tailored to local conditions, particularly in challenging mountainous terrain or in the periphery of the state that has different ethnic, religious, or territorial groups whose identities differ from the "national" identity projects routinely advanced by the centers of power.

Third, developing the border for reasons of security and stability must include developing certain aspects of the local community, access to medical care, and food and water security, and treatment for addiction. This will decrease the need for the local community to look outside of the state apparatus for money to feed their family, treat medical conditions, or buy drugs. If the local community is both marginalized from the process and lacking in basic needs, it will look elsewhere for social and economic support.

In the final analysis, developing institutions at the border is a tricky business and one that is mired in assumptions that are unfounded, such as the assumption that increasing border controls will under all circumstances increase border and state security. My research shows that this is not necessarily the case and that it is even more so when the local context is not included in the development process.

Further research

There are several veins of research that deserve further exploration. One vein would be to study any border that has conditions similar to the borderlands of Badakhshan, such as marginalized religious and ethnic groups and a history of being autonomous. The question would be whether border development has caused the same types of issues or whether the border development projects are being approached differently and therefore, different issues have occurred.

Studying different border development projects that have taken into account the local context as well as including the local leaders and organizations in the process in order to see if these have indeed been more sustainable and stable over time, could be a second vein of study. As for my future research, I plan to continue studying the social organization of the areas in the borderlands of Badakhshan. I plan to conduct additional in-depth research (in order to add to my already completed fieldwork) about the role of the local leaders and local organizations to border stability in the borderlands of Badakhshan, and I plan to continue studying the relationship among the state institutions, the local organizations, and the places in-between, which the locals accept as the state to which they belong but still mediate around.

Notes

1 Finding 1a: If the state increases authority through formalization of institutional infrastructure at the border, then local leaders will be marginalized and the local population will be alienated from the state and this will decrease overall stability in the long run. Moreover, national identity will weaken while (some) local identities will strengthen. Finding 1b: If the state works to monopolize power at the border, the stability in the border region (Badakhshan) decreases as local groups assert alternative forms of identity and local control as a means of rejecting the imposition by the state and as a form of silent protest.

2 Finding 2: If local leaders and organizations are given semi-autonomy in coordination with state border forces, then the borderlands in Badakhshan will be more stable and national identity will be more broadly accepted.

Bibliography

Abaeva, T.G. (1964) *Ocherki Istorii Badakhshana* (History of Badakhshan). Tashkent: Uzbek Soviet Socialist Republic.

Abdelal, R., Herrera, Y.M., Johnston, A. and McDermott, R. (eds) (2009) *Measuring Identity: A Guide for Social Scientists*. Cambridge and New York: Cambridge University Press.

Adams, L. (2009) 'Techniques for Measuring Identity in Ethnographic Research', in Y. Abdelal, R. Herrera, A. Johnston and R. McDermott (eds) *Measuring Identity: A Guide for Social Scientists*. Cambridge and New York: Cambridge University Press, pp. 316–341.

Ahmed, A.S. (1977) *Social and Economic Change in the Tribal Areas, 1972–1976*. Oxford: Oxford University Press.

Anderson, B. (1983) *Imagined Communities*. London and New York: Verso Press.

Andreas, P. (2000) *Border Games*. Ithaca, NY and London: Cornell University Press.

Andreas, P. (2008) *Blue Helmets and Black Markets: The Business of Survival in the Siege of Sarajevo*. Ithaca, NY and London: Cornell University Press.

Andreas, P. (ed.) (1999) *The Illicit Global Economy and State Power*. Lanham, MD, Boulder, CO, New York and Oxford: Rowman and Littlefield Publishers.

Andreas, P. and Wallman, J. (2009) 'Illicit Markets and Violence: What is the relationship?' *Crime Law Social Change*, 52: 225–229.

Andreas, P. and Nadelmann, E. (2006) *Policing the Globe: Criminalization and Crime Control in International Relations*. Oxford: Oxford University Press.

Anonymous (Producer). (2012) *Youtube of Alinazorov – Protest*. Retrieved from: www.youtube.com/watch?v=PpclU16mP0k. Retrieved from: Protest: Vigil: www.youtube.com/watch?v=660fsBhbDuU (accessed April 13, 2013).

Ansari, B. (2009) *The Crisis of National Identity in Afghanistan*. Retrieved from: www.bashiransari.com (accessed January 15, 2012).

Anzurat, A. (2012) *Medical Plants of Rushan District, GBAO, Tajikistan: Medicinal Plants Use and Their Conservation Status in Rushan District of Gorno-Badakhshan Autonomous Oblast (GBAO)*. Saarbrücken: Lambert Academic Publishing.

Appadurai, A. (1990) *Disjuncture and Difference in the Global Cultural Economy*. Retrieved from: www.intcul.tohoku.ac.jp/~holden/MediatedSociety/Readings/2003_04/Appadurai.html.

Aronoff, M. and Kubik, J. (2012) *Anthropology and Political Science: A Convergent Approach*. Oxford: Berghahn Press.

Atkin, M. (1992) 'Religious, National, and Other Identities in Central Asia', in J. Gross (ed.) *Muslims in Central Asia: Expressions of Identity and Change.* Durham, NC: Duke University Press.

Barfield, T. (2010) *Afghanistan: A Cultural and Political History.* Princeton, NJ: Princeton University Press.

Barkey, K. (1994) *Bandits and Bureaucrats: The Ottoman Route to State Centralization.* Ithaca, NY: Cornell University Press.

Barry, M. (2010) *Compilation of Afghan Primary Source Materials (1700–2001).* Princeton, NJ: Princeton University Press.

Barth, F. (1959) *Political Leadership among Swat Pathans.* London: The Athlone Press.

Barth, F. (1966) *Models of Social Organization.* London: Royal Anthropological Institute.

Barth, F. (1969) *Ethnic Groups and Boundaries. The Social Organization of Culture Difference.* Oslo: Universitetsforlaget.

Barth, F. (1973) 'Descent and Marriage Reconsidered', in J. Goody and M. Fortes (eds) *The Character of Kinship.* Cambridge: Cambridge University Press, pp. 3–19.

Barth, F. (1981) *Features of Person and Society in Swat: Collected Essays on Pathans.* London and Boston, MA: Routledge & K. Paul.

Barth, F. (1993) *Balinese Worlds.* Chicago, IL: University of Chicago Press.

Bartold, V.V. (1918 [1934; 2009]) *Mussulman Culture* (S. Suhrawardy, trans.). Calcutta and Oxford: Oxford University Press.

Bartold, V.V. (1920) *A Short History of Turkestan* (V.T. Minorsky, trans.). Leiden: E.J. Brill.

Bekhradnia, S. (1994) 'The Tajik Case for a Zoroastrian Identity.' *Religion, State, and Society,* 22(1): 109–121.

Bergne, P. (2007) *The Birth of Tajikistan: National Identity and the Origins of the Republic.* London: I.B. Tauris.

Bleuer, C. and Nourzhanov, K. (2013) *Tajikistan: A Political and Social History.* ANU E-Press.

Bliss, F. (2005) *Social and Economic Change in the Pamirs.* London: Routledge.

Borneman, J.A.H. (ed.) (2009) *Being There: The Fieldwork Encounter and the Making of Truth.* Berkeley, CA: University of California Press.

Bosworth, C.E. (1968) *The Political and Dynastic History of the Iranian World (A.D. 1000–1217).* Cambridge: Cambridge University Press.

Bosworth, C.E. (ed.) (1971) *Iran and Islam in Memory of Vladimir Minorsky.* Edinburgh: Edinburgh University Press.

Bosworth, C.E. (ed.) (1998) *History of Civilizations of Central Asia – The Age of Achievement: 750 to the End of the Fifteenth Century* (Vol. IV). UNESCO.

Bourdieu, P. (1984) *Distinction: A Social Critique of the Judgement of Taste* (R. Nice, Trans.). Cambridge, MA: Harvard University Press.

Bourdieu, P. (1989) 'Social Space and Symbolic Power.' *Sociological Theory,* 7(1) Spring: 14–25.

Bowen, E. (1747) *A Complete System of Geography.* London: Innys, R. Ware.

Braithwaite, R. (2011) *Afgantsy: The Russians in Afghanistan, 1979–1989.* Oxford: Oxford University Press.

Bregel, Y. (1996) *Notes on the Study of Central Asia.* Bloomington, IN: Research Institute for Inner Asian Studies, Indiana University.

Brubaker, R. and Cooper, R. (2000) 'Beyond "Identity"', *Theory and Society,* 29: 1–47.

Carter, D. and Poast, P. (2015) 'Why Do States Build Walls.' *Journal of Conflict Resolution*, September 1, online.

Chandra, K. (ed.) (2012) *Constructivist Theories of Ethnic Politics.* Oxford and New York: Oxford University Press.

Chilton, P. (2004) *Analysing Political Discourse: Theory and Practice.* London: Routledge.

Clastres, P. (1987) *Society Against the State: Essays in Political Anthropology* (R. Hurley, trans.). New York: Zone Books, MIT Press.

Cobbold, R.P. (1900) *Innermost Asia: Travel & Sport in the Pamirs.* London: W. Heinemann.

Collins, K. (2004) 'The Logic of Clan Politics Evidence from the Central Asian.' *World Politics*, 56(2): 224–261.

Collins, K. (2006) *Clan Politics and Regime Transition in Central Asia.* Cambridge: Cambridge University Press.

Cumot, F. (1903) *The Mysteries of Mithraism.* Chicago, IL: The Open Court Publishing Company. Retrieved from: www.sacred-texts.com/cla/mom/mom04.htm.

Cooper, H. and Slackman, M. (2007) 'U.S. and Syria Discuss Iraq in Rare Meeting', *New York Times*, May 3.

Curzon, G.N. (1896) 'The Pamirs and the Source of the Oxus.' *Proceedings of the Royal Geographical Society*, 8(1).

Daftari, F. (ed.) (2011) *A Modern History of the Ismailis.* London: I.B. Taurus.

Daftary, F. (2005) *Ismailis in Medieval Muslim Societies.* Ismaili Heritage Series, 12, London: I.B. Taurus.

Dagiev, D. (2013) *Regime Transition in Central Asia: Stateness, Nationalism and Political Change in Tajikistan and Uzbekistan.* Routledge Advances in Central Asian Studies. London: Routledge.

Dalrymple, W. (2013) *Return of a King: The Battle For Afghanistan (1939–42).* New York: Knopf.

Danspeckgruber, W. (ed.) (2002) *The Self-Determination of Peoples: Community, Nation, and State in an Interdependent World.* Boulder, CO: Lynne Rienner Publishers.

DeWeese, D. (ed.) (2001) *Studies on Central Asian History in honor of Yuri Bregel.* Bloomington, IN: Indiana University.

Dhalla, M.N. (1938) *History of Zoroastrianism* (Vol. V). New York: Oxford University Press.

Dhingra, P. (2007) *Managing Multicultural Lives: Asian American Professionals and the Challenges of Multiple Identities.* Stanford, CA: Stanford University Press.

Dodikhudoeva, L. (2004) 'The Tajik Language and the Socio-Linguistic Situation in the Mountainous Badakhshan.' *Iran & the Caucasus*, 8(2): 281–288.

'Drugs in Tajikistan – Addicted: Heroin Stabilises a Poor Country' (2012) *The Economist*, April 21. Retrieved from: www.economist.com/node/21553092.

Dupee, M. (2008) 'Coalition and Taliban Vie for Control of Southwestern Afghanistan in Farah Province.' *The Long War Journal*. Retrieved from: www.longwarjournal.org/archives/2008/06/coalition_and_taliba.php#ixzz2UqCmGbYW.

Dupee, M. (2012) Afghanistan's Conflict Minerals: The Crime-State-Insurgent Nexus, *Combating Terrorism Center Sentinel*, February 16.

Elnazarov, H. and Aksaqolov, S. (2011) 'The Nizari Ismailis in Central Asia in Modern Times', in F. Daftari (ed.) *A Modern History of the Ismailis*, London: I.B. Taurus.

Emelianova, N. (2007) *Darwaz: Religioznaia I Kulturnaia Zhizn' Tadzhiko-afganskogo prigranich'ia* (Darwaz: Religious and Cultural Life of the Tajik-Afghan Border). Moscow.

Encyclopaedia of Islam. (2013) (Second edn). Brill Online.

Fernandes, L. (2006) *India's New Middle Class: Democratic Politics in an Era of Economic Reform.* Minneapolis, MN: University of Minnesota Press.

Foucault, M. (1995) *Discipline and Punish: The Birth of the Prison* (A. Sheridan, trans., Second edn). New York: Vintage Books.

Fredholm, M. (2014) 'Uzbek Islamic Extremists in the Civil Wars of Tajikistan, Afghanistan, and Pakistan: From Radical Islamic Awakening in the Ferghana Valley To Terrorism with Islamic Vocabulary in Waziristan', in A. Krawchuk and T. Bremer (eds) *Eastern Orthodox Encounters of Identity and Otherness: Values, Self-Reflection, Dialogue.* New York: Palgrave Macmillan, pp. 320–351.

Gardizi, A. and Thuess, M. (2006) 'What Is It All About? A Tale of Two Afghan Frontier Borders.' *CSCCA.*

Gavrilis, G. (2008) *The Dynamics of Interstate Boundaries.* Cambridge: Cambridge University Press.

Geertz, C. (1973) *The Interpretation of Cultures.* New York: Basic Books Classics.

Gellner, E. (ed.) (1980) *Soviet and Western Anthropology.* New York: Columbia University Press.

Gellner, E. and Smith, A.D. (1996) 'The Nation: Real or Imagined? The Warwick Debates on Nationalism.' *Nations and Nationalism*, 2(3): 357–370.

Gilboa, E. (2008) 'Searching for a Theory of Pubic Diplomacy.' *The Annals of the American Academy*, March: 55–78.

Giustozzi, A. (2009) *Empires of Mud: Wars and Warlords in Afghanistan.* New York: Columbia University Press.

Giustozzi, A. and Isaqzadeh, M. (2013) *Policing Afghanistan: The Politics of the Lame Leviathan.* New York: Columbia University Press.

Giustozzi, A. (2011) *The Art of Coercion: The Primitive Accumulation and Management of Coercive Power.* New York: Columbia University Press.

Goertz, G.E. (2009) 'Making Room for Interpretivism? A Pragmatic Approach.' *Qualitative & Multi-Method Research*, 7(1): 3–8.

Goertz, G.E. (2009) 'Symposium: Teaching Interpretive Methods.' *Qualitative and Multi-Method Research*, 7(1) Spring.

Goertz, G. (2005) *Social Science Concepts: A User's Guide.* Princeton, NJ: Princeton University Press.

Golden, P. (2011) *Central Asia in World History.* Oxford and New York: Oxford University Press.

Golden, P. (2013) [Emails].

Goody, J. (ed.) (1975) *The Character of Kinship.* New York: Cambridge University Press.

Greenfield, V.A., Paoli, L., Rabkov, I. and Reuter, P. (2007) 'Tajikistan: The Rise of the Narco-State.' *Journal of Drug Issues*, 37: 951.

Greenhouse, C.J., Mertz, E. and Warren, K.B. (eds) (2002) *Ethnography in Unstable places: Everyday Lives in Contexts of Dramatic Political Change.* Durham, NC and London: Duke University Press.

Grierson, G.A. (1920) *Ishkashmi, Zebaki, and Yazghulami: An Account of Three Eranian dialects.* University of Michigan Library.

Gross, J. (1992a) *Muslims in Central Asia: Expressions of Identity and Change.* Durham, NC: Duke University Press.

Gross, J. (1992b) 'Approaches to the Problem of Identity Formation', in J. Gross (ed.) *Muslims in Central Asia: Expressions of Identity and Change.* Durham, NC: Duke University Press.

Gross, J. (2013) 'Foundational Legends, Shrines, and Isma'ili Identity in Tajik Badakhshan', in M.J. Cormack (ed.) *Muslims and Others in Sacred Space.* Oxford: Oxford University Press.

Habberton, W. (1937) *Anglo-Russian Relations Concerning Afghanistan 1837–1907.* Urbana-Champagne, IL: University of Illinois at Urbana-Champagne.

Haqnazarov, I. (1998) *Reflections: Critical Insights into the Realities of Life of the Ismaili Jamat and the Impact of AKDN Institutions on the Economy of GBAO.* (S. Khojaniyozov, ed. and trans.). Khorog. Unpublished Report.

Harris, C. (2004) *Control and Subversion: Gender Relations in Tajikistan.* London and Sterling, VA: Pluto Press.

Harris, C. (2006) *Muslim Youth: Tensions and Transitions in Tajikistan.* Boulder, CO: Westview Press.

Helmke, S. and Levitsky, G. (2004) 'Informal Institutions and Comparative Politics: A Research Agenda.' *Perspectives on Politics,* 2(4): 725–741.

Hoffmann, B., Kauz, R. and Ritter, M. (2008 [1970]) *Iran und iranisch geprägte Kulturen.* Wiesbaden.

Holvino, E. (2011) 'I Think it's a Cultural Thing and a Woman Thing.' *Cultural Scripts in Latinas' Careers, CGO Insights,* 30.

Marsden, M. and Hopkins, B.D. (2012) *Fragments of the Afghan Frontier.* New York: Columbia University Press.

Hughes, J. and Sasse, G. (ed.) (2002) *Ethnicity and Territory in the Former Soviet Union: Regions in Conflict.* London: Routledge.

Human Rights Watch (2016) 'Tajikistan: Severe Crackdown on Political Opposition US, EU Should Urgently Raise Abuses', February 17. Retrieved from: www.hrw. org/news/2016/02/17/tajikistan-severe-crackdown-political-opposition.

Hunsberger, A. (2000) *Nasir Khusraw, The Ruby of Badakhshan: A Portrait of the Persian Poet, Traveller and Philosopher.* London: I.B. Tauris in association with The Institute of Ismaili Studies.

Hylland, E.T. (2001) 'Ethnic Identity, National Identity, and Intergroup Conflict: The Significance of Personal Experiences', in R. Ashmore, L. Jussim and D. Wilder (eds) *Social Identity, Intergroup Conflict, and Conflict Reduction.* Oxford: Oxford University Press.

Isaqzadeh, A. (2013) *Policing Afghanistan.* New York: Columbia University Press.

Iskandarov, B.I. (1996) Истёрия Памира (History of the Pamirs). Khorog.

Jackson, P.T. (2010) *The Conduct of Inquiry in International Relations: Philosophy of Science and Its Implications for the Study of World Politics.* London: Routledge.

Karmysheva, B.K. (ed.) (1969) *Etnograficheskie ocherki Uzbekskogo sel'skogo naseleniya* (Ethnographic Sketches of the Uzbek Rural Population). Moscow.

Keyes, C. (1981) 'The Dialectic of Ethnic Change', in C. Keyes (ed.) *Ethnic Change.* Seattle, WA: University of Washington Press, pp. 3–30.

Kipling, R. (1891) *Life's Handicap: Being Stories of Mine Own People.* London: Rudyard Kipling Centenary Edition.

KLMA. (2013) History of Badakhshan. *World History at KLMA.*

Koen, B.D. (2009) *Beyond the Roof of the World: Music, Prayer, and Healing in the Pamir Mountains.* Oxford and New York: Oxford University Press.

Kubik, J. (1994) *The Power of Symbols Against the Symbols of Power: The Rise of Solidarity and the Fall of State Socialism in Poland.* Pittsburgh, PA: Pennsylvania State University Press.

Kubik, J. (2009) 'Ethnography of Politics: Foundations, Applications, Prospects', in E. Schatz (ed.) *Political Ethnography: What Immersion Contributes to the Study of Power.* Chicago, IL: The University of Chicago Press, pp. 25–52.

Kubik, J. and Linch, A. (eds) (2013) *Postcommunism from Within: Social Justice, Mobilization, and Hegemony.* New York: Social Science Research Council/New York University Press.

Kunitz, J. (1935) *Dawn Over Samarkand: The Rebirth of Central Asia.* New York: Covici Friede Publishers.

Kushkeki, B. (1926) *Kattagan-I Badakhshan (Rahnama-I Badakhshan).* Tashkent: Mellor.

Kushlis, P.K. (2009, February 6) 'The Public Diplomacy Hard Part: Getting from Here to There', *Whirled View.* Retrieved from: http://whirledview.typepad.com/whirledview/2009/02/the-public-diplomacy-hard-part-getting-from-here-to-there.html.

Laitin, D. (1986) *Hegemony and Culture: Politics and Change among the Yoruba.* Chicago, IL: University of Chicago Press.

Laruelle, M. (2007) 'The Return of the Aryan Myth: Tajikistan in Search for a Secularized National Ideology.' *Nationalities Papers*, 35(1): 51–70.

Lewis, B. (2002) *The Assassins.* New York: Basic Books.

Levi-Sanchez, S. (2008) *Myth Objectives: The Social Construct of Narrative Influence in Iran.* San Francisco, CA: San Francisco State University Press.

Lorey, D. and Ganster, P. (ed.) (2005) *Borders and Border Politics in a Globalizing World.* Lanham, MD: SR Books.

Lorimer, D.L.R. (1958) *The Wakhi Language, Volume 1: Introduction, Phonetics, Grammar and Texts.* London: School of Oriental and African Studies, W. C. I.

Lubin, N., Nunn, S.S. and Rubin, R. (1999) *Calming the Ferghana Valley: Development and Dialogue in the Heart of Central Asia* (Vol. 4). New York City: The Century Foundation Press.

Luigi De Martino, E. (2004) 'Tajikistan at a Crossroad: The Politics of Decentralization.' *Situation Report.*

Luong, P.J. (2008) *Institutional Change and Political Continuity in Post-Soviet Central Asia: Power, Perceptions, and Pacts.* Cambridge: Cambridge University Press.

Lustick, I. (1996) 'Hegemonic Beliefs and Territorial Rights.' *International Journal of Intercultural Relations*, 20: 1–14.

Mahler, Joseph L.M. and Auyero, J. (ed.) (2007) *New Perspectives in Political Ethnography.* New York: Springer.

Maisky, P.M. (1935) 'Traces of Ancient Belief Systems in the Pamirs.' *Soviet Ethnography*, 3: 50–58.

Mansfield, D. (2004) *Coping Strategies, Accumulated Wealth and Shifting Markets: The Story of Opium cultivation in Badakhshan 2000–2003*, Report for Aga Khan Development Network.

Mahmood, Z., Usmanghani, M., Jahan, S. and Zaihd, Z. (2009) 'Review: Kohl (Surma): "Retrospect and Prospect".' *Pakistan Journal of Pharmaceutical Sciences*, 22(1): 107–122.

Masson, V.M. and Sariandi, V.I. (1972) *Central Asia: Turkmenia before the Achaemenids* (R. Tringham, trans.). New York and Washington, DC: Praeger Publishers.

McDermott, R. (2002) 'Border Security in Tajikistan: Countering the Narcotics Trade.' *Conflict Studies Research Center K36*: 1–20.

Middleton, R. and Thomas, H. (2008) *Tajikistan and the High Pamirs.* Hong Kong: Odyssey Books.

Midgal, J.S. (1988) *Strong Societies and Weak States.* Princeton, NJ: Princeton University Press.

Migdal, J.S. (ed.) (2004) *Boundaries and Belonging.* Cambridge: Cambridge University Press.

Monogarova, L.F. (1972) *Transformation in Family Structures of the Pamiri Tajiks.* Moscow: Institute of Ethnography.

Mostowlansky, T. (2011) 'Paving the Way: Isma'ili Genealogy and Mobility along Tajikistan's Pamir Highway.' *Journal of Persianate Studies*, 4(1): 171–188.

Naim, M. (2006) *Illicit: How Smugglers, Traffickers, and Copycats are Hijacking the Global Economy.* New York: Anchor.

Noelle-Karimi, C. (1997) *State and Tribe in Nineteenth-century Afghanistan: The Reign of Amir Dost Muhammad Khan (1826–1863).* London: Curzon Press.

Noelle-Karimi, C. (2008) 'Khurasan and Its Limits: Changing Concepts of Territory from Pre-Modern to Modern Times', in M. Ritter, R. Kauz and B. Hoffmann (eds) *Iran und iranisch geprägte Kulturen. Studien zum 65*, 30: 9–19.

Nordstrom, C. and Robben, A.C.G.M. (ed.) (1996) *Fieldwork Under Fire: Contemporary Studies of Violence and Culture.* Berkeley, CA: University of California Press.

North, D.C. (1982) *Structure and Change in Economic History.* New York: W.W. Norton & Company.

North, D.C. (1990) *Institutions, Institutional Change and Economic Performance (Political Economy of Institutions and Decisions).* Cambridge: Cambridge University Press.

Norton, A. (2004) *95 Theses on Politics, Culture, and Method.* New Haven, CT and London: Yale University Press.

OECD. (2005) *Fighting Corruption in Transition Economies: Tajikistan.* Paris: OECD.

Olufson, O. (1904) *Through the Unknown Pamirs: The Second Danish Expedition 1898-99.* London: William Heinemann.

Orwell, G. (1961) *1984.* New York: Signet Classics.

Ostrom, E. (1990) *Governing the Commons: The Evolution of Institutions for Collective Action.* Cambridge: Cambridge University Press.

Ostrom, E. (2005) *Understanding Institutional Diversity.* Princeton, NJ: Princeton University Press.

Ostrom, E. (2006) 'A Frequently Overlooked Precondition for Democracy: Citizens Knowledgeable About and Engaged in Collective Action', in G. Tampere (ed.) *Preconditions of Democracy.* Finland: Tampere University Press.

Ozodi, R. (2013) 'Head of Tajik Prison Asked to Resign Over Torture', *Radio Ozodi*, March 13.

Pangborn, C.R. (1983) *Zoroastrianism.* New York: Advent Publishing.

Payne, J. (1989) 'Pamir Languages', in R. Schmitt, *Compendium Linguarum Iranicum.* Wiesbaden: Reichert.

Peter, T.A. (2011) *Loya Jirga: Afghans Question Karzai's Motives in Calling the Meeting*, November 15. Retrieved from: www.csmonitor.com/World/Asia-South-Centra l/2011/1115/Loya-jirga-Afghans-question-Karzai-s-motives-in-calling-the-meeting.

Pettigrew, J. (1995) *The Sikhs of the Punjab: Unheard Voices of State and Guerilla Violence.* Atlantic Highlands: Zed Books.

Philips, C.H. (ed.) (1951) *Handbook of Oriental History*. London: Offices of the Royal Historical Society.

Postnikov, A. (2000) 'Istoricheskaya pravda' sosednikh gosudarstv i geografiya pamira kak argument v 'bolshoy igre' britanii i rossii (1869-1896).' *Acta Slavica Iaponica*, 17: 33–99.

Poteete, A., Janssen, M. and Ostrom, E. (2010) *Working Together: Collective Action, the Commons, and Multiple Methods in Practice*. Princeton, NJ: Princeton University Press.

Rashid, A. (2000) *Taliban*. New Haven, CT: Yale Nota Bene.

Rashid, A. (2009) *Descent into Chaos: The U.S. and the Disaster in Pakistan, Afghanistan, and Central Asia*. New York: Penguin Press.

Roy, E. (1924) 'The Revolution in Central Asia: The Struggle for Power in Holy Bokhara.' *Labour Monthly*, 6(7): 403–410.

Roy, O. (1986) *Islam and Resistance in Afghanistan*. Cambridge: Cambridge University Press.

Roy, O. (1992) Ethnic Identity and Political Expression in Northern Afghanistan, in J. Gross (ed.) *Muslims in Central Asia: Expressions of Identity and Change*. Durham, NC: Duke University Press.

Roy, O. (2000) *The New Central Asia, the Creation of Nations*. London: Tauris.

Rubin, B. (1993) 'The Fragmentation of Tajikistan.' *Survival: Global Poltics and Strategy*, 35(4): 71–91.

Russell, Z. and Sahadeo, J. (ed.) (2007) *Everyday Life in Central Asia: Past and Present*. Bloomington, IN: Indiana University Press.

Sarianidi, V.I. (1972) *Central Asia: Turkmenia Before the Achaemenids* (R. Tringham, trans.). New York: Praeger.

Sartori, G. (1970) 'Concept Misformation in Comparative Politics.' *The American Political Science Review*, 64(4): 1033–1053.

Schatz, E. (2004) *Modern Clan Politics: The Power of "Blood" in Kazakhstan and Beyond*. Seattle, WA: University of Washington Press.

Schatz, E. (ed.) (2009) *Political Ethnography: What Immersion Contributes to the Study of Power*. Chicago, IL: The University of Chicago Press.

Schwartz-Shea, P. and Yanow, D. (2012) *Interpretive Research Design: Concepts and Processes*. London: Routledge.

Scott, J.C. (1985) *Weapons of the Weak: Everyday Forms of Peasant Resistance*. New Haven, CT: Yale University Press.

Scott, J.C. (1999) *Seeing Like a State: How Certain Schemes to Improve the Human Condition Have Failed*. New Haven, CT: Yale University Press.

Scott, J.C. (2009) *The Art of Not Being Governed: An Anarchist History of Upland Southeast Asia*. New Haven, CT: Yale University Press.

Shaban, M.A. (1970) 'Khurasan at the Time of the Arab Conquest', in *The Abbasid Revolution*. Cambridge: Cambridge University Press.

Shokhumurov, A. (1997) *Pamir – The Land of Aryans*. Dushanbe.

Shokhumurov, A. (2008) *Razdilenie badakhshana i sudbi ismailizma* (The Region of Badakhshan and the State of Ismailis). Moscow: Moscow State University.

Shughnan Rebellion of 1925 and Verdict. *Collection 62, list 2, file 243* (pp. 53–55, 61). London: Access to this document provided by the Institute for Ismaili Studies.

Schurmann, A.H.F. (1962) *The Mongols of Afghanistan: An Ethnography of the Moghôls and Related Peoples of Afghanistan* (Vol. IV). The Hague: Mouton.

Smith, A.D. (1991) *National Identity*. Reno, NV: University of Nevada Press.

Sneath, D. (2007) *The Headless State: Aristocratic Orders, Kinship Society, & Misrepresentations of Nomadic Inner Asia.* New York: Columbia University Press.

Sodiqov, A. (2012, May 9) 'Explaining the Conflict in Eastern Tajikistan.' *Central Asia-Caucasus Institute.* Retrived from: http://old.cacianalyst.org/?q=node/5831.

Steinberg, J. (2011) *Isma'ili Modern: Globalization and Identity in a Muslim Community.* Berkeley, CA: University of North Carolina Press.

Tambiah, S.J. (1996) *Leveling Crowds: Ethnonationalist Conflicts and Collective Violence in South Asia.* Berkeley, CA: University of California Press.

Tanner, S. (2002) *Afghanistan: A Military History from Alexander the Great to the Fall of the Taliban.* Boston, MA: Da Capo Press.

Tilly, C. (1978) *Mobilization to Revolution.* Boston, MA: Addison-Wesley.

Tilly, C. (1981) *As Sociology Meets History.* New York: Academic Press.

Tilly, C. (2005a) *Trust and Rule.* Cambridge and New York: Cambridge University Press.

Tilly, C. (2005b) *Identities, Boundaries & Social Ties.* Boulder, CO: Paradigm Publishers.

Togan, Z.V. (2011) *Memoirs: National Existence and Cultural Struggles of Turkistan and Other Muslim Eastern Turks.* Createspace Publishing.

Tomsen, P. (2011) *The Wars of Afghanistan: Messianic Terrorism, Tribal Conflicts, and the Failures of Great Powers.* New York: Public Affairs.

United Nations Development Program (UNDP) in Tajikistan and the EU Border Management of Central Asia (BOMCA) (2009) *Workplan: Project Number 5*: "Assisting Tajikistan in Securing the Tajik-Afghan Border in Gorno-Badakhsan."

United States Department of State (2008) *Foreign-Operations Report.*

UNODC. (2011) *World Drug Report.* Retrieved from: www.unodc.org/documents/data-and-analysis/WDR2011/The_opium-heroin_market.pdf.

UNODC. (2012) *Afghan Opium Survey 2012.*

USSR (1921 [1946; 1948]) *Protocol Number 354 and Agreement Number 855: "Agreement between the Government of USSR and Royal Government of Afghanistan on the Status of the Soviet-Afghan State Border," original Protocol (1921), revised Protocol (1950), and Re-Demarcation Agreement (1946, 1948).* Accessed 2009 at OSCE, Dushanbe Office.

Vesperi, M.D. and Waterston, A. (ed.) (2011) *Anthropology off the Shelf: Anthropologists On Writing.* Chichester: Wiley-Blackwell.

Viola, L. (2000) 'The Role of the OGPU in Dekulakization, Mass Deportation, and Special Resettlements in 1930.' *Carl Beck Papers in Russian and East European Studies 1406*, 8(12).

Viola, L. (2007) *The Unknown Gulag. The Lost World of Stalin's Special Settlements.* Oxford: Oxford University Press.

Vogelsang, W. (2002) *The Afghans.* Oxford and Malden, MA: Blackwell Publishers.

Walsh, K.C. (2004) *Talking About Politics: Informal Groups and Social Identity in American Life.* Chicago, IL and London: University of Chicago Press.

Warikoo, K. (ed.) (2011) *Central Asia an South Asia: Energy Cooperation an Transport Linkages.* New Delhi: Pentagon Press.

Wedeen, L. (1999) *Ambiguities of Domination: Politics, Rhetoric, and Symbols in Contemporary Syria.* Chicago, IL: University of Chicago Press.

'We Will Help Tajik Border Guards Says Russian Border Service'. (2011) Retrieved from: http://news.tj/en/news/we-will-help-tajik-border-guards-says-russian-border-service-head.

Wierzbicka, A. (2006) *English: Meaning and Culture*. Oxford: Oxford University Press.

Williams, J. (2006) *The Ethics of Territorial Borders: Drawing Lines in the Shifting Sand*. Basingstoke: Palgrave Macmillan.

Wimmer, A. (2008) 'The Making and Unmaking of Ethnic Boundaries: A Multilevel Process Theory.' *American Journal of Sociology*, 113(4) January: 970–1022.

Zamonov, S. (2007–2010) *Badakhshan*. Retrieved from: www.freewebs.com/beep-sino/badakhshanpamir.htm.

Zerell, B. *et al.* (2005) *Documentation of a Heroin Manufacturing Process in Afghanistan*. Wiesbaden: Federal Criminal Police Office, Germany.

Index

For Product Safety Concerns and Information please contact our EU representative GPSR@taylorandfrancis.com Taylor & Francis Verlag GmbH, Kaufingerstraße 24, 80331 München, Germany

Printed and bound by CPI Group (UK) Ltd, Croydon, CR0 4YY

08/05/2025

01864528-0001